How It Works®

Science and Technology

Third Edition

Marshall Cavendish
99 White Plains Road
Tarrytown, NY 10591

Website: www.marshallcavendish.com

Third edition updated by Brown Reference Group plc.

Library of Congress Cataloging-in-Publication Data
How it works: science and technology.—3rd ed.
p. cm.
Includes index.
ISBN 0-7614-7314-9 (set)   ISBN 0-7614-7329-7 (Vol. 15)
1. Technology—Encyclopedias. 2. Science—Encyclopedias.
[1. Technology—Encyclopedias. 2. Science—Encyclopedias.]
T9 .H738 2003
603—dc21   2001028771

Consultant: Donald R. Franceschetti, Ph.D., University of Memphis

Brown Reference Group
Editor: Wendy Horobin
Associate Editors: Paul Thompson, Martin Clowes, Lis Stedman
Managing Editor: Tim Cooke
Design: Alison Gardner
Picture Research: Becky Cox
Illustrations: Mark Walker, Darren Awuah

Marshall Cavendish
Project Editor: Peter Mavrikis
Production Manager: Alan Tsai
Editorial Director: Paul Bernabeo

Printed in Malaysia
Bound in the United States of America
08 07 06 05 04   6 5 4 3 2

Title picture: Astronauts capture *Intelsat VI*, see *Satellite, Artificial*

How It Works®

Science and Technology

Volume 15

Salvage, Marine

Space Probe

Marshall Cavendish

New York • London • Toronto • Sydney

Contents

Volume 15

Salvage, Marine

Marine salvage is the recovery of objects lost or damaged in the oceans, and the salvaging techniques may apply also to lakes and rivers. In modern times, many objects, ranging from treasure to hydrogen bombs, as well as wrecked ships, have been recovered by salvage operations.

Towing

If a ship is disabled, for example, because of failure of the main engines or the steering gear, or damaged by a collision so that it is unable to proceed under its own power, it can be towed to a port or sheltered location by a salvage tug. These tugs are specifically designed for towing, with their strong cable attachment points. Tugs intended for deep sea salvage may be more than 250 ft. (76 m) long with engine ratings of more than 15,000 horsepower (11,250 kW) to give a pulling effort of more than 100 tons (90 tonnes).

Grounded ships

A ship that has run aground may seem at first to be a simple salvage job, but each salvage operation is different, and ingenuity is always important. If a ship has simply run aground, it may be

necessary only to wait for the next high tide and pull it afloat again, but each decision depends upon the circumstances. If a ship goes aground in a rocky, treacherous terrain, its hull may be broken when the tide goes out. If the hull suffers some damage from running aground, it may be possible to make temporary repairs with steel or wooden patches, which the water pressure will help to hold in place when the ship is afloat.

If a vessel has been driven high aground by winds and waves, it may still be possible to refloat it by lightening the ship. Freight, fixtures, and even the ship's superstructure may be removed and transferred to waiting barges, but it is important to anchor the ship in the direction of deep water before lightening begins so that in its lightened condition, it does not go further aground.

Sunken ships

Whether sunken ships can be salvaged depends upon a combination of factors: depth of water, size of the ship, weather conditions, availability of equipment, estimated cost, and so on. The larger the ship to be salvaged, the more difficult the job will be at a given depth, because the amount of lift

▲ Salvage work is often linked with archaeology when ancient wrecks are found. Here, divers are location-tagging artifacts from an 11th century Turkish ship, the *Glass Wreck*, before they are brought to the surface for examination and restoration. Whole cargoes of early Chinese pottery have been raised from the seabed by salvagers and sold for profit.

◀ Raising the final starboard section of the hull of the *Mary Rose* on October 11, 1982. The hull, supported by a steel cradle, is suspended beneath a lifting frame. The salvage of the *Mary Rose* was particularly difficult because the 16th century vessel was extremely delicate and likely to break up when disturbed. Even a modern, steel-hulled vessel is likely to break up if it is lifted too quickly.

available from the different types of equipment used is limited.

If the ship has sunk in shallow water so that the main deck is out of water, it can usually be refloated by patching any holes and pumping the water out. When the ship is completely under-water, however, more elaborate techniques have to be used, and effective salvage operations became possible only during the past 100 years with the development of suitable technology.

Often the location of the vessel to be salvaged is known from the records of the sinking, but abandoned vessels may eventually sink some distance from where they were left. With aircraft (which often have to be recovered to establish the causes of a crash), precise location may be more difficult. Accordingly, the first operation is usually to find the wreck. If the wreck lies in shallow water, it may be possible to see it from the air, and in deeper water sonar is used.

Sonar (*s*ound *na*vigation *r*anging) operates on the principle that sound travels through a medium at constant, measurable velocity; thus, the time it takes for a sound signal to reflect from an under-water object can be translated into a measurement of distance. Computer processing of the sonar signals allows a picture of the seabed to be built up with unexpected shapes possibly indicating the presence of a wreck. Problems can occur, though, if a vessel or aircraft has sunk in an area where

▼ The hull of the *Mary Rose* breaking the surface of the water. Protective sandbags had to be placed under the hull to keep it from being crushed by the cradle.

the ocean floor is naturally rough, because it will be difficult to distinguish between natural and unnatural projections from the seabed.

Once the wreck is located, the work of the divers begins. Mechanical lifting by floating cranes is still the most popular method, as it has been since the invention of the diving suit made it possible to attach cables and chains to the hulk. The laying of cables is done so that the sunken vessel is cradled by supporting gear that leads to the surface; the cables are frequently positioned by dredgers with the assistance of divers, and the chief considerations are the size of the hulk, the power and buoyancy of the surface vessels, and the unpredictability of the weather. If the cables are improperly positioned or if the weight of the hulk shifts as it is being lifted, weeks of work may be wasted, and the stricken vessel may break its back or slip out of the matrix of cable and go back to the bottom.

A sunken vessel is likely to be mired in mud at the bottom, and the effect is a powerful force of static friction, or suction. The force required to break the suction will be many times the force required to lift the vessel once it is free, resulting in a sudden increase in the rate of the vessel's motion. Such a change in lifting power can break the ship's hull or at least cause it to be difficult to control.

Ingenious methods have been devised to deal with this problem. Cables from the positive and negative terminals on a generator on the surface vessel can be directed to two sides of a sunken hull so that they become positive and negative electrodes. When the power is turned on, the water between the electrodes acts as a conductor; electrolysis results, and the water is broken up into

hydrogen and oxygen; hydrogen bubbles attach themselves to the hull, displacing the mud and destroying the static friction.

Other lifting methods

Mechanical lifts are often aided by other devices, such as pontoons. Pontoons are empty metal tanks or rubber bags that are flooded, sunk, arranged around the hulk, and finally pumped free of water with compressed air, resulting in buoyancy of the wreck. Pontoons were developed especially for rescuing submarines.

Compressed air is often used without pontoons. Apertures and leaks are sealed by divers so that the vessel becomes relatively airtight; most seagoing vessels have been constructed in compartmented form anyway, so it is often not necessary to seal up the whole of a wreck before pumping in compressed air.

Mechanical lifting can be aided by the tides as well. Partially flooded vessels are attached to the sunken hull at low tide and pumped free of water as the tide rises, providing extra lift. This method is particularly successful where the lifting equipment is insufficiently powerful for the job.

Polyurethane foam has been used to raise vessels. Polyurethane components are sent down in a hose to a mixing chamber that divers have installed near the wreck. Another agent with a low boiling point is also sent to the chamber, and the materials are mixed and expelled with pressurized nitrogen. The low-boiling agent volatilizes because of the sudden decrease in pressure, and a froth of polyurethane bubbles is produced inside the hull. The bubbles cure to form a rigid, cellular material; each cubic foot of this foam weighs 2 lbs. (0.907 kg) and displaces 64 lbs. (29 kg) of water. Polyurethane beads or pressure-injected spheres are even better, because they are easier to remove from the recovered hull than solid foam. They are pumped into the hull through a pipe. The pressure-injected spheres are 11 in. (28 cm) in diameter, providing 30 lbs. (13.6 kg) of buoyancy; they are pressurized to synchronize with ambient pressure at a given depth and are equipped with valves that allow internal pressure to adjust as necessary when the ship rises.

The prop wash is an elbow-shaped aluminum tube that fits on the transom of a boat. The wash from the ship's propeller is directed through it to the sand at the bottom, so digging operations that used to take days for divers can sometimes be accomplished in a few minutes. Pumps are also used to provide the necessary water flow. The air lift is used to recover small objects. It is an open-ended pipe; a hose from the surface supplies compressed air to a perforated chamber at the lower

◀ A World War II Wellington bomber, which crashed into Loch Ness, Scotland, is recovered using land-based lifting gear. Floats have been attached to raise the airplane closer to the surface.

end of the pipe. The air bubbles rush upward, creating suction, which carries small objects with it.

If the cargo is a potential pollutant, such as oil or chemicals, the salvager may have to transfer the cargo before the wreck can be salvaged. Old wrecks with weapons on board are a particular hazard, as the structure may be badly corroded.

Submersibles

Increasing use is being made of both piloted and remote-controlled submersibles for salvage in deep water. These craft are operated from a mother ship, and the most advanced designs are capable of working at depths greater than 15,000 ft. (4,570 m), though most have a more restricted working depth of around 6,000 ft. (1,830 m). External manipulator systems allow objects to be recovered or worked on and cables attached for lifting, though the lifting capacity is generally limited. Sonar systems and magnetometers are fitted to allow examination and searches of the seabed, along with lighting systems and cameras. Remote-controlled units are connected to the mother ship by control and power cables and have low-light television cameras to allow the operator to view the working area.

Destroying wrecks

Salvage companies are often asked to destroy or remove a wreck rather than to recover it; during wartime, scuttled or sunken ships often blocked ports, for example. Sometimes the wreck is recovered and towed to deeper water to be sunk again, but explosives are also used. A ring of explosives is placed around the wreck and detonated; tons of water suddenly converge on the hulk, crushing it.

SEE ALSO:	ARCHAEOLOGICAL TECHNOLOGIES • COMPRESSOR AND PUMP • CRANE • HYDRAULICS • MAGNETOMETER • SHIP • SUBMERSIBLE

Satellite, Artificial

In general, a satellite is any object that follows an orbital path around a larger celestial body—the Moon is a satellite of Earth, for example. Artificial satellites are objects that are built and put into orbit by humans. To date, the only space vehicles to maintain long-term orbits have been satellites of Earth; other space probes and missions have entered temporary orbits around other planets and the Moon, but these orbital phases were short stages of longer journeys, and such vehicles are not considered to be satellites.

Since the first artificial satellite, *Sputnik I*, was launched by the USSR on October 4, 1957, thousands of satellites of various sizes and complexities have been put into Earth's orbit. Most of them have since fallen into disuse as their onboard energy supplies have become depleted or they have dropped into Earth's atmosphere to be vaporized in the heat of reentry. A few satellites have been recovered by plucking them out of orbit and carrying them back to Earth on NASA's space shuttles, and others have been deliberately "deorbited" by firing retromotors to reduce their orbital energy and so cause their demise.

The satellites that are currently operational perform a variety of roles. Some act as relay transmitters for telecommunications systems, others as navigational beacons for terrestrial travelers. Yet other satellites act as observation platforms for recording features of Earth's surface and atmosphere, while some gaze out into space using powerful telescopes that would be impeded by interference from Earth's atmosphere. Some satellites are in open public service, while others perform secret military work.

Mechanics of satellites

Motion in a circular orbit at constant speed can only occur when the object experiences a constant force directed towards the center of the orbit. In this respect, the mechanics of a satellite's orbit are identical to those of a stone whirled around in a slingshot: the force for the stone's motion is provided by tension in the slingshot, the force that keeps a satellite in orbit is gravitational attraction.

In 1666, the British mathematician and physicist Isaac Newton proposed a law of gravitation that he based on his observations of the motions

▲ The free-flying satellite *Spartan* leaving the cargo hold of the space shuttle *Discovery*. The satellite spent several days gathering data on the solar wind and the Sun's corona before it was recaptured by the shuttle and returned to Earth.

of celestial bodies. According to this law, the force of attraction, F, between two bodies is related to the distance between them, r, by the formula

$$F = \frac{GmM}{r^2}$$

where G is the gravitational constant. In the case of a satellite in orbit, m is the mass of the satellite, and M is the much greater mass of the planet.

Newton's laws of motion can be manipulated to show that the force required to keep an object—in this case, the satellite—in circular motion is given by the equation

$$F = m\omega^2 r$$

where ω is the angular velocity of the satellite in radians per second (a full circle is 2π radians).

Since the gravitational force is identical to the force that keeps the satellite in orbital motion, the above equations can be combined:

$$m\omega^2 r = \frac{GmM}{r^2}$$

This expression is simpler when both sides are divided by mr to give an equation that relates the angular velocity of a satellite to its orbital radius:

$$\omega^2 = \frac{GM}{r^3}$$

Since both G and M are constant for a satellite in orbit around Earth, the square of angular velocity is proportional to the inverse cube of orbital radius—the closer the satellite is to Earth, the shorter the time it takes to complete an orbit. Interestingly, the mass of a satellite has no effect on its angular velocity in orbit.

Another feature of a satellite's motion is that it is in constant free fall toward Earth: its downward acceleration is what keeps it in orbit, rather than allowing it to hurtle into space, and creates a condition of apparent weightlessness, even though the satellite and its onboard equipment are responding to Earth's gravity.

Orbital types

At one particular orbital radius, any satellite will travel at the same angular velocity as a point on Earth's surface, completing an orbit in the period of one day. The altitude at which this phenomenon occurs is around 22,300 miles (35,900 km), and when such an orbit is directly over Earth's equator, it is called a geostationary equatorial orbit (GEO), or parking orbit. A satellite in a GEO—and traveling in the same sense as Earth's rotation—remains permanently stationed over a set point on Earth's equator, a position useful for certain telecommunications applications.

One application of satellites in geostationary orbits is the transmission of television signals: since the satellite is geostationary, dish-shaped receiving antennas on Earth can be pointed at a fixed point in the sky location to receive the strongest signal at all times.

Geostationary orbits are examples of high Earth orbits (HEOs). Satellites that orbit much closer to Earth's surface—at altitudes less than 1,200 miles (1,930 km)—are said to occupy low Earth orbits (LEOs). As dictated by the relationship between angular velocity and orbital radius, these satellites complete several orbits within the space of a day, and they are therefore useful for scanning Earth's surface. Consider the example of an LEO satellite that passes over both poles in a single orbit, photographing a band of Earth's surface as it goes. By the time one orbit is complete, Earth will have rotated by an amount that depends on the period of orbit, and so the satellite starts to photograph an adjacent band.

Medium Earth orbits (MEOs), at altitudes around 6,000 miles (9,700 km) correspond to slow sweeps over Earth's surface. Examples of satellites that occupy MEOs include global positioning system (GPS) satellites, such as those of

◀ The *Spacenet 1* civil telecommunications satellite was launched aboard the French Ariane V9 rocket from French Guyana in May 1984.

the U.S. NAVSTAR system. Dozens of such satellites—around 24 for NAVSTAR—form a network of intercommunicating beacons. At any given time, three or four such beacons are "visible" over the horizon, and a receiver on Earth can calculate its position by comparing their signals. By the time one satellite has set below the horizon, another has risen to take its place.

Not all orbits are circular, however. Some satellites enter temporary elliptical orbits, in which their speed rises to a maximum at the closest distance to Earth, and then falls to a minimum at the greatest distance from Earth. In this way, energy exchanges between its kinetic and potential forms during a single orbit. Elliptical orbits are used to move between circular orbits at different altitudes, as will be discussed.

Launch techniques

A satellite in orbit has a combination of kinetic energy and potential energy much greater than it has on Earth, and this energy must be supplied by the burning rockets of a launch vehicle. Early satellites used unpiloted single-use multistage rockets to get into orbit. This continues to be the preferred method for European space agencies—in particular, the French agency, which keeps the unit costs of its Ariane launch vehicles low by producing large numbers of standardized vehicles.

In this approach, two rocket stages suffice to enter low Earth orbit; if necessary, a third stage can be used to boost the satellite into an elliptical transfer orbit that passes through both LEO and HEO altitudes. When the appropriate point is reached, booster rockets fire to establish a circular orbit at the required altitude.

Since the 1980s, NASA has used its space shuttles to put satellites into orbit. Most of the space shuttle can be reused with a limited amount of refurbishment between launches, thus helping cut the cost of launches. Furthermore, the shuttle accompanies a satellite into orbit, ensuring the accuracy of its orbit and the correct functioning of its equipment before the astronauts leave the satellite to its own devices.

The use of the space shuttle reduces overall costs by reducing the likelihood of abortive satellite commissionings. Furthermore, the shuttle can collect malfunctioning satellites and mend them before putting them back in orbit, or it can take a satellite back to Earth for detailed examination and recovery of its expensive equipment.

Working environment

Satellites have to operate in a harsh environment that cannot be entirely reproduced in ground tests. Equipment must work in zero gravity, under high-vacuum conditions, and with wide and frequent temperature fluctuations caused by extreme variations in exposure to sunlight. Onboard equipment must be able to withstand powerful vibrations transmitted from the launch vehicle during the ascent as well as the sudden increases in thrust that occur when an upper stage takes over from a depleted lower stage.

Materials that emit dissolved gases or partially vaporize under hard vacuum must be avoided, as the particles they give off could confuse star sensors or contaminate solar arrays. Two similar metal surfaces may weld together under pressure in a vacuum, and conventional lubrication systems would not work, as the oil would evaporate. Surfaces in contact are therefore made of dissimilar materials, and solid-film lubricants, such as polytetrafluoroethylene (PTFE, or Teflon), are used to provide slip where it is needed. Highly reflective foil cladding helps reduce the heating effect of sunlight without adding much weight.

Construction

The design of a satellite involves a number of subsystems: structure, thermal control, attitude control, power, electricity distribution, telemetry and command, and an operational payload. The payload may be a number of scientific instruments, telecommunications amplifiers, or cameras to photograph the terrain below.

So that the satellite can carry the maximum payload, its construction must be as light as possible while being sturdy enough to maintain its integrity under the strains of launch. Aluminum alloy and conventional aerospace building techniques are generally employed. Floor panels, side walls, and solar array frameworks are made from aluminum or glass-fiber laminate-faced honeycomb panels. Equipment is held in place on the

▶ This tethered satellite is deployed by astronauts on board the space shuttle. It is used as a free-flying observation platform at distances up to 62 miles (100 km) from the shuttle.

◀ Three shuttle crew members hold the 4.5 ton (4 tonne) *Intelsat VI* telecommunications satellite. The satellite was captured from its orbit using the remote manipulator system arm and a new vertical perigee stage attached before it was released back into space.

honeycomb panels by inserts that thread through the honeycomb. Machined parts are made from aluminum alloy, titanium, or beryllium—materials chosen for their nonmagnetic properties as well as for their high ratios of strength to density and for their thermal stability.

Sensitive electronic equipment usually requires an operating temperature within a few degrees of 77°F (25°C). The satellite's environment, however, can vary from full sunlight to full eclipse, and it may or may not be illuminated by light reflected from Earth, so the temperatures on the satellite body exterior can be as high as 320°F (160°C) and as low as −220°F (−140°C). The apparatus on board can vary in its heat output as well, and yet the interior of the satellite must be kept in thermal balance. If the experiments are not too demanding, a passive control system may be used: the exterior finish of the satellite is chosen to absorb or emit radiation, and no further temperature control is needed. For example, a light, shiny finish absorbs and emits little heat by radiation, whereas a matt-black finish would exchange a great deal of heat with the surroundings, thereby emphasizing temperature fluctuations. Thermal blankets of multilayer aluminized plastic film are used to insulate the more heat-sensitive areas of satellites.

For complex satellites, an active thermal control system is used. A louver system on the spacecraft wall can control the inside temperature, or a heat-exchange fluid can carry heat away from localized hot spots to the wall of the satellite.

Finally, at least part of the external surface of satellites is made highly reflective to ensure that a satellite remains visible for tracking by optical telescopes on Earth long after its power sources have died and its transmissions ended. The ability to track defunct satellites is important when planning launches, since an orbiting satellite could cause a great deal of damage if it were to hit an ascending launch vehicle.

Electric power

Satellites rely heavily on solar panels for their electricity, since they require no fuel and sunlight is in plentiful supply. Solar cells can be mounted around the body of the satellite or on panels that extend from the sides of the satellite on light-weight spars. These panels can be of extremely flimsy construction, since they will experience neither air resistance nor the effects of gravity once the satellite is in orbit. A solar panel of 21.5 sq. ft. ($2 m^2$)—the size of a typical tabletop—can provide 500 watts of power all the time it is in

sunlight. Some of this energy charges a battery that provides power for emergencies and for the time the craft is in Earth's shadow.

Attitude control

The orientation of a satellite about three perpendicular axes is called its attitude, and it must be controlled so that its solar arrays point toward the Sun and its cameras, telescopes, and antennas point unwaveringly at their targets, be they on Earth or in the depths of space.

The main source of stability is the gyroscope effect, which operates independent of gravity. Some satellites have three perpendicular gyroscopes that maintain the correct attitude; simpler satellites of cylindrical construction depend on the rotation of the whole satellite to provide spin stabilization about a single axis.

Changes in attitude are effected by the deployment of control jets fixed to the body. Onboard monitoring systems identify the current attitude from the positions of astronomical bodies such as the Sun, Earth, and certain stars. The attitude-control system receives this information or an overriding ground command and demands pulses from the control jets to realign the satellite as required. The usual propellant system for these

▲ One of the major uses of satellites is to monitor weather patterns in the upper atmosphere. They are particularly useful in following the path of hurricanes so that warnings can be given in areas likely to be affected.

FACT FILE

- Solar Max, *a satellite launched in 1980 to monitor solar flares, had to be repaired in orbit by the crew of NASA's* Challenger *space shuttle after blowing fuses ten months into its mission. Using a backpack propulsion unit, the astronaut George Nelson stabilized the satellite's wobble so that it could be captured, repaired, and relaunched.*

- *The U.S. Navy's LEASAT satellites, which occupy geostationary equatorial orbits at an altitude of 22,300 miles (35,900 km) above Earth, were the first satellites specifically designed for shuttle launch. With a diameter of 14 ft. (4.2 m), they are too large for any other launching vehicle.*

- *NASA's first satellite-salvaging operation took place in November 1984, when the Palapa B–2 satellite was coaxed into* Challenger's *cargo hold by spacewalking astronauts. Two days later, a second satellite—Westar 6—was also rescued. Both these satellites had been launched unsuccessfully the previous February.*

control jets combines nitrogen tetroxide (N_2O_4) and monomethylhydrazine ($H(CH_3)NNH_2$). Future satellites may use ion propulsion, which is extremely efficient in using fuel.

Working life

Satellites have limited lifetimes for a number of reasons, two of which are limits in the availability of power for proper functioning. First, the efficiency of solar cells decreases with time, although this limitation can be compensated for to some extent by specifying excess power at the start of working life and reradiating unused electrical energy into space as heat. Second, the attitude-control systems have only a certain amount of fuel, so a satellite can stray uncorrected from its required attitude once this fuel is depleted. Some specialists are now advocating that all traces of fuel and compressed gases be discharged at the end of the working lifetime to eliminate energy sources that could cause explosions and generate large quantities of dangerous space debris.

Another limiting factor in the lifetimes of satellites is the gradual dissipation of their orbital energy through collisions with particles—a very dilute form of air resistance. As orbital energy decreases, so does the orbital altitude, and the satellite gradually falls into Earth's atmosphere. Given these limitations, current working lifetimes range from two to ten years. This range is set to increase as maintenance by space shuttle encounters becomes more commonplace.

Applications

Communications satellites are an important part of the information revolution. Telephone calls, computer data, television, and still pictures are transmitted across the world via satellite. Cheaper global communications become available as each new satellite is launched.

Weather satellites are in constant use providing pictures of cloud cover over Earth. These satellites can operate at night by observing infrared wavelengths, since there is a temperature difference between cloudy and clear areas. Other systems measure the concentration of ozone (O_3) in Earth's atmosphere, monitoring the evolution of ozone holes and helping forecast the risk of sunburn where low ozone coverage allows heavy doses of ultraviolet light to reach Earth's surface.

Other satellites help oceanographers construct accurate profiles of currents, temperatures, and densities of the oceans—a task that would be almost impossible by conventional means. Such information helps identify such phenomena as El Niño and La Niña—ocean-current systems that have widespread impacts on climate and even the movements of deep-sea fish.

Earth's resources can be studied from space far more effectively than they can from ground level. By using cameras that take images in several different color bands, crop diseases can be spotted by their effect on the reflectivity of plants. Mineral resources, cattle densities, forestry, and water supplies can be surveyed rapidly from space, and satellites can also detect environmental hazards such as fires in the Amazon rain forest, oil spills, and deliberate dumping at sea.

Satellite-borne telescopes, such as the Hubble Space Telescope, are able to receive much clearer images than could be observed from Earth and detect radiation at frequencies that are absorbed by Earth's atmosphere. Closer to home, the average consumer benefits from satellite-borne navigation systems, television, and mobile phone links. In the near future, it is likely that networks of LEO satellites will provide the communications links for rapid wireless Internet access in areas far from cable networks.

SEE ALSO: ENVIRONMENTAL SCIENCE • GLOBAL POSITIONING SYSTEM • METEOROLOGY • SPACE STATION • TELESCOPE, SPACE

Schlieren Techniques

Many problems of science and engineering involve substances that are colorless, transparent, and nonluminous, so their observation by direct visual or photographic methods is difficult. Examples include the motion of air over models of aircraft wings, problems of convection, the mixing of liquids or gases, and the detection of faults in windows.

In such cases the phenomena that are of interest frequently involve changes of refraction index. The refractive index of a material is simply the ratio of the speed of light in a vacuum to the speed of light in the material. It is a measure of how much the material will bend a light ray traversing it. Several methods are available for revealing small changes in refractive index, and those most frequently adopted are called schlieren methods, because they were originally used in Germany for detecting regions of enhanced density in optical glass, which are often in the form of streaks (in German, *Schliere*).

Suppose that a beam of light is passed through a transparent material in which the refractive index changes at right angles to the beam. The beam will be deflected by refraction from its undisturbed path. With schlieren methods, several techniques may be used to detect these deflections and enable changes in refractive index to be observed or recorded.

The arrangement of the apparatus depends on the nature and scale of the phenomena to be observed. Assume that the experiment is two dimensional, in other words, imagine that the event to be studied is contained between flat parallel windows perpendicular to the light beam and that between these windows the conditions are constant along the undisturbed path of each light ray. This situation would, for example, occur approximately in a wind tunnel experiment if a model of the section of an aircraft wing completely spanned the wind tunnel in a direction parallel to the light beam between glass windows in the side walls. Lenses or mirrors may be used as the main optical components, and it will be assumed here that mirrors are used because, if a light beam of large diameter is required, mirrors are easier and cheaper to manufacture.

A concave mirror has a focal point to which all parallel rays of light coming in along its axis are reflected, forming an inverted image. If this situation is reversed and a point source of light is placed at the focus, it will produce a beam of parallel light just like a searchlight. In practice, the mirror is tilted slightly so that the light source

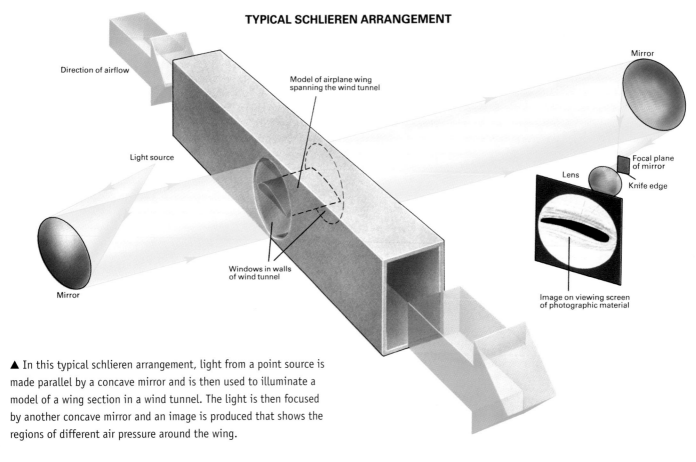

TYPICAL SCHLIEREN ARRANGEMENT

Direction of airflow

Model of airplane wing spanning the wind tunnel

Mirror

Light source

Lens

Focal plane of mirror

Knife edge

Windows in walls of wind tunnel

Mirror

Image on viewing screen of photographic material

▲ In this typical schlieren arrangement, light from a point source is made parallel by a concave mirror and is then used to illuminate a model of a wing section in a wind tunnel. The light is then focused by another concave mirror and an image is produced that shows the regions of different air pressure around the wing.

lies outside the parallel reflected beam. If a second concave mirror is now used to intercept the parallel light, it will form an image of the point source at its focus.

If the aircraft wing section is located between the two mirrors, it is possible to form an image of it by putting a lens beyond the image of the light source and to project the wing section's image to a viewing screen or photographic film. Because the light between the two mirrors is parallel, each point around the wing section itself can be considered to form a separate image of the light source at the focal point of the second mirror. If the light is undisturbed on its path, all these images will coincide, producing a point image. But if there are variations in the refractive index gradient (such as those caused by changes in air density and pressure as air flows across the wing section), some light rays will be deflected slightly and will not come to the same focal point as the rest of the light. They will, however, be imaged by the lens in the normal way.

Because the light has been displaced and because the displacement is evident at the image in front of the lens, it is possible to reveal the deviations that have taken place. A sharp straight edge, usually called a knife edge, is placed at the focal point of the second mirror in such a way that if there were no deviations, most of the light would reach the viewing screen, the total intensity being slightly reduced. If, however, the light is deflected, it may be blocked off completely by the knife edge or will pass completely unhindered. In the first case, the image of the wing at a certain point will be reduced in brightness, and in the second case, it will be increased. In this way, the slightest deviation of light across the wing section will show up as a lighter or darker region. A rectangular light source of small size is used for this arrangement. If instead of a knife edge, an optical filter with bands of different colors is used, deflection of the light rays will displace the image onto a different band of the filter so that, to the observer, the color of the light on the viewing screen changes.

Practical uses

By using discharge tubes, spark gaps, or pulsed lasers as light sources, exposure times well below a millionth of a second can be produced for schlieren photography, and various techniques are available for motion picture photography. These methods may be used to study rapidly moving phenomena, such as explosion waves or the shock waves produced by projectiles moving at high speeds. They produce no disturbances to the flow field or other event and are limited only by the

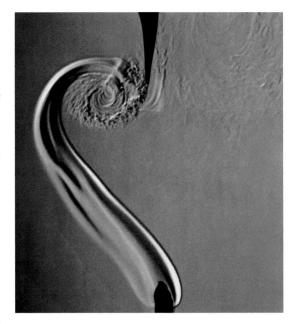

◀ A schlieren photograph of the vortex formed by a fan spinning over an alcohol lamp.

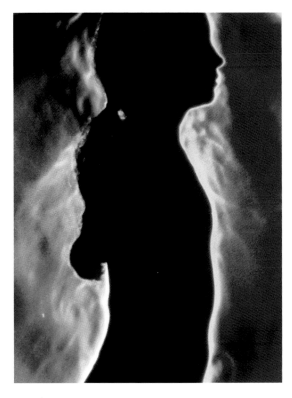

◀ This schlieren photograph of a girl shows the thin layer of air attached to her skin.

size of the optical components. Typical systems use mirrors 1 to 3 ft. (0.3–1 m) in diameter.

A development of schlieren techniques is the use of schlieren interferometry, where polarized light is used to create images that show disturbances of the light wave as a series of alternating light and dark fringes. Another system, the Foucault test, used in optics production, tests not the refractive index of the air but the quality of a single mirror. Errors on the mirror surface produce easily visible effects using this system.

SEE ALSO: CAMERA • LIGHT AND OPTICS • MIRROR • WIND TUNNEL

Screw Manufacture

The origins of the screw are not known exactly, but some types of screw devices, such as the screw auger (a kind of drill) and the Archimedes' screw, were in use in Greece and Egypt before the third century B.C.E. By the first century B.C.E., heavy wooden screws were used in presses for making wine and olive oil. The character of the screw had thus been given a new dimension and was used to exert a force, the ancient counterpart to the modern power screw or screw jack. Metal screws and nuts first appeared in the 15th century and can be seen in some medieval armor.

In the United States, in 1794, the machinist and inventor David Wilkinson designed and built a screw-cutting lathe, and later, in 1845, Stephen Fitch built the first turret lathe specifically to produce screws for an arms contract. Shortly after the American Civil War, Christopher Walker invented the completely automatic lathe solely to make screws to improve the assembly of his repeating rifles. As with many other inventions, the development of the lathe was largely inspired by the production of weapons.

A screw consists of a circular, cylindrical barrel onto which is formed a spiral ridge, which is generally of roughly triangular cross section. There are two broad categories, machine screws and wood screws. Both are generally made of metal, but whereas the machine screw is of constant diameter and mates with a threaded nut or hole, the wood screw tapers to a point, and the wood into which it is turned is deformed into a mating thread. The latter must usually be started in a hole made by an awl or a drill. The principle of operation in both cases is that, as the screw is turned, the spiral thread translates the rotation into an axial movement. This ability makes the screw useful for a variety of applications.

There are many varieties of machine screw, used to clamp machine parts together. These screws stretch when tightened so that the axial tensile load holds the parts together. The heads of smaller screws generally contain screwdriver slots, Phillips-type heads, or hexagonal recesses to take an Allen key. The larger types have hexagonal heads to which very large torques can be applied with open-ended or box-end wrenches.

Threads

The basic thread form used in the United States is the Unified Thread series developed in association with Britain and Canada. In this series, the

◄ Automatic lathes like this one are used in the manufacture of high-quality, precision screws for use in aircraft manufacture.

Unified Coarse (UNC) threads are recommended for general use, while the Unified Fine (UNF) threads are used where the screw is subjected to strong vibration or where extra strength is required. Metric threads are increasingly used and generally conform to the International Standards Organization (ISO) standards.

Self-tapping screw

Beside the woodscrew and the machine screw is a third class of screw fastener—the self-tapping screw. It forms its own mating thread in materials such as metals, plastics, glass-reinforced plastics, asbestos, and resin-impregnated plywood when driven into a drilled hole of which the diameter is less than the overall diameter of the screw. The threads are formed in the hole by the displacement of material adjacent to the hole so that it flows around the screw. A further refinement is the thread-cutting tapping screw, which has cutting edges and chip cavities that produce a mating thread by removing material.

Screw jacks

Screws that modify force and motion are known as power screws, one form being the screw jack, which converts torque (turning movement) to thrust. In one version, the thrust, used to lift a heavy object, is created by turning the screw in a stationary nut. By using a long bar to turn the screw, a small force at the end of the bar can create a large thrust force, and the screw jack can then be said to have a high mechanical advantage.

Screw production

The production of screws by machining is a fairly limited technique, employed only on fasteners of unusual design or those too small or too large to be processed by other methods. Both standard automatic lathes and special automatic screw machines are employed, using hexagonal or round stock in cut lengths. Although this method produces an excellent finish, machining of screws is slow and wasteful of metal.

Screws are produced in a wide range of sizes, head styles, and materials, all of which are determined by their applications. Until quite recently, thread forms were equally numerous and thus created problems in both standardization and manufacture. Accordingly, in 1966, the International Standards Organization proposed the restriction of threads to ISO metric and inch, coarse and fine pitches, in what is known as the preferred range of sizes. These proposals have been generally adopted throughout the world, and the advantages to manufacturing are considerable. The pitch, also called basic pitch, is the

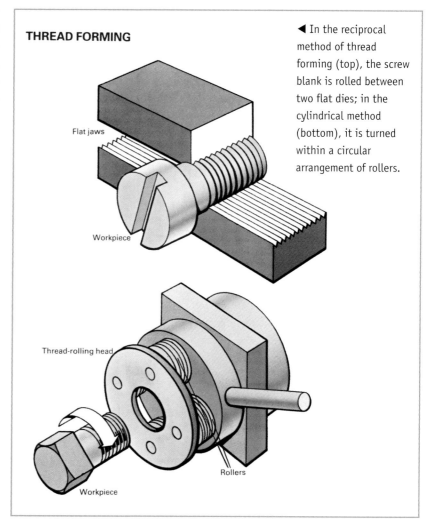

THREAD FORMING

Flat jaws

Workpiece

Thread-rolling head

Rollers

Workpiece

◄ In the reciprocal method of thread forming (top), the screw blank is rolled between two flat dies; in the cylindrical method (bottom), it is turned within a circular arrangement of rollers.

distance between a point on one thread to the corresponding point on the next thread. Pitch is also taken to mean the number of threads per inch or per centimeter. For example, the Unified Standard pitches for a ¼ in. screw are ¼ 20 (coarse), ¼ 28 (fine), and ¼ 32 (extra fine).

Screws are made from specific heading qualities of low-to-medium-carbon steel wire, stainless steel, nickel alloys, brass, and aluminum alloy. Although some of these materials are more difficult to process than others, the production methods remain much the same.

Cold heading

Cold heading is a widely used method of forming, or upsetting, a head of predetermined size and shape on one end of a cut blank of rod or wire. Production is a relatively high-speed continuous process; the wire is fed from coil mounted on a swift, or pay-off, unit. The end of the coil may be welded to the end of the next one. The wire passes through a prestraightening unit into the machine where, in a predetermined sequence, it is cut to the correct length, and depending on the number of blows required to form the head, it is punched into a tungsten-carbide die so that the head takes up the required shape, for example, hexagonal, round, recessed, and so on. After forming, the blank is automatically ejected into a receiver for further processing.

The two basic types of cold-heading machines are those fitted with split (open) dies and those fitted with solid (closed) dies. Split dyes are used for making screws with wide tolerances and greater than average lengths; solid dies are designed to achieve greater accuracy (closer tolerances) and also allow a degree of extrusion, that is, a reduction in the shank diameter of the screw blank. Extrusion is achieved within the die and is necessary so that when the threads are rolled into the metal at a later stage of production, the correct major diameter is accomplished.

In screw manufacture, the cold-heading machines are also classified as either single blow or double blow. The single-blow header applies the heading punch once for each revolution of the machine's flywheel to produce one screw for each stroke of the punch ram. The double-blow header is fitted with an indexing head containing two punches, each of which is applied once during the cycle. Thus, two strokes of the ram are required to produce one screw blank. As an alternative, the die itself may be indexed automatically, instead of the punch. Production speeds, depending on the diameter and length of the screw, can range from about 100 to 550 parts per minute.

A more advanced type of cold header is the transfer machine, which is rather like a series of single-blow, single-die headers, each linked to the other by means of a transfer mechanism. In this machine, the blank is ejected from the die after each blow, and transferred to the next station for progressive forming. One of the advantages of this type is that trimming, reduction, and pointing are all carried out by one machine.

There are many advantages of cold heading, including the high volume of production achieved and the complete elimination of material wastage. (For that reason, cold heading is called a chipless method of production.) Also, cold heading causes the metal grain to follow the contours of the head, thus avoiding stress, particularly where the underside of the head joins the shank. The process allows the use of low-carbon steels for highly stressed application, because the cold working that takes place during heading actually improves the mechanical qualities of the metal.

The disadvantages of this method are generally restricted to size. For example, very small or very large screws tend to be uneconomic to manufacture with this method, the former because of handling problems and the latter because large screws demand large and powerful machines.

The intermediate stages in manufacture between cold heading of the screws and the thread-rolling operation may include slotting of the head, trimming, and pointing.

Thread rolling

Thread rolling is also a cold-forming process. The thread form is impressed in the screw shank by rolling it in a single operation under controlled pressure between two hardened dies having the reverse profile of the specified thread. The indentation of the die thread crests causes the metal to fill the area between the thread flanks by plastic deformation. Since it is displaced from the screw blank rather than removed, the blank diameter on which the thread is rolled must be slightly undersize, about equal to the thread pitch diameter.

The pitch diameter is also called the simple effective diameter. It is the diameter of an imaginary cylinder, the surface of which would pass through the thread profiles at such a point as to make the width of the remaining groove equal to one half the basic pitch. On a perfect thread (where the groove and the thread are the same size), this will be the point at which the widths of the thread and the groove are equal.

There are three types of thread-rolling processes, the flat (reciprocating) die, the centerless cylindrical die, and the planetary rotary die. The first two processes have production speeds in the range 60 to 250 parts per minute, depending on blank diameter, while the planetary die type achieves speeds of between 60 and 2,000 parts per minute. In the reciprocating-die method, there are two flat dies, one of which is stationary while the other reciprocates, rolling the screw blank between them. With centerless cylindrical dies, there are two or three round dies, and the blank is rolled between them. In the planetary-die method, the blank is held while the dies roll around it.

In most thread-rolling operations, the screw blanks are fed automatically to the dies down a guide chute from a vibrating hopper feeder; this method ensures that the blanks are correctly presented and at the correct feed rate.

Arguably, the rolled screw thread is superior to the cut thread, since it has the same characteristics as a cold-headed product in that the fibers of the metal follow the contour of the thread and are not discontinued or severed as in the case of cut threads. The roots of rolled threads are stressed in compression, thus improving the fatigue strength, particularly in medium-carbon steels.

 SEE ALSO: Machine tool • Metalworking • Tool manufacture

Seaplane and Amphibian

◀ A Canadair water bomber, a firefighting seaplane that fills its water tanks when skimming along the surface of a lake.

The practice of flying aircraft off water is almost as old as aviation itself and results from the number of good natural runways available from the world's rivers, lakes, and harbors. It releases the aircraft from its greatest limitation, the need for specially prepared strips of ground for takeoff and landing. If, however, the seaplane is fitted with retractable wheels to exploit landing strips as well, it becomes an amphibian.

The true water plane is the flying boat. Its fuselage is designed to operate on water with most of the characteristics of a boat. Most small landplanes can be fitted with minihulls or floats instead of wheels and, as such, earn the separate designation of floatplane.

The first recorded successful flight from water was made in March 1910 by Henri Fabre of France, just over six years after the Wright brothers achieved the first sustained powered flight of a heavier-than-air aircraft. The aircraft, with its three flat-bottomed floats, was primitive, but it initiated two decades of aircraft evolution in which seaplanes played the leading role.

The next step, in 1911, introduced one of the great names of seaplane development when Glenn Curtiss of the United States flew a novel craft with a single float—to which wheels were soon added to produce the first amphibian. His first real flying boat came out the following year,

and suddenly seaplanes gained acceptance. In 1914, the world's first scheduled airline began in Florida, operating between St. Petersburg and Tampa, using Benoist flying boats.

The famous Schneider Trophy races for seaplanes were held between 1913 and 1931. Their role in stimulating high-performance technology is reflected in the progress of winning average speeds from 47.75 mph (76.8 km/h) for the first meeting to 340 mph (547 km/h) for the last. The final winner, Britain's Supermarine S.6B, later set a world record of 407 mph (655 km/h) and evolved directly into the Spitfire fighter plane of World War II fame.

Britain's efforts, in fact, led seaplane developments of all kinds through the 1920s and early 1930s, culminating in the huge Short Sarafand of 1935, which, with its 215 ft. (65.7 m) wingspan, was the largest ever biplane. By then, such devotion to biplanes had already cost Britain the lead, as faster monoplane flying boats were developed in Europe and the United States. Germany's 12-engined Dornier Do X, although never entering service, introduced the age of the giants, dominated by the great Sikorsky boats and Martin Clippers of America. Finally came the Boeing 314 Clipper, which, in 1939, established scheduled transatlantic passenger services. Largest of all was the U.S. industrialist and aviator Howard

Hughes's 460,000 lb. (208,650 kg) *Hercules*, with a 320 ft. (97.5 m) wingspan, which made its first and only flight in 1947, and could have carried 700 passengers. It is the largest aircraft ever to fly, with an overall length of 219 ft. (66.7 m).

Among the most famous aircraft of World War II are America's Consolidated Catalina and Britain's Short Sunderland flying boats, used unceasingly for maritime patrol in the Atlantic and the Pacific Oceans. The year 1953 saw the appearance of the British 310,000 lb. (140,610 kg) Saunders Roe Princess, the last of the giants, which never entered service. Several attempts were made at building smaller, jet flying boats, notably the elegant Saunders Roe SR-A1 fighter and the four-engined Martin P.6M Seamaster.

Design

Seaplane designers must understand hydrodynamics as well as aerodynamics and must appreciate the complex forces of wind on water. The variations and conflicts in design, both past and present, are as numerous as those of the boat industry. The aerodynamic factors differ little except for a preference for keeping wings, tailplane, and engines high and as far as possible from spray. The seaplane's greater bulk forward usually calls for a larger vertical tail area to control it, but the landing floats require unique considerations, such as good flotation and stability,

ruggedness and lightness, plus hydrodynamic lift with minimal spray.

A flying boat, like an ordinary boat, must have its center of buoyancy beneath its center of gravity (cg), enough displacement for its gross weight, enough freeboard to prevent swamping, and a high bow for low-speed taxiing. It differs only in the greater stability offered by wing-tip floats or other outrigger-type stabilizers, which compensate for a high cg and a minimal keel.

For takeoff, the hull must rise quickly out of the water and start planing like a speedboat if flying speed is to be attained, and so the hull bottom is designed to push the water downward. A shallow V-shaped bottom is now almost standard, often slightly concave to flatten out the spray and improve lift. Fluted bottoms with an intermediate chine, or ridge, running between keel and side improve these characteristics and are now popular on floats and small flying boats.

Unlike a speedboat, where the cg is near the stern or transom, an aircraft also needs hull support well behind the cg, to cope with displacement when at rest and to give lift during early acceleration. So, slightly behind the cg, the flying boat hull has a sharp up-break called the step, corresponding to the transom of a boat. The step reduces skin friction on the hull afterbody while planing and allows the aircraft to tilt up at liftoff to achieve a suitable flying angle for the wings.

◄ The water in a Canadair water bomber is mixed with a chemical to form a smothering foamy-white blanket, which is released onto a forest fire.

THE LAKE BUCCANEER AMPHIBIAN

The Lake Buccaneer amphibian has a fully retractable wheeled undercarriage for use on land and wing floats to provide stability on water. Steering on land is by means of the nose wheel, and a retractable rudder is used for steering on water. The engine pod is mounted on the fuselage to prevent water ingress.

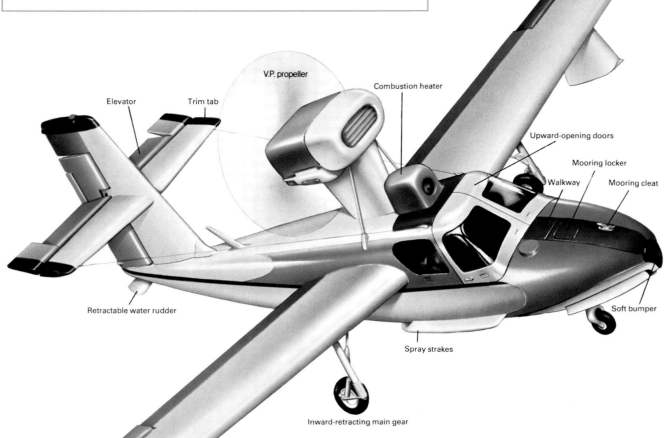

When planing, the airplane is described as being on the step and can also taxi at speed in this mode with low throttle setting while maneuvering tightly yet safely.

The floats fitted to landplanes to convert them into floatplanes are little more than small, sealed hulls. Modern floats also have some aerodynamic shape to give lift and reduce the weight penalty. Twin floats are now standard, although a single float was popular before World War II and a tail float was carried on some early seaplanes. The high stance of floatplanes, however, gives them a high cg and sensitivity to crosswinds.

Helicopters, not needing hydrodynamic gear, are often fitted with light, inflated-rubber pon-toons or have these strapped to landing skids ready for inflation by compressed gas. Some larger modern helicopters even have full boat hulls for amphibious operation.

Although seaplanes and amphibians are no longer the most common form of aircraft, they are still used in situations where landing strips are rare and where large bodies of calm water are common. In Alaska, for example, small float-planes, such as the De Havilland Beaver are still in use despite manufacture of this model having ceased. Their ability to perform short takeoff and landing (STOL) and their sturdy construction make them ideal for use in remote locations. Many small seaplanes and floatplanes are currently manufactured for leisure purposes. Some of these airplanes are microlights, which are relatively inexpensive to purchase and are therefore suitable for large numbers of enthusiasts.

SEE ALSO: AERODYNAMICS • AIRCRAFT DESIGN • AIRLINER • HYDRODYNAMICS • ULTRALIGHT AIRCRAFT

Sea Rescue

◀ For some rescue missions, helicopters are the best means of transportation. Equipped with a rescue basket and winch, they can respond quickly and fly long distances to the scene of accidents. Helicopters are also used by the coast guard to patrol the coastline and prevent people from getting into difficulties.

In the West, the first steps toward establishing sea rescue services were taken at the end of the 18th century, although by that time the Chinese had already been operating red boats (specially built rescue boats) for several hundred years. Initial efforts were concentrated on building unsinkable open boats, the first lifeboats, which were fitted with buoyancy tanks to keep them afloat. A boat of this type was successfully tested in France in 1765, and another was constructed in Britain in 1785. In the United States, a lifeboat equipped with hydrogen-filled buoyancy tanks was designed and constructed in 1816.

Today, most seafaring nations have some system for making rescues at sea, whether operated by volunteers, government agencies, or the armed forces. One of the earliest such organizations was the British Royal National Lifeboat Institution, which was formed in 1824 and is still funded by voluntary contributions—even most of the crew members are volunteers. In the United States, the responsibility for sea-rescue operations lies with the coast guard, which, when it was established in 1915, took over the duties of the older Life Saving Service, and which itself had grown out of a fleet of cutters brought in to protect the revenue at the end of the 18th century.

In many countries the efforts of such services are supplemented by the armed forces, who have the equipment and trained personnel to carry out large-scale search and rescue (SAR) operations, particularly those needing airborne support.

▶ Helicopters have an advantage over lifeboats in that they can be positioned right over the emergency. This ability is very useful, as a rescuer can be winched down to pluck someone who is hurt from the sea or rescue someone who is stranded on a vessel that cannot be boarded because of stormy conditions.

Techniques

When a vessel or individual requires rescue, the immediate action is to attract attention. This action may be done by firing distress flares or by radio. The alarm may also be raised by nearby observers, as is often the case when people get into trouble in coastal waters or estuaries. Most rescue organizations maintain a constant radio watch on the distress frequencies so that they can respond as quickly as possible.

Other vessels may be able to provide assistance or pass on the distress call, but usually it is the onshore coast guard who receives the message or spots the flares and alerts the appropriate rescue service. Generally, a helicopter or a lifeboat is alerted, though these services frequently work together. On long searches, such as when a vessel is reported missing, fixed-wing aircraft may also be used together with surface ships.

Rescue by helicopter can be quicker than by lifeboat, and if the rescued person is injured, minutes may be vital. Lifeboats are able to stay out longer without refueling and can take people from vessels that helicopters are unable to approach because of masts, rigging, or fires; they are also better able to effect searches and rescues at night. Because a helicopter can also carry more people, when large numbers are involved, it may transfer the survivors to a lifeboat and then continue the rescue operation without having to return to land.

Lifeboats are normally based in one place and may lie afloat, be launched down a slipway, or transported on a carriage down to the sea. The carriage launch uses specially designed tractors with watertight engines. The tractors may be submerged up to the driver's neck without stalling, as the air intake and exhaust pipes are extended above this level. In some countries, such as Norway, there are some cruising lifeboats that accompany fishing fleets.

Once at the scene of the casualty, the coxswain of the lifeboat must quickly assess the situation and decide which equipment will best help. The main purposes of lifeboat equipment are to help a lifeboat to reach a casualty, to allow survivors to be taken off, to maintain communications with other vessels, aircraft, and the shore, and to give protection to the survivors and the crew. One of the great advances in sea rescue has been in communications. To maintain liaison between the shore, the sea, and the air, VHF and MF radio equipment is used.

Helicopter rescue

Helicopter rescues are made using a winch system with the helicopter hovering above the vessel and lowering a cable with a sling to pick up the survivors one at a time and take them into the helicopter. Frequently, a crew member is first lowered to the ship to take charge of the opera-tion. Stretcher systems can be used for casualties, again with a helicopter crew member being lifted along with the casualty to control the movement of the stretcher.

Problems can arise when deck cranes and the superstructure prevent the helicopter from taking up a suitable position, and considerable demands are placed on the flying skill of the pilot, especially in adverse weather conditions. Individuals can also be lifted directly from the sea or from lifeboats and rafts.

Shore rescue

When a ship is in difficulties or aground on the shore, the survivors may be taken off using breeches-buoy equipment. A rocket is used to carry a light line from the shore to the vessel, and the crew uses this line to pull over the main cable and a pulley block system, which are secured to the ship, the other end of the cable being similarly secured on shore. The breeches buoy itself consists of a canvas seat arrangement in which one of the survivors sits and is pulled to shore along the fixed cable; the buoy is returned repeatedly until everyone has been taken off the ship.

Lifeboats

Some of the modern lifeboat's equipment is traditional and has been proved by years of experience. The drogue, a hooped canvas cone streamed from

◀ Far left: This tanker has run aground off Britain's southwestern coast. A lifeboat stands by as the crew is winched to safety aboard a helicopter of the RAF Inshore Rescue Service. The lifeboat can do little in such treacherous, rocky waters.
Top left: A line-throwing gun—one of the essentials carried aboard every RNLI lifeboat.
Bottom left: The introduction of high-speed inflatable lifeboats has made it easier for the rescue services to reach people in trouble in shallower coastal waters.

MODERN LIFEBOATS

The Royal National Lifeboat Institute's Arun class lifeboat is typical of the type of boat used for sea rescue by many countries around the world. The majority are self-righting, an important feature for boats that have to tackle heavy seas at speed. The Arun's hull has 26 foam-packed compartments that keep it afloat even if it is holed below the waterline. Modern boats are fitted with sophisticated tracking instruments and global-positioning equipment to help them locate stranded vessels. Satellite communications also help the rescue to be coordinated between the coast guard, armed forces, and any other vessels that might be in the immediate area that could assist in saving lives.

the stern of the boat to steady it when it is running before a sea and the breeches buoy are familiar items. The echo sounder, which tells a coxswain the exact depth of water under the boat, and the radio direction finders are among the items of electronic equipment. For some years after the invention of radar, no sets were available for boats as low in the water as lifeboats, but today radar is one of several items fitted as standard equipment.

Modern lifeboats are self-righting and have much greater stability than the nonself-righters designed between the world wars. They rely on the buoyant force provided by watertight compartments, including the engine casing and superstructure. Although the first boats to have this sort of righting arrangement also had a system of water-ballast transfer, it is no longer necessary, because watertight cabins and additional closed watertight doors have been introduced.

The main boat in use in the United States is the 44 ft. (13.4 m) Motor Lifeboat (MLB), which has a maximum range of 215 miles (345 km) and will self-right in 30 seconds or less. Its steel hull is designed to withstand the most severe conditions. The MLB is gradually being replaced by a more up-to-date 47 ft. (14.1 m) version that can self-right in 8 seconds.

In Britain, the biggest lifeboat in current use is the 52 ft. (16 m) Arun class, which has a glass fiber hull and a superstructure of welded aluminum. Seats in the wheelhouse for the five crew members are equipped with safety belts. The vessel can be controlled either from the wheelhouse or from a flying bridge above the wheelhouse. Access to the wheelhouse is through a coffer dam entrance that has two doors, as in an airlock, to prevent flooding if the vessel should capsize.

One of the limitations of these boats is that they cannot be launched down slipways. Coastlines vary greatly, and in many places, there will be no harbor with a sufficient depth of water at all states of the tide to moor a lifeboat afloat, and so a slipway is necessary.

To protect the screws and prevent cavitation, a certain hull form, with propellers in tunnels, was necessary. In Britain, the Tyne class of lifeboat, with its semiplaning hull, was designed for slipway launch and is capable of speeds up to 18 knots.

Some rescue services also use large vessels that can spend extended periods at sea. For example, the U.S. Coast Guard Reliance class cutters have a range of 6,000 miles (9,700 km) and are specially designed for search-and-rescue operations. Special features include a bridge with 360-degree visibility and a helicopter flight deck, and they are also able to tow ships of up to 10,000 tons (9,000 tonnes) to safety.

Inshore rescue

One of the most important recent innovations in sea rescue techniques has been the development of inshore lifeboats. Increasing numbers of people in all developed countries are taking their leisure on the sea, and naturally some of them get into difficulties in shallow waters that are difficult for the deep-hulled lifeboats to reach. Small dinghies, yachts, swimmers, and children on air beds may all need very quick assistance, and therefore, inshore lifeboats were introduced by the RNLI.

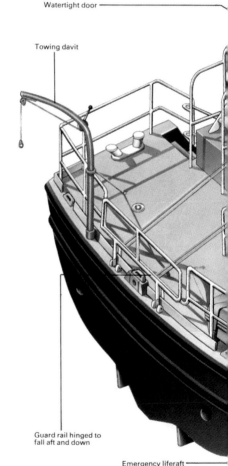

Watertight door

Towing davit

Guard rail hinged to fall aft and down

Emergency liferaft

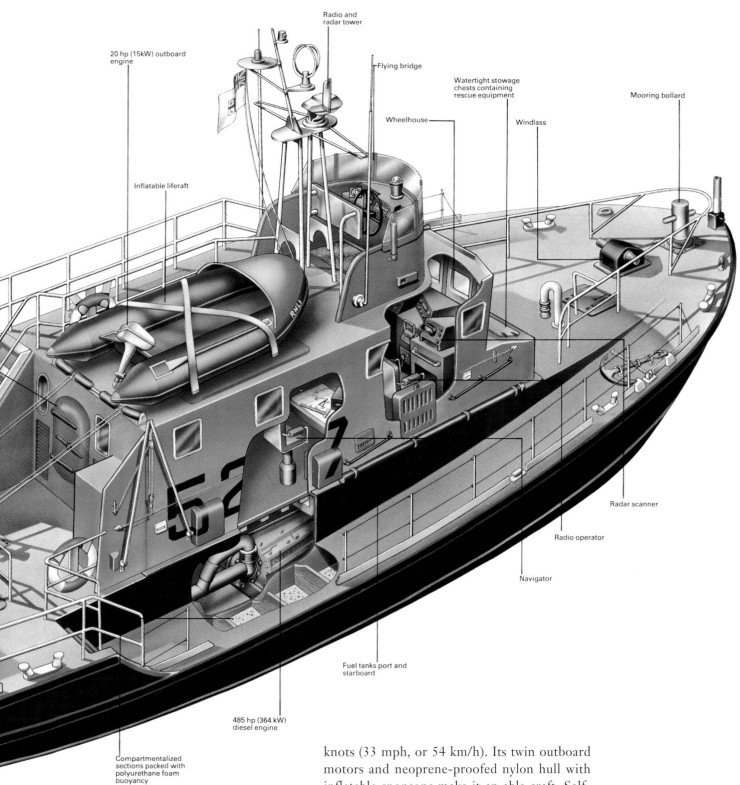

20 hp (15kW) outboard engine

Radio and radar tower

Inflatable liferaft

Flying bridge

Wheelhouse

Watertight stowage chests containing rescue equipment

Windlass

Mooring bollard

Radar scanner

Radio operator

Navigator

Fuel tanks port and starboard

485 hp (364 kW) diesel engine

Compartmentalized sections packed with polyurethane foam buoyancy

At first, these tiny inflatable dinghies powered by a small outboard engine were not taken seriously, but they soon proved their worth.

Inshore lifeboats can be launched quickly from a beach and are capable of high speeds once in the water. A typical design, the Atlantic 21, is highly maneuverable and can reach about 29 knots (33 mph, or 54 km/h). Its twin outboard motors and neoprene-proofed nylon hull with inflatable sponsons make it an able craft. Self-righting is achieved by means of an air bag fitted on a frame over the stern. If the lifeboat should capsize, the air bag is inflated from the upturned position, the stern is pushed up, and the boat rights itself.

SEE ALSO: GLOBAL POSITIONING SYSTEM • HELICOPTER • RADIO • SELF-RIGHTING BOAT

Security System

A typical security system is a device or installation that helps protect people, property, and buildings from theft, fire, aggression, or intrusion. Some security systems help in law enforcement by providing information on the location of individuals who have had their movements restricted, such as early-release convicts on a tagging program.

Some security systems are acquired and operated privately, such as household intruder alarms. Others are maintained and operated by security firms that charge for their services, as is the usual case for the defense of a large commercial building. Public security systems are operated by the police and other security forces as a deterrent against crime, and as a means of collecting video evidence to help secure convictions.

Although many aspects of security systems are automated and secure against tampering, there are frequently human elements, such as security guards, that could be vulnerable to blackmail, corruption, or temptation. Hence, careful selection of personnel of high integrity is fundamental to an effective security system.

One form of selection technique is vetting, whereby a candidate's integrity is investigated by interviewing family, associates, and former employers, as well as by consulting police records if available. Other techniques include polygraph (lie-detector) tests and psychometric analysis, which can provide some indication of character through a person's responses to a series of apparently neutral questions.

Depending on the sensitivities of their positions, other employees can be subjected to vetting as part of their appointment procedure. Also, the hiring contracts of many manufacturing and retail companies include clauses that allow the security personnel of the company to inspect the employees' baggage, vehicles, and even homes for evidence of pilfering or theft of information.

Protection against intruders

A major part of the security of a building is its resistance to unauthorized access. The precise details of security systems vary to suit different applications, but most systems include some means to defend the perimeter of a secure location; they may be combined with motion sensors that detect intruders and other systems to detect when doors open or windows break.

Perimeter defense. Perimeter fences or walls are physical barriers that keep casual or accidental intruders out, and they may be supplemented by motion-sensitive floodlights or audible alarms

◀ This tower contains equipment for emitting and detecting microwave beams. Several such towers around the perimeter of a site form a system for intruder detection—an alarm is activated if one of the beams is interrupted.

that warn potential intruders that further ingress is likely to meet resistance from security guards, often accompanied by trained guard dogs.

Alternatively, the perimeter defense system might give the intruder no indication that he or she has been detected, alerting instead a security guard stationed in a central control room. The guard can then proceed to inspect the area where the intruder has been detected or view the images from closed-circuit television (CCTV) cameras in that area. At night, these cameras may use light from constantly lit lamps, or they can use image intensifiers to make the meagre ambient light sufficient to illuminate the intruder. Alternatively, the intruder can be viewed using both invisible infrared light from appropriate lamps and infrared-sensitive CCTV cameras.

Motion sensors. A variety of techniques can be used to detect moving intruders, either in the grounds of a building or within the building itself. Beams of infrared light can span the gaps between sources and photocell detectors, so the passage of an intruder through the beam temporarily interrupts the current from the detector, so triggering the alarm. Microwave and ultrasound transceivers can detect moving objects by the frequency shift of reflected radiation, just as Doppler radar does. Other detectors, called passive infrared detectors, sense the presence of humans by the infrared radiation given off by a warm body.

Many motion sensors can operate over a range of sensitivities and must be set according to the environment where they will be used. This feature helps minimize the number of false alarms caused by movement of leaves and wildlife and even drapes or sheets of paper in drafty rooms.

Other detectors. Various electromechanical devices can detect when windows are broken and doors forced or when a window or door is opened outside normal working hours and the alarm system has been armed. Thin strips of conducting foil attached to a window can split if a window is broken, triggering an alarm when the current that they carry is interrupted. Opening doors and windows can be detected by a simple switch in the frame, similar to the switches that operate refrigerator lights. Also, the impact that breaks a window or door lock can be detected by vibration sensors similar to those of car alarms.

Patrols. Another approach to the protection of buildings is a security patrol, whereby one guard or more makes regular inspections of vulnerable premises. The effectiveness of such patrols can be improved by using a network of checkpoints, where the guard registers his or her presence by entering a secure code on a keypad or turning a key. The alarm is raised if a guard fails to report on time at any point along the route, indicating a possible attack. The patrol system has several weaknesses, however. Determined intruders can often establish the patrol pattern by observation and then attack when no patrol is due; also, guards can be coerced into giving up the key or code for the checkpoint, rendering the checkpoints useless.

Personal identification

Entrance to a building or to a secure area within a building, must often be restricted to authorized personnel. Where few people are authorized to enter, it might be sufficient to rely on a security guard to recognize authorized personnel and challenge unfamiliar persons. Where a large number of people are authorized for access, it is

▼ The integrated security system of a commercial property comprises several elements. Loop detectors foil attempts to remove tagged items without authorization, while video surveillance can deter the theft of untagged items. A network of sensors detect intruders out of working hours, and fire sensors raise the alarm in case of fire. The fire and burglary alarm systems can be linked by telephone to the monitoring post of a security firm or to a police or fire department, as appropriate to the event.

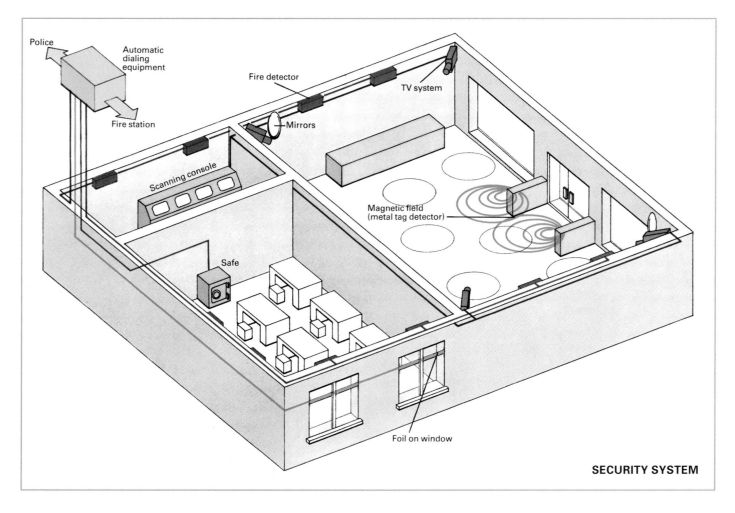

Police
Automatic dialing equipment
Fire detector
TV system
Fire station
Mirrors
Scanning console
Magnetic field (metal tag detector)
Safe
Foil on window

SECURITY SYSTEM

This CCTV camera surveys the grounds of a factory, transmitting images to a central control, where guards watch for intruders.

usual to rely on an automated system to control access. In one such system, authorized personnel are issued with plastic cards that usually carry a photograph and sometimes a fingerprint of the bearer. A magnetic strip on the card carries a code that can be identified by card readers at automatic turnstiles or lock-controlled doors, allowing or denying access according to the code. In some cases, the card reader also requires a secure code to be typed on a keypad before entry is allowed.

Some systems dispense with identity cards, relying instead on some form of automatic recognition to identify an individual by comparison with database entries. Some systems use voice recognition; others use optical recognition of fingerprints or faces, for examples. Optical recognition of the patterns on the irises of eyes have proven to be particularly foolproof.

Video surveillance

Closed-circuit television (CCTV) cameras are used to protect the security of crowds in public spaces, such as streets, malls, and sports arenas. Mounted on posts, CCTV cameras afford better views than those available to guards on foot, and video recordings of the views from such cameras are useful in identifying perpetrators of assaults, kidnappings, and robberies, for example.

A combination of CCTV, optical recognition, and a database of images of known offenders can be used to detect when a suspected individual is in the view of a camera, alerting an operator to the presence of that person. Such systems are particularly useful in controlling crowd violence at sports events and public demonstrations.

Monitors in this subway control room show images from key points of the network. They are used to help controllers react to station congestion, assaults, and other platform incidents.

While video surveillance is undoubtedly useful in security and law enforcement, it is not without critics. Some people have the opinion that CCTV is an excessive invasion of privacy or that optical recognition could result in reformed offenders being harassed. Others point out that the clarity of CCTV images is not always adequate to be admissible as evidence in court.

Tagging

Various forms of electronic tags are used to prevent theft. All use radio-frequency (RF) transceivers to detect the presence of a tagged object.

The simplest form of tag is the ferrite strip inserted in the spines of books to prevent their theft from libraries. The strip is cut to such a length that, when it passes through an arch-shaped RF antenna at the exit of the library, it retransmits a signal at half the original frequency. When a book is properly checked out, the librarian passes it around the antenna for collection. If a person tries to smuggle the book out, however, the transceiver antenna detects the lower frequency and triggers an audible alarm.

Articles in shops are protected using stud or adhesive strip tags that contain circuits that emit radio signals when energized by a radio signal from loop antennas at the shop doorway. After purchase, studs are removed using a powerful electromagnet that releases the stud from its clasp. In the case of strips, the sales assistant passes the item over a strong radio source that overloads and deactivates the circuit in the strip.

More expensive items, such as computer equipment in offices, can be protected by RFID (radio-frequency identification) tags. These tags emit coded signals in response to radio pulses from a transceiver. Each code is unique, so it allows equipment to be identified against a database. Transceivers at access points raise the alarm if an attempt is made to smuggle equipment out of a building. If the whole of a building is equipped with transceivers, the system can be

used to locate equipment and track its movements between departments. The system can also be configured so that equipment emits a distress signal if its power supply fails or is disconnected.

Tags can also be used to keep low-risk offenders under house arrest rather than in prison for part of their sentence, thereby allowing convicts to make a living during their sentences. In such systems, an RFID tag is securely attached to the convict's wrist or ankle, and a transceiver with a telephone connection is installed in the convict's home. The convict must report in by telephone at the start of each detention period, the RFID tag confirming that he or she is within the specified range of the transceiver. The central control registers these reports and makes random calls to check that the offender is abiding by the terms of the house arrest. Failure to do so results in the convict having to return to prison.

A variant of the tagging system is used to protect vulnerable vehicles, such as the secure trucks that collect takings from stores and deliver cash wages. Such devices use signals from global positioning system (GPS) satellites to ascertain the location of the vehicle and then transmit that information via a cellular telephone network. In this way, the location of a stolen vehicle can be monitored and reported to the police.

Store detectives

While tags are useful in protecting high-value items such as clothing and compact discs, disposable adhesive tags are too expensive to be used with low-value items, such as cans of food. Hence, stores that trade in low-value goods, such as grocery stores, use uniformed and plainclothes detectives to deter shoplifters. CCTV, ceiling-mounted mirrors, and direct observation, are used to spot potential shoplifters.

When a person has been seen putting an item in his or her clothing, for example, the detective must watch that person pass through the checkout to see whether payment is made. If not, the guard challenges the shoplifter to provide proof of purchase as he or she leaves the store.

In some cases, high-value display items cannot be tagged, for example, electronic goods and domestic appliances, where adhesive tags would leave unacceptable marks. Such items are protected by electric cables that typically thread through a door handle or some other opening in the device. Any attempt at theft results in a plug-and-socket connection being broken, and the break in the circuit raises the alarm.

Plainclothes detectives are sometimes required to check the integrity of sales assistants rather than customers. For this purpose, the detective makes trial purchases and watches for irregularities in till transactions and for attempts to remove money that has not been registered.

Fire protection

Building fires endanger life and property, and their detection and extinction is therefore an important function of security systems. Some fire-detection systems merely raise the alarm, either at a central control room or at the local fire department; others operate in conjunction with automatic firefighting systems.

The detectable sign of a fire is the production of ions by combustion processes. These ions trigger ionization detectors when they pass through a detection chamber, causing changes in electrical conductivity. As a fire progresses, smoke can be detected by the drop in current from a photoelectric cell as its light source is obscured, and flames can be detected by infrared heat detectors. Usually, circuitry in such detectors monitors the flicker rate of flames to prevent false readings from normal infrared sources, such as heaters.

The heat of a fire can also be detected using a bimetallic strip made of two metals of different thermal expansion characteristics. As temperature rises, the strip bends until it touches an electrical contact that completes the alarm circuit.

Once a fire is detected, a central control releases electromagnetic catches on any fire doors that have them and opens smoke vents where installed to release the heat and fumes of a fire. Water can be pumped to the fire zone if appropriate. Where water-sensitive chemicals or electrical equipment is present, some systems sound an evacuation alarm first and then seal and flood the fire with carbon dioxide, an extinguishing gas.

▲ A bank customer uses her magnetic card to gain access to a lobby that contains automatic teller machines (ATMs). The same card, together with a personal identification number (PIN), allows a customer to withdraw money and perform other transactions by ATM.

 SEE ALSO: BURGLAR ALARM • LOCK, SECURITY • OPTICAL SCANNER

Seismology

▲ Puu Oo crater erupting in Hawaii's Volcanoes National Park. Volcanoes and earthquakes both tend to occur in the same regions, commonly where tectonic plates meet or diverge or, as in the case of the Hawaiian Islands, within a plate at an intraplate hot spot.

Seismology is the study of earthquakes. Because humans first lived in earthquake-prone areas such as Ethiopia, Mesopotamia, and Indonesia, they have always known and feared earthquakes. Over the past 100 years, however, scientists have learned to use earthquakes as a powerful tool for investigating Earth's interior.

In 132 B.C.E., a device for registering seismic activity was made by Chang Hâng in China. It had a number of metal balls arranged around the rim of an urn so that an earth tremor would disturb a central column and thus operated a mechanism that dropped one of the balls into a metal holder causing a noise. The direction of the earthquake was worked out by observing which balls fell and which did not. From this simple device, today's sensitive seismometers have developed into complex instruments, and a science has grown up with them. There is now an industry involved in using artificially generated seismic shocks to search Earth's crust for minerals. The data collected from these shocks have so far provided a wealth of knowledge on conditions near Earth's surface. A technique called seismic tomography, developed in the 1980s, uses seismic waves to construct three-dimensional images of Earth's interior. A similar technique is employed on the *Solar and Heliospheric Observatory (SOHO)* space probe, which collects data on solar waves that pass through the Sun and uses the information to create internal images. This technique has resulted in a new science called helioseismology.

Seismographs

In the past 100 years, there have been many advances in the design of seismographs, which record the movements of Earth's crust at a given location. There are now seismic recording devices fixed in countries throughout the world making continuous recordings. Portable equipment is available that can be installed for temporary projects, while remote locations may be monitored using telemetric devices that record and transmit information to a central collecting station. Any device that measures seismic activity is a seismometer; those that record the activity, for example, by means of a pen recorder are known as seismographs.

It has not proved possible to design a seismograph to measure faithfully the movement of Earth's crust in every direction at once in response to seismic waves. What invariably happens is that each seismic observatory has at least two seismographs, one each for the horizontal and vertical parts of the movement. Often there are three—the horizontal component is measured in two directions.

The horizontal-component seismograph consists of a pendulum with a heavy weight. Just as the French physicist Léon Foucault's pendulum, which is extremely long, always swings in the same direction in space, thus showing the rotation of Earth beneath it, the seismograph pendulum tends to stay in the same place by virtue of its inertia while the ground vibrates beneath it. The difference is that the seismograph pendulum is not set swinging—it is restrained from swinging by means of damping of some kind. The pendulum has a resonant period—the time it would normally take to complete a whole swing—and if the period of the earthquake waves happens to coincide with it, the result will be meaningless.

Periods expected from seismic activity are approximately ¹⁄₁₀₀ to 3,000 seconds, and one seismograph will not be suitable for the entire range. Consequently, a range of seismographs is needed, including some with a long resonant period to measure the longer-period waves. A true pendulum with a period of many seconds would be impractical, so a practical pendulum seismograph consists of a weight on a horizontal beam, pivoted at the end, suspended by a wire from a point not quite above the pivot. The pendulum is slightly out of balance and if pushed will swing with a period of up to a minute.

The vertical-component seismograph is essentially a weight on the end of a spring. As in the case of the horizontal-component device, the period of vibration of the spring is increased by holding the weight out at a slight angle by means of a horizontal bar. The ground movement is measured by the extension of the spring. The exact value of the disturbance, typically less than 0.04 in. (1 mm), can be found only if the physical characteristics of the seismograph are available.

More recent seismographs use electromagnetism. They are made of electrically inductive material and are surrounded by coils so that an electric current is produced when the pendulum moves. The damping is also carried out electromagnetically. This is a very sensitive arrangement and also gives a tape output, which can be readily used with computers, allowing the information to be more easily analyzed.

▲ A solar-powered earthquake-monitoring station, which transmits a continuous record of seismic activity to a central collecting station.

▼ Deep-focus quakes have little effect at the surface, but their location can be discovered by comparing information recorded at different stations.

A specialized type of seismograph, first introduced in 1935, allows the strain in Earth's materials to be measured directly. This instrument is useful in earthquake areas and works by recording the variation in distance between two points some 60 ft. (18 m) apart. Also providing information are tiltmeters, which show the buildup in tilt before large earthquakes.

Today, seismographs may be positioned at remote sites and linked together by radio or satellite to form huge arrays that are much more powerful than any one single unit. The resulting data is stored in large computers, which give fine details of how the ground actually breaks, as well as the size of the earthquake and its precise location. The farther away one is from an earthquake, the less one will be shaken. Pictures of very serious damage reveal that it is usually the result of poor construction or building on soft ground. Soft ground can increase shaking by many times—it caused buildings to collapse in the bayside Marina district of San Francisco 50 miles (80 km) from the center of the 1989 Californian (Loma Prieta) earthquake.

Earth studies

Waves from earthquakes and artificial explosions can reveal a great deal about Earth's interior. The waves generated are of three main types. The first are surface waves, which are very strong close to the earthquake's epicenter, where they cause most of the quake damage. These waves are attenuated

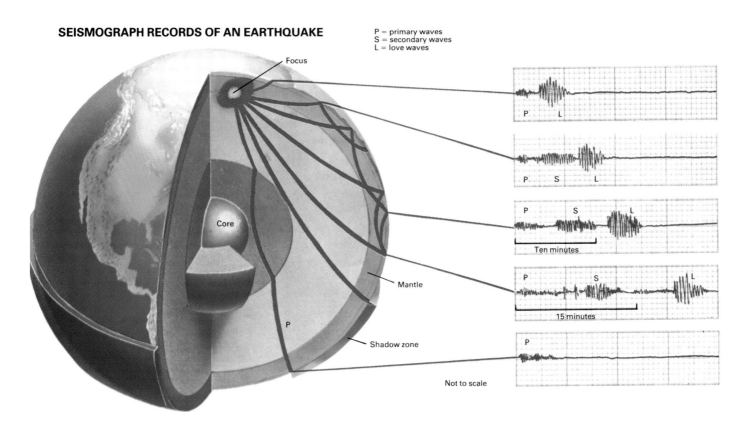

SEISMOGRAPH RECORDS OF AN EARTHQUAKE

P = primary waves
S = secondary waves
L = love waves

Focus

Core

Mantle

P

Shadow zone

Not to scale

P L

P S L

P S L
Ten minutes

P S L
15 minutes

P

(reduced in intensity) rapidly, however, and become undetectable in most cases about 200 miles (320 km) from the epicenter, though there are some much weaker waves, known as Love waves that can travel great distances. Another type of surface wave is the Rayleigh wave, which combines longitudinal and vertical vibrations. At a distance from the epicenter, the waves observed are generally those that have traveled through the body of Earth itself, normally called P-waves and S-waves, being primary and secondary respectively. P-waves are associated with "push-pull," and S-waves with "shake." They differ because in P-waves the particles of the material through which the wave passes are moved backward and forward along the line of travel, and in S-waves the movement is perpendicular to the line of travel. It is a rule that P-waves travel faster than S-waves, and thus they arrive at an observing station sooner and are therefore called primary. In addition, S-waves are attenuated so heavily by liquids that they will effectively not pass through liquids at all. Every major property change inside Earth, such as the division between the crust (the outermost layer) and mantle (the bulk of Earth), will transmit P- and S-waves at different speeds and refract them at different angles, so that the various layers of Earth are distinguishable by the location and strength of waves arriving from their upper and lower surfaces. In addition, the outer part of Earth's central core is known to be liquid because it does not transmit S-waves.

In the late 19th century, it was observed that earthquake waves, apart from surface waves, received very close to the epicenter (the point on the surface vertically above the earthquake center, or focus) are heavily attenuated and altered or

▲ This sophisticated apparatus to monitor changes in Earth's crust, the tilt of the landscape, and even such things as Earth's gravity and magnetism has been set up in Tokyo, an area prone to earthquakes. In densely populated urban areas, advance warnings of quakes would prevent the loss of thousands of lives.

completely lost, causing an apparent shadow. Other shadow zones are observed at different distances from the epicenter, and during the early years of the 20th century, this fact was used to discover the nature of the various interior layers of the Earth. The core, for example, was discovered in 1906 as a result of a shadow zone on the opposite side of Earth to the epicenter in which few waves are received. It almost certainly consists of liquid iron and nickel, first, because these metals are major constituents of metallic meteorites from which the planets are believed to have accumulated and also because the pressure and temperatures present in Earth's core would not allow any other likely liquid to exist.

The IDA network

In the early 1980s, the International Deployment of Accelerometers (IDA) Seismic Network was set up. The IDA network is an array of specially designed ultralong-period seismographs arranged around Earth, dividing the crust into 20 equal-area triangles. The aim of the IDA Network is to study Earth tides—distortions of Earth's crust caused by the interaction of Earth's and the Moon's gravitational fields—and Earth's normal modes. In the period following a large earthquake, the whole planet is set into oscillation, like a bell. The oscillations, which occur at a discrete set of resonant frequencies, are the normal modes. The longest period mode is 54 minutes; the shortest, 30 seconds.

The sensors (La Coste and Romberg gravity meters) have detection periods longer than 20 seconds. Employing a zero-length spring—corresponding to a regular pendulum with an extremely long period—they have a low mechanical drift, allowing the minute movements of the crust to be measured accurately.

◄ Studying a trace of the North Sea made by setting off a series of arc discharges underwater and then detecting the echoes from the rocks. This technique is useful for detecting the type of rock formations where oil may be found.

Causes of earthquakes

Earthquakes are caused by some adjustment of Earth's material and may be deep or shallow. The shallow earthquakes, within 30 miles (50 km) of Earth's surface, are by far the most numerous and mainly occur in zones of geological activity, for example, the midocean ridges, edges of continents, and large volcanic areas, such as Hawaii. They are caused by friction in bodies of magma—molten material—welling up to the surface at the centers of oceans or by material moving back down into the Earth at the edges of continents. As the magma makes its way to the surface, it must alter its chemical form many times. These changes of state involve changes in crystal structure and hence in volume. This change always results in expansion, because the temperature and pressure of the material are falling steadily and forcing surrounding rocks to move aside, the disturbance sending the waves through Earth.

Heat is also released by the changes in state undergone by the minerals; it helps to drive the volcanic activity in the midocean ridges, the result being increased heat flow along these ridges and their landward extensions, such as the central part of Iceland and the rift valley of Ethiopia.

At the edges of the oceans (in cases where material is moving downward), the situation is almost exactly the opposite. Material is carried deep into Earth's crust, where it remelts, and as it is carried downward, corresponding changes of state occur. Hence, at the edges of oceans, the deeper earthquakes occur away from the ocean

EARTHQUAKE WAVES

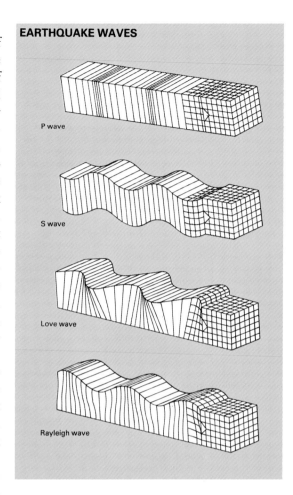

P wave

S wave

Love wave

Rayleigh wave

◄ Earthquake waves travel in different modes and at different velocities through Earth's crust. The intervals between the arrival of each type of wave at a seismic station can tell scientists where a quake occurred and how strong it was.

and close to the nearby continental land mass. Here, too, volcanoes are driven by the accompanying heat, so that island chains, such as Japan, are built of volcanic material. The earthquakes to the southeast of Japan, in the deep ocean trench where the material sinks, are only a few miles down, while those below Tokyo are many tens of miles down.

Earthquakes are measured on scales of intensity, one of them being the Mercalli scale, which has a range of 1 to 12. The lower figures measure mild quakes, and the larger, increasingly strong ones. However, the Mercalli scale lacks precision, and the Richter scale is often used instead, particularly for measuring severe earthquakes, which on the Mercalli scale would all be classified as 12. The Richter scale, named after the U.S. scientist who invented it, Charles F. Richter, is an open-ended scale, though the maximum so far recorded on Earth is around 9. The intensity measured may be quoted either as its strength at the observing station or as the intensity that it would have had at the epicenter. Many earthquakes take place in remote regions where there are no seismographs to record them, but their strengths are known from the records at distant stations.

FACT FILE

■ At a depth of 3,700 miles (6,000 km), the pressure at Earth's core, measured by changes in seismic wave velocity, is 3.5 million times as high as the atmospheric pressure at Earth's surface.

■ The greatest depth at which earthquakes have been detected by seismologists is 435 miles (700 km). At this depth, descending slabs of Earth's mantle become a part of the surrounding material.

■ In order to reproduce deep mantle and core pressures in the laboratory, seismologists use the diamond-anvil cell, in which materials are compressed between the sharp points of diamonds, thus giving enormous pressures over small areas.

SEE ALSO: EARTH • EARTHQUAKE • GEOPHYSICS • PLATE TECTONICS

Self-Righting Boat

Safety on the water is important to any sailor. One of the biggest dangers is the risk of capsizing in rough weather conditions. Even big boats are susceptible to swamping, which can sink smaller vessels in a matter of minutes. Just keeping the hull afloat can make a great deal of difference to the survival of anyone thrown into the sea while waiting to be rescued.

Boats capsize when they are tipped at 90 degrees to the vertical. Dinghy sailors can usually right the boat by climbing over the side and standing on the center plate to bring it back to an upright position, but they have to take care not to turn the boat over the other way. The weight of the mast and wet sails can add to the difficulties of righting the boat in rough weather.

Most small boats are built with buoyancy mechanisms that will help them stay afloat long enough for the crew to try to right them. However, there is an increasing trend among small-boat manufacturers to design craft with mechanisms to right themselves if they should capsize. Adding ballast to the keel and buoyant materials to the hull has proved successful in some designs when combined with rapid drainage and watertight cockpits. These boats are almost unsinkable unless prevented from righting by crew error. There are bigger boats, however, that

need to be able to survive capsizing in extreme conditions and quickly bring themselves back to an upright position—they are the rescue boats.

Lifeboats

All modern lifeboats are built to a self-righting design that makes them virtually unsinkable. Self-righting lifeboats of the 19th century were not liked by many crews, as the main buoyancy for righting was provided by high end boxes. They could not be built too high, otherwise they obstructed vision, so the boats had to be kept fairly narrow, reducing their initial stability and increasing the tendency to capsize.

Developments after World War II to make lifeboats safer relied on the buoyant force provided by watertight compartments, including the engine casing and superstructure. The Oakley self-righting system—named for its inventor, Richard Oakley—had a ballast tank in the bottom of the hull that was normally filled with water. A second tank—the righting tank—was mounted on the port side. If the lifeboat capsized, water rushed from the ballast tank into the righting tank so that either the turning movement was checked or the boat was turned through 360 degrees. Once the lifeboat returned to its normal position, water flowed back from the righting tank into the

▲ This Hawk 20 sailboat has been designed to right itself if it should capsize and is unsinkable. Its sealed buoyancy compartments are filled with closed-cell foam, which will keep the hull afloat even if it is punctured. The Hawk self-rights because of its ballast ratio, which is nearly half the weight of the whole boat and has been carefully shaped and positioned along the keel to pull the boat back upright.

SELF-RIGHTING BOAT

There are a number of mechanisms for capsized boats to right themselves. The Oakley mechanism shown right has an ingenious system of tanks and valves that brings it the right way up almost immediately. Every new lifeboat must undergo a self-righting trial before it can be granted a certificate of seaworthiness. A boat should be able to right itself within 5 to 8 seconds.

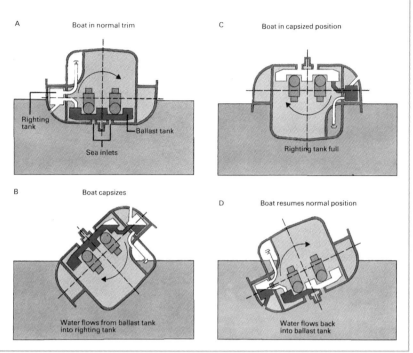

A   Boat in normal trim

Righting tank
Ballast tank
Sea inlets

C   Boat in capsized position

Righting tank full

B   Boat capsizes

Water flows from ballast tank into righting tank

D   Boat resumes normal position

Water flows back into ballast tank

Testing

One of the first tests every new lifeboat has to undergo is a righting trial. Trials usually take place on a calm but reasonably deep stretch of water such as a harbor. The boat is positioned about 50 ft. (15 m) away from the quayside with a couple of mooring ropes to stop her from drifting away. Then a parbuckle—a huge, double-thickness length of rope suspended from a crane—is attached to the craft. The two loose ends of the rope are secured to the nearside deck, while the rest of the rope is passed under the keel and attached to a quick-release mechanism.

As the crane begins to lift, the parbuckle heels the boat over onto its beam end and then farther still until it is floating upside down in the water. At this point, the quick-release mechanism is unhooked, the parbuckle falls free, and the boat is left, one hopes, to right itself. If all goes well, then within 5 to 8 seconds, the boat will be back right side up with water flowing off its decks and housetop.

ballast tank once again. The whole operation was controlled by specially designed valves. The introduction of watertight cabins and additional closed watertight doors eventually rendered this system out of date.

Constructional development of lifeboats has brought several completely new concepts. Designs have always been tied to the requirements of strength and ability to stand the worst weathers, because lifeboats put to sea when other vessels are seeking shelter. As a result, airtight buoyancy compartments have been incorporated in the hulls so that if the hull is punctured in several places, the lifeboat will remain afloat.

The 44 ft. (13.4 m) steel-hulled lifeboat developed in the United States and used by the coast guard rescue service has been widely adopted by other countries. Capable of speeds of about 15 knots, it is exceptionally maneuverable, self-bailing, and self-righting. The larger, 52 ft. (15.9 m), British Arun class lifeboat, initially built in wood, is constructed in GRP (glass-reinforced plastic) or glass fiber, which had to be stringently tested before acceptance. Boats of this class have speeds in excess of 20 knots, are self-righting, and like the 44 ft. lifeboats, lie afloat. They have double-skinned hulls, the spaces between the inner and outer skins being filled with expanded polyurethane foam, which keeps the lifeboat afloat even if all 26 of the watertight compartments are punctured at the same time.

Smaller inshore rescue craft are fitted with inflatable air bags mounted on the stern of the craft. The bags are slightly off center so that the boat is righted immediately.

▼ The boats used by the U.S. Coast Guard are designed to right themselves even in the roughest of seas.

SEE ALSO: BOAT BUILDING • SAILING • SEA RESCUE • SHIP • SPEEDBOAT • WATER • WAVE MOTION

Semiconductor

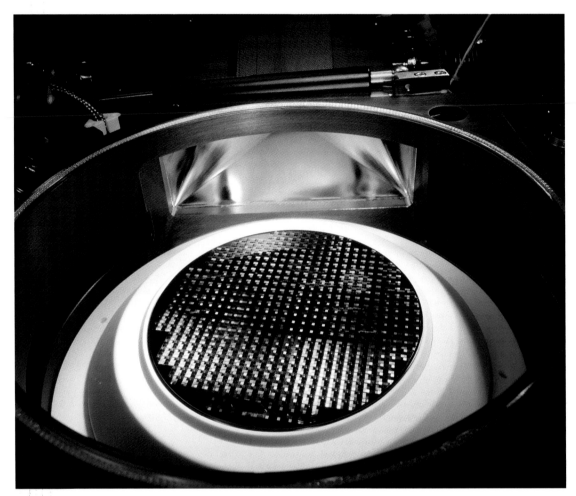

◀ A circular wafer of semiconductor material being etched to produce microchips. Extremely clean and dust free conditions must be maintained in the manufacture of these devices.

Materials can be divided into three main types according to the way in which they allow the flow of electricity when a potential difference (voltage) is applied across them. With insulators there is no current flow, while with conductors a comparatively large current flow will occur, the magnitude of the flow (for a given potential difference) depending on the conductance of the material. The third type of material is the semiconductor, which as the name suggests, has properties that lie between those of conductors and insulators with a limited flow of current occurring. Semiconductors possess conductivities (represented by the Greek letter σ, sigma) within the range of 10^{-8} and 10^3 siemens per cm, their conductivity varying considerably with the purity of the material and with external factors such as temperature, magnetic field, and incident light. The control of such variables allows a wide range of electronic devices to be produced.

A large number of chemical elements and compounds have semiconductor properties, with the most important being germanium and silicon (group IV) and the III–V compounds formed from elements such as gallium, arsenic, indium, and phosphorus (the numerals refer to groups in the periodic table). In these materials, the electric conductivity is determined by the number of elementary positive charges (holes) and negative charges (electrons) that are free to move and so can take part in conduction. The density of these free carriers and, hence, the conductivity, depend on the material structure, the presence of certain impurities, and the temperature.

Although the concept of a positive-charge carrier—a hole—is difficult to explain rigorously, being based on quantum mechanics, it can be considered as simply being an electron vacancy (that is, the absence of an electron from a valency bond of the semiconductor crystal). For example, silicon is a tetravalent compound with each of the four electrons in the outer shell being shared by the four neighboring atoms to give four covalent bonds. With a pure, defect-free crystal at low (absolute) temperatures, these bonds are intact, but as the temperature rises, some of the bonds will be broken, releasing electrons and creating holes.

The electrons can move through the crystal, as in a conductor, and so can the holes. This movement is achieved by the transfer of an electron from some other area to fill the original hole, while creating a hole at its original position. In a pure semiconductor, the number of holes produced is equal to the number of electrons, and such a material is known as an intrinsic semiconductor. When a potential difference is applied across the semiconductor, the electrons move toward the negative potential, and the total current flow is the sum of the electron and hole currents.

The number and type of the charge carriers in an extrinsic semiconductor are controlled by the addition of impurities, with the number of valence electrons of the impurity determining the type of carrier produced—a technique known as doping. Only very small amounts of impurities are needed to increase the conductivity of a semiconductor. In some cases, for example, an addition of around 0.01 percent of an impurity will result in a fourfold increase in conductivity. With impurities such as phosphorus and arsenic, which have five valence electrons, four of the electrons can bond normally to the tetravalent silicon crystal structure, leaving a free electron. The effect is to increase the number of free electrons, giving an *n*-type (*n* for negative) semiconductor with a preponderance of free electrons. In contrast, doping with boron, which is trivalent, results in an excess of holes and gives a *p*-type (*p* for positive) semi-

conductor. Free electrons still exist in *p*-type semiconductors and are known as minority carriers, as are free holes in *n*-type semiconductors, while the holes (or electrons in *n*-type semiconductors) are known as majority carriers.

A *p-n* semiconductor junction is produced when there is a change from one type of impurity to the other within the same crystal structure. Semiconductor devices such as diodes and transistors are based on the use of such junctions to give specific current-flow characteristics.

Development and applications

The first applications of semiconductors was in the fabrication of metal rectifiers. These devices used semiconducting copper oxide or selenium, which formed a rectifying contact with a metal electrode. Later, germanium was used with a point contact consisting of a thin metal whisker. This device also acts as a rectifier but at a much lower current level. Another important development was the use of semiconductors to make electronic devices called diodes, which allow electricity to flow in only one direction. They are formed by putting *n*-type and *p*-type semiconductors together. One use of diodes is in the protection of electronic equipment susceptible to damage from current flowing in the wrong direc-

▼ Impurities in the lattice produce an excess or lack of electrons. Mobile electrons drift through the material. Holes seem to move like positive charges as they appear to jump from one atom to its neighbor. These properties are used for the *p-n-p* transistor shown here with a low forward bias.

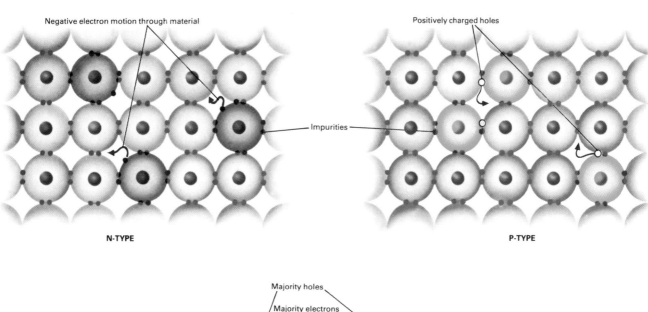

NEGATIVE electron motion through material — Impurities — N-TYPE

Positively charged holes — Impurities — P-TYPE

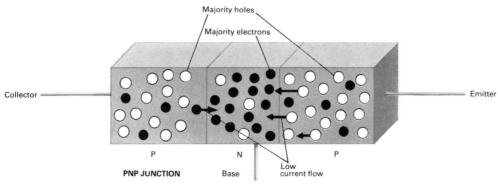

Majority holes
Majority electrons
Collector — Emitter
P — PNP JUNCTION — N — Base — Low current flow — P

other arrangements, ultimately leading to integrated circuits containing large numbers of interconnected components.

The material used for most semiconductor devices is silicon, which has to be produced to a high standard of purity. Semiconductors made of silicon are used to create highly miniaturized microprocessors that are now capable of containing tens of millions of transistors on a very small area. The level of miniaturization is constantly improving, allowing further reductions in the sizes of electronic equipment.

Although the greatest usage of semiconductors is in the manufacture of silicon transistors and integrated circuits, many other devices and materials are of great commercial importance.

The dependence of a semiconductor's electric properties on illumination by light or by other forms of radiation has led to the development of a wide range of photosensors. Different materials have sensitivity in different parts of the wavelength spectrum, extending out to the infrared region. Photosensors are used in a number of applications, including security devices and automatic-switching systems for street lighting. A similar device is the solar cell used for power generation. Solar cells were first developed to provide an energy source for spacecraft, such as satellites, but are now also used on Earth for power generation. Electronic devices, such as calculators, that require only small amounts of electricity are often powered by solar cells.

Semiconductor elements are also widely used in strain and pressure transducers, enabling the measurement device to be fully integrated with a sensitive amplifier, with a consequent improvement in performance.

tion. Some diodes can also generate light. Indicators and displays are available in many colors using a light-emitting diode (LED), in which current through a *p-n* junction of relatively complex semiconducting compounds causes radiation of a color that is characteristic of the material. Coherent light can also be produced by semiconductor lasers for use in fiber-optic communications systems. The most important materials for light emission are III–V binary and ternary compounds.

The most important use of semiconductor technology, however, is in transistors, which consist of two adjacent *p-n* junctions in a *p-n-p* or an *n-p-n* arrangement with three connecting electrodes. Ordinarily no current would be able to pass through these three layers, but if a third electrode is attached to the center layer and a small current is applied, a much larger current is then able to pass through the three layers, thus permitting this device to be used as a switching component in electronic circuits. Subsequent development of transistors resulted in a number of

▲ An astronomer refilling a charge-coupled device (CCD) with coolant. CCDs use semiconductors to turn light into an electronic signal that is then used to produce a digital image.

▶ Pure silicon wafers in a quartz tube prior to diffusion, which involves melting a wafer with the right amount of dopant and cooling it to form a single crystal with the right orientation.

SEE ALSO:

ATOMIC STRUCTURE • CHARGE-COUPLED DEVICE • CONDUCTION, ELECTRIC • DIODE • INTEGRATED CIRCUIT • MICROPROCESSOR • PHOTOELECTRIC CELL AND PHOTOMETRY • SILICON • SOLAR ENERGY • TRANSDUCER AND SENSOR

Servomechanism

The word *servomechanism* is derived from two roots: the Latin *servus*, "a slave," and the Greek *mechanema*, "a contrivance." Put together, they suggest the concept of a slave mechanism, something that will perform a particular function with little effort from the controller.

Servomechanisms are defined as closed-loop control systems in which a small input power controls a much larger output power in a strictly proportional manner. The means by which this control is obtained may be mechanical, electric, hydraulic, pneumatic, or electronic or any combination. In principle, control is effected by comparing the desired value to the actual value, and the difference (or error) between them is then used to bring the actual value closer to the desired value. Many different servomechanisms may be brought together to form a complex automatic control system to control, for example, a nuclear reactor or a chemical processing plant.

History

The history of servomechanisms is largely one of development and invention to solve some specific engineering problems. Thus, engineers with a need to automatically control the speed of steam engines developed speed regulators, while chemists developed temperature control for ovens and processes. The first servomechanism is credited to the Scottish inventor James Watt, who invented a governor in 1775 to provide automatic speed regulation for a steam engine. In this mechanism, two heavy balls are attached to the drive shaft of the engine in such a manner that they rotate with the shaft, moving away from the shaft as the speed increases, causing a sliding collar to move along the shaft.

This sliding-collar movement is connected via a rod to the input steam valve. As the speed increases, so the extra movement of the collar decreases the amount of steam entering the

▲ Full-authority digital engine control (FADEC) servomechanism units being fitted to a Lynx helicopter engine.

engine, slowing it down. The ball then moves closer to the shaft and displaces the collar in the other direction, thus admitting more steam and causing the engine to speed up. The speed excursions and sliding-collar movements diminish until the engine is running at a constant speed.

Dampers or the use of a feedback path linked to the governor mechanism may be used to prevent a phenomenon called hunting, in which the engine speed oscillates continually around the desired speed, never settling into a stable position.

Electronics and servomechanism

Perhaps the greatest contribution to a theory of servomechanisms came with the development of electronics. The theory of electronic amplifiers and associated circuits was developing very quickly. The principle of negative feedback was established, and the realization that negative feedback was a specific example of the action of a servomechanism opened the way to the fundamentals of automatic control theory. The deep and far-reaching ideas developed to explain the behavior of electronic circuits could now be applied across the entire spectrum of servomechanisms.

All servomechanisms are control systems, but not all control systems are servomechanisms. Servomechanisms have two dominant features. First, the control is actuated by a quantity that is affected by the result of the control operation. Second, they allow a low-power unit to control a high-power operation at a distance. In regulators or self-operated controllers, there is no separate control power, the force for the control action being derived from the controlled system.

Basic elements

Although the details vary according to the application, all servomechanisms consist of the same basic functional elements and work in the same manner. The set input is compared with the sensed output, and the difference between these signals gives an error signal, which is normally amplified and used to drive an actuator system. This actuator works to alter the controlled quantity, the value of which is measured by a feedback sensor to give the output signal supplied for comparison with the desired input. When the required setting has been achieved, the input and output are equal, so there is no error signal to drive the actuator, and movement stops. This sequence forms a closed loop; each of the operations affects and is dependent on the other.

The accuracy of such a control system depends on the precision with which the set input and achieved output can be measured and compared, and since these units do not have to handle the full power of the system, they can be more

▼ These two robot arms used on the space shuttle and the International Space Station both use servomechanisms to amplify the action of the operators inside the spacecraft.

readily produced to high standards of accuracy. Problems can occur if the output of the actuator system is not powerful enough to alter the output as required; this deficiency can be overcome by higher amplification of the error signal to give a greater operating force for a given error, so long as the actuator has sufficient capacity.

If the level of amplification is too great, the actuator may overcorrect and drive the output beyond the required level. The control system will then act to reduce the set level, when the same effect may again occur to give an output value that is now less then required, leading to a further control action to increase the level, and so on. Such a sequence of over- and undercorrection is known as hunting, and the system is unstable. Instability is clearly undesirable, and various techniques are used to provide stability to the system. The simple system described above is proportional, the error signal being simply amplified to give the correcting action. One solution is to add damping to the system so as to slow and smooth the output fluctuations. Alternatively, a control unit may be used to modify the error signal so as to obtain the required actuator response.

Servomechanisms may be entirely mechanical in character, but electric sensors and actuators are more often used. Hydraulic and pneumatic systems are also employed for some applications.

Applications

The applications of servomechanisms are to be found in many industries. For example, the modern airplane could not fly without using these devices. Consider the strain on a pilot who has to fly a set course on a particular compass bearing and has to contend with a variable crosswind. The physical strain of flying with a few degrees of rudder would be intolerable after a short time. One way of solving this problem is to use actuators.

The pilot flies onto course and switches on a servomechanism consisting of a rate gyro, amplifier, actuator, and feedback loop. From now on, the gyro senses any deviation of the airplane from the original course and adjusts the length of the actuator; this action has the effect of shortening or lengthening the control rod to the rudder and so moving it one way or the other to remedy the deviation. The stabilizer is designed to have only a limited effect, say five degrees, of rudder deflection and is capable of being overridden by the pilot at any time. Actuators can be fitted to all the control surfaces of an airplane, but they are not the same as automatic pilots.

An autopilot is a more complex mechanism that will sense yaw, pitch, and roll and will fly an airplane to a particular height at a particular speed on a particular heading. The first servo system is controlled by the rate gyro plus another unit, which is connected also to the rudder bar and consists of a heading gyro and another actuator, amplifier, and feedback loop. The second actuator is capable of much greater movement and can exercise complete yaw control of the airplane in response to the signals from the heading gyro. When the autopilot is switched on, the pilot has no need to control the airplane, as servomechanisms exercise similar control over the other flying control surfaces, deriving their signals from the artificial horizon, the altimeter, and similar instruments.

Other uses of servomechanisms include satellite-tracking antennas, where, to maintain a strong signal, the ground-based antenna must be able to move automatically to follow the position of a satellite above. Servomechanisms are also used extensively on robots to enable the accurate positioning of robot arms, for example, and accurate performance of tasks.

▼ A scheme for a position-control mechanism. A to B is the distance to be maintained. Any variation in the distance alters the slider, which sends a compensating voltage to X.

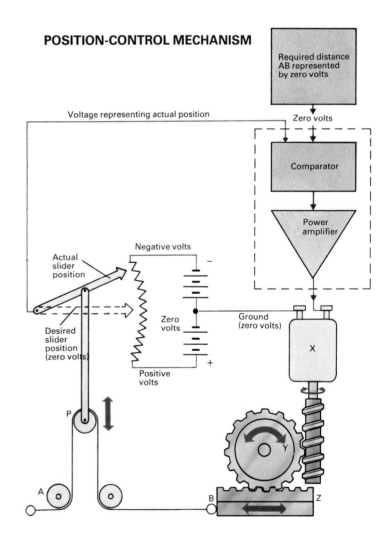

POSITION-CONTROL MECHANISM

SEE ALSO: FEEDBACK • GOVERNOR • GYROSCOPE • HYDRAULICS • LINEAR MOTOR • ROBOTICS

Sewing Machine

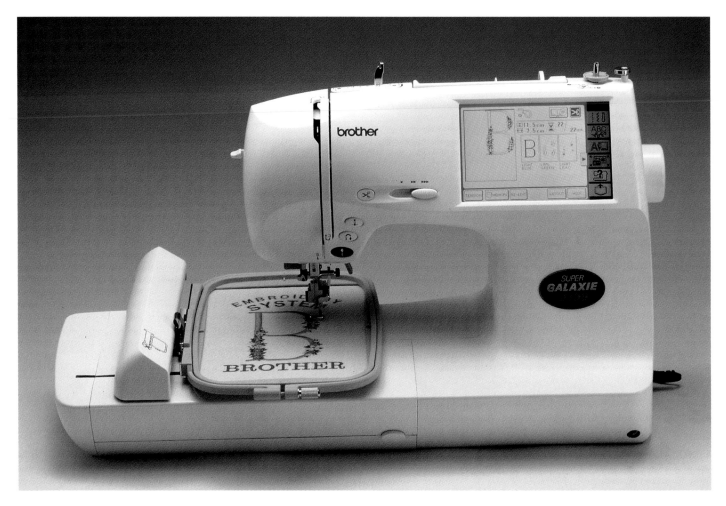

The sewing machine works on a different principle from that of hand sewing. In hand sewing, the needle and the free end of the thread are passed right through the fabric and pulled through to the other side. No normal sewing machine could do this, because its needle is attached to the mechanism and cannot be released. Furthermore, hand sewing is done with a limited length of thread, the whole of which is pulled through the fabric at each stitch (except for the part that has already formed stitches). This approach would not be practical for a high-speed machine, which must be able to draw thread continuously from a spool or bobbin or both.

There are now a few highly complex machines that can imitate hand sewing, thanks to a free-floating double-pointed needle and other devices, but the most popular designs of the machine use either chain stitch or lock stitch.

Chain stitch

In the simplest form of chain stitch, only one thread is used. The thread is pulled off a reel above the fabric and threaded through the eye of the needle; some machines have a built-in needle threader for automatic threading. All sewing machine needles have the eye at the same end as the point.

The needle enters the fabric, pulling a loop of thread through with it. It then withdraws slightly, but friction against the fabric prevents the thread from withdrawing so that it broadens out into a loop under the fabric. A looper—basically an oscillating hook—then comes across and catches the loop, after which the needle withdraws fully, and the fabric moves on one stitch length.

The looper holds the loop under the fabric in such a position that when the needle descends again, it passes through the held loop before forming a new loop, which is caught in turn by the looper. Thus, a succession of loops is formed under the fabric, each one laced through the previous one.

Lockstitch

Two threads are used in basic lockstitch, one above the fabric, pulled continuously off a spool, and the other below it, taken from a small bobbin mounted in a bobbin case, or shuttle. The upper thread, or needle thread, is carried down through

▲ The modern domestic sewing machine is a very advanced piece of technology, with computerized touch screens, automatic needle threading, embroidery options, and a huge range of stitches.

the fabric as before, but the loop it forms is caught by a hook traveling on a curved path (either oscillating or revolving fully) that passes the loop around the bobbin, looping it around the bobbin thread. The needle then withdraws, pulling the intersection of the threads into the fabric. In this way, a stitch is created that looks the same from above and below; each thread runs across the surface of the fabric and dips into it at intervals to loop around the other thread halfway through the fabric.

Relative merits

Chain stitch can be executed quickly, typically at 7,000 stitches per minute, corresponding to 8 ft. (2.4 m) per second at 12 stitches to the inch. Lockstitch cannot match this speed, because it puts a greater strain on the thread, but single-thread chain stitch can be unraveled by simply pulling apart the end of an unfinished seam or cutting one stitch and pulling. The latter stitch is therefore used only on certain industrial machines, such as button sewers and tacking machines, where this weakness does not matter. It was also used on the earliest machines. Other chain-stitch machines use two-thread chain stitch, where a separate underthread is interlooped with the ordinary loops under the fabric, making the stitch secure. This method, however, results in excessively high thread consumption: about five inches of thread are used for every inch of seam.

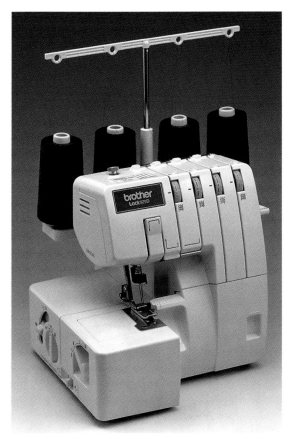

◄ Overlocking machines are specially designed to sew over the raw edges of cut material to prevent them fraying. Industrial overlockers can also trim excess material from the edge as it passes through the machine.

Lockstitch is secure and uses about half as much thread, but its use is restricted by its maximum speed and also by the fact that the needle thread has to pass right around the bobbin at each stitch. This movement makes it impossible for the bobbin thread to be drawn from a large fixed spool, and since the size of the bobbin is restricted by the size of the loop that can be drawn from the needle thread, its capacity is severely limited. (The underthread for two-thread chain stitch, however, can be drawn from a fixed spool.) For this reason, lockstitch is most suitable for home sewing machines, where speed and thread capacity are less important than they are in industry, where chain stitch is generally preferred. Chain stitch was also used in many home machines during the 19th century.

Feed

The fabric is advanced at each stitch by a feed mechanism, which consists of a toothed bar under the fabric gripping it by pressing it up against a smooth spring-loaded presser foot. The feed bar moves in a four-stop motion: up, forward, down, and back. This motion can normally be reversed to move the fabric the other way (to secure the end of a seam by backstitching) and its travel can be altered to change the length of the stitch.

History

The first patent for a sewing machine was taken out in 1790 by Thomas Saint, an English cabinetmaker. It used single-thread chain stitch and had a forked needle that went through a hole previously made by an awl. It was probably never built, since minor design faults in the patent specification would have made it unworkable.

In 1810, a German, B. Krems, invented the eye-pointed needle, again without commercial success. The first commercial machine, built in France in 1841 by Barthélemy Thimonnier, a tailor, had a barbed needle, which tended to catch in the cloth. It also had no feed, and the fabric was moved by hand. Nevertheless, Thimonnier set up a business making military uniforms and operated successfully until his machines were destroyed by handworkers who feared they would lose their jobs. After this setback, Thimonnier abandoned any further development of his design.

The first lockstitch machine was invented in the early 1830s in New York by Walter Hunt. Again, it was not commercially exploited, but in 1846, Elias Howe patented a fairly similar machine. It had an inconvenient feed mechanism whereby the edge of the cloth was held vertically on spikes on a baster plate, which then carried it through the machine. At the end of its travel, the baster plate had to be moved back and the next length of cloth put on the spikes. Moreover, the machine needed a specially curved needle.

The first machine to have the general form of a modern one was produced by the American Isaac M. Singer in 1851. It was a lockstitch machine with a straight, vertically sliding needle and a spring-loaded presser foot. It was the first machine to be foot-powered by a treadle.

In 1852, another American, Allen B. Wilson, invented the rotary hook, which took the needle thread around a stationary bobbin (Singer's machine had had a straight-line oscillating shuttle). In 1854, he invented the four-motion feed. This development completed the basic equipment of the modern machine, and later improvements were mainly in detail.

Modern machines

Most modern household machines have a swing needle, which produces a zigzag stitch. There is an elongated hole in the needle plate under the fabric, and the needle moves left and right at alternate stitches. The width of zigzag can be set from zero (resulting in a straight stitch) to 0.2 or 0.3 in. (5–7 mm). Adjusting the stitch length can give a long, loose zigzag for sewing stretch fabrics or finishing raw edges to stop fraying or a very short, tight stitch, for making buttonholes or doing satin stitch, which is a simple embroidery stitch. If the forward motion is completely stopped, the machine will sew on buttons or make bar tacks (reinforcements at points of strain). The zigzag can also be used for blind hemming (turning up the bottom of a garment so that stitches do not show from the outside) by folding the fabric right sides (outsides) together and stitching so that the point of each zigzag just catches the fold without passing through the thickness of the fabric. Fancy stitches are produced by cam boxes that vary the width of the zigzag and the direction of the feed in a set pattern.

Most machines come with a number of easily interchangeable parts to increase functionality. Different presser feet are available to make hemming, embroidery, and inserting zippers easy. Needles come in different gauges to cope with light or heavy fabrics and as ready-paired twin needles for double seaming. Special ball-pointed needles were developed for jersey fabrics, which risk snagging and running if a normal sharp needle is used. Part of the bed is usually removable, leaving a narrower column that makes inserting tightly curved sleeves or cuffs much easier.

As with other modern machinery, the domestic sewing machine has benefited from microchip technology. Top-of-the-range machines boast over 1,200 built-in stitches and the ability for the user to create customized stitches that can then be held in the sewing machine's memory.

▼ This handheld scanner allows the home sewer to make his or her own embroidery designs and download them into the sewing machine's memory. The machine then converts them into a stitching pattern.

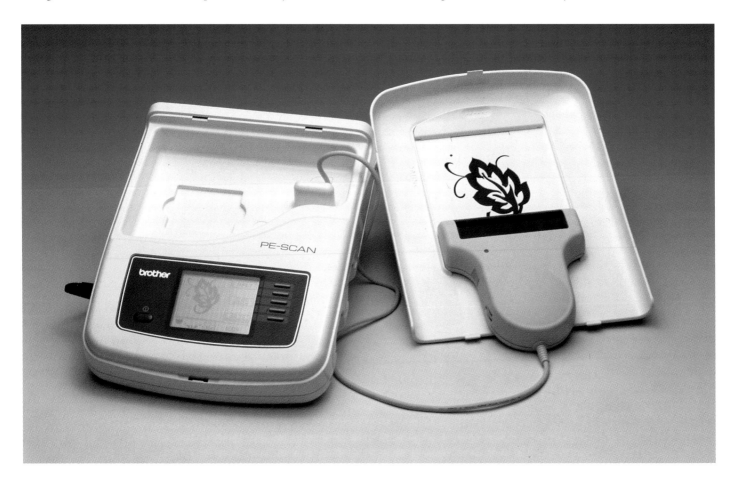

▲ Industrial sewing machines are designed for specific tasks rather than the multifunctionality of domestic machines. This man is using a heavy-duty machine set into a recess in the floor to sew sails for a dinghy.

Multidirectional feed mechanisms allow straight stitches to be sewn in eight directions without turning the fabric. The greatest advantage has been with embroidery programs. A number of designs and lettering now come built-in to the machine and can be sized, rotated, or added to. The design can then be previewed and altered on a color-touch screen before sewing commences. Some even have a handheld scanner that allows the machinist to scan in his or her own design, which the machine converts into a stitch pattern.

Industrial sewing machines

The greatest use of sewing machines is in the footwear, clothing, and furnishing industries. Because the materials employed by these industries can range from the finest silk gauzes to leather, plastics, and heavy sailcloth, sewing machines are designed for specific stages in the production of a particular garment or item. There are thought to be around 10,000 different models of industrial sewing machine, classified by the type of stitch they make and the shape of the machine's bed or frame.

Bed shapes affect the passage through the machine of the material being sewn. There are seven basic bed types: flatbed, cylinder, raised bed, post, closed vertical, open vertical, and off-the-arm. Machines are also classified by the degree of operational control the machinist needs to carry out the task into fully automatic, manual paced, automatic cycle with manual, and automated loading and extraction.

Garment production can require the use of a number of specialist machines, depending on the complexity of the item. They can include over-

lockers, automatic buttonholers, button stitchers, pocket seamers, contour seamers for the curves around armholes, and zip inserters. Some machines sew in automatic sequences—a set of buttonholes at preset intervals down the front of a shirt, for example—before the next piece is fed in. In many cases, two or more machines are synchronized so that when one machine has performed its operation on the garment, it feeds it to a second machine for the next stage. Only one operator is needed to mind the sequence, saving time and labor costs.

Industrial sewing machines can be fitted with different attachments to save downtime between operations. Needle positioners ensure that the needle is in or out of the material when the machine stops as required. Sewn items are removed from the machine by stackers that flip, slide, lift, or convey the item on to the next operation. Some machines are programmable; the garment is positioned under the needle, sewn, and repositioned if necessary; the threads are cut; and the garment is ejected, all in a single timed cycle.

The majority of industrial machines use chain stitch. There are many complex multiple versions of chain stitch for extra-strong stitching on heavy fabrics; up to nine threads may be used at once. Two or three needles may be used together for lap-seam felling work, where the edges of two pieces of material are turned under each other in a pair of interlocking U shapes and then two parallel lines of stitching secure the raw edges inside, similar to a French seam. This type of seam is commonly used in making shirts, overalls, and trousers and saves the manufacturer from having to overlock each piece separately.

There have also been experiments with threadless machines with hollow needles that inject a fluid into the material to be sewn—this fluid is hardened by heat treatment to form a seam. These are really no longer sewing machines.

▶ Jam-proof rotary hooks, found on many domestic sewing machines, ensure perfect stitch formation whatever the sewing speed.

SEE ALSO: CLOTHING MANUFACTURE • KNITWARE AND HOSIERY MANUFACTURE • MASS PRODUCTION • OPTICAL SCANNER

Sextant

Since the earliest ocean voyages navigators have had to fix their position at sea by means of measuring the angles above the horizon of heavenly bodies: the Sun, Moon, and stars. The simplest, and least accurate, of these methods is to measure the altitude (angle above the horizon) of the Pole Star (in the Northern Hemisphere). More accurately, the altitude of the Sun at local noon or of bright stars whose position is known at their highest point will give the latitude after simple calculations from tables.

The first instruments to be used for measuring these angles were astrolabes, cross staffs, back staffs, and quadrants—all variations on the theme of a sighting bar moved along a scale of degrees. In most cases, it was necessary to view both the star and the horizon at the same time from the deck of the ship, and it is not surprising that the observations were inaccurate. In the case of the quadrant, the reference point was not the horizon but a plumb line attached to the scale. This instrument made it possible to concentrate on the star only, but the plumb line could easily swing about, leading to further errors.

The device that replaced these instruments, the forerunner of the sextant, was the reflecting octant invented by an Englishman, John Hadley,

▲ An early model of a sextant. This nautical instrument was introduced in the 18th century and revolutionized travel by enabling accurate mapping of the world.

in 1731. The principle and design of the octant was the same as that of any sextant in daily use today: the main difference is that the octant had a scale that was one-eighth of a circle, 45 degrees, and a sextant has a scale of one-sixth of a circle, 60 degrees. Because both devices measure an angle that is reflected by a mirror, the octant will measure angles up to 90 degrees, and the sextant, angles up to 120 degrees.

Hadley's invention used a pair of small mirrors to reflect the image of the star to be observed so that it appeared to be on the horizon. The navigator could keep both in view at the same time, and as the ship rolled, both would move together. The movable mirror was attached to the pivot of the movable index bar at the radius of the scale or arc, so that, as the angle was changed, the mirror would move. This mirror reflected the star's image to a second mirror, permanently set to view the first one. The navigator looked through a sight to the second mirror, past which he could see the horizon. He moved the first by moving the index bar until the star's image reflected by both mirrors exactly touched the horizon. The angle was then read off the arc, which was graduated in degrees (but twice as closely as a true scale of degrees, to allow for the mirror's reflection).

Hadley's octant was immediately accepted by navigators. In 1757, John Campbell introduced the true sextant, which was capable of measuring a greater angle. Captain Cook, the English explorer, was probably the first to fully apply the potential of the sextant for measuring not only vertical angles but also angles at any inclination. By measuring the angle between the Moon and a given star, he could calculate the precise time using tables of the Moon's motion, thus enabling him to find his longitude as well as his latitude—he used this method for the charting of New Zealand during the voyage of 1768–1771. The invention of accurate timekeepers made the procedure unnecessary, and the sextant was then used to measure the altitude of stars or the Sun at precise times, thus giving the longitude whenever it was required.

Although the earliest sextants and octants had simple sighting devices, the accuracy was much improved by the use of a small telescope instead. The second mirror, the horizon mirror, would be silvered only across half its width so that the telescope would show both the horizon and the star side by side. Dark filters could be moved into the light paths to cut down the brightness of the Sun or horizon.

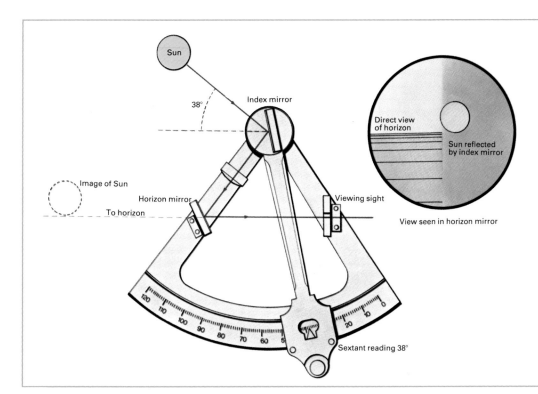

SEXTANT OPERATION

Despite the introduction of modern technology, ship's officers and other navigators are still required to learn how to check their position using a sextant. A sextant is an instrument for measuring the angle of stars or the Sun at precise times to give a location at sea. The procedure is to move the the index mirror until the bottom of the image of the Sun or star just touches the line of the horizon, as shown in the inset. This reading is corrected to give the position of the center of the Sun or star.

The sextant has remained basically unchanged from 1800 to the present day, but there have been some changes to the way in which the arm of the sextant is made to travel along the arc. In the early days, there was no fine-adjustment screw, and the navigator merely moved the arm along the arc and clamped it to the frame so that the reading could be taken. On a moving deck, this procedure was rather difficult, so in the 1760s a fine-adjustment tangent screw was added. With this improvement the operator could quickly take his sight to the nearest degree and then, by using the tangent screw, make the final close adjustment. The only drawback with the clamping type of sextant was that the tangent screw frequently had to be returned to its starting position; otherwise it would come to the limit of its thread as a sighting was being taken. The problem was solved in the 1920s. A toothed rack was cut into the sextant frame, and the tangent screw was now meshed into this rack. The arm could be moved along the arc by pressing a quick-release catch, and the tangent screw could travel the full length of the arc without needing to be reset.

The sextants of this period were still using the finely engraved scale, which had to be read with a magnifier, as they had been over the previous 100 years. Around 1933, the micrometer sextant was evolved, which is still in use today. Instead of engraving the fine divisions on the arc, they were transferred to an enlarged tangent screw head, thus doing away with the magnifier and making the sextant easier to read.

Other types of sextants

The sextant may still be used for air navigation far from the busy air corridors. In this case, the horizon cannot be used as it is below the true horizontal, and a system that reflects the image of a bubble level into the field of view is used. Astrodomes, small transparent domes into which the sextant will fit, may be set into the top of the airplane, or in the case of the faster airplane, a periscope system will be fitted. Land sextants, in which the horizon is provided by a small trough of mercury in the sextant, have also been made.

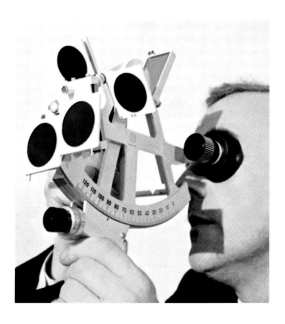

◄ The general design of the sextant has not changed, although advanced optical technology has made it possible to shorten the length of the telescope.

SEE ALSO: Global positioning system • Inertial guidance • Latitude and longitude • Navigation • Telescope, optical

Sheet Metal

Refrigerators, office furniture, cars, and many other consumer products use sheet metal in their manufacture. Most of this sheet metal is steel, but copper, brass, aluminum, and other metals are also formed into various shapes by pressing them between dies in a power press.

Presses

The power press is used in forging and drawing metals, minting coins, forming automobile body parts, and many other industrial processes. The press has tools called dies installed in it; the material to be shaped is placed in the machine between the dies, and the machine closes, forming the material.

In many cases, the press is powered by hydraulic mechanisms or by steam pressure. For example, some types of forging require a slow, steady squeeze on a piece of metal heated to a state of plasticity; hydraulic actuators provide the pressure. Other types of forging require repeated heavy hammer blows—the hammer may be lifted by means of steam pressure and dropped, the pressure being provided by the weight of the tool itself or, in a double-acting hammer, forced down by the steam pressure as well. For ordinary sheet-metal forming, the machine is often a simple mechanical press.

The lower part of the press is a table called the bolster plate on which the lower die, or female, is installed. The upper part of the machine, which

▲ Die makers finishing a 25-ton (22.5-tonne) die set for drawing automobile floor pans. Drawing involves stretching and bending the sheet metal—mild steel—into the correct shape in the dies.

goes up and down between guides installed in the frame, is called the ram. The punch, or male die, is installed on the ram. In a mechanical press, the ram is connected by means of one or more connecting rods to a crankshaft, which turns in bearings installed, like the guides, in the frame of the machine, one on each side. On the side of the machine, a clutch, a brake, and a flywheel are connected to the end of the crankshaft. An electric motor drives the flywheel, either by means of several rubber V-belts running in grooves around its perimeter or by means of gear teeth, in which case the flywheel is in effect a large gear with teeth around its perimeter. When the operators push all the buttons, the clutch is activated, the crankshaft makes one revolution, and the ram makes one trip down toward the bolster plate and back up again. The upper die strikes the piece of metal placed on the lower die, forming it by means of the pressure or impact. The pressure provided by the various types of presses varies from less than 1 ton to more than 5,000 tons (0.9–4,500 tonnes). Some hydraulic forging presses have a capacity of up to 50,000 tons (45,000 tonnes).

Some presses have a geared flywheel on each side and intermediate geared shafts, pulleys, or gearwheels between the motor and the flywheel. There are also presses with eccentric shafts instead of crankshafts; an offset section of the shaft functions like a cam. Some presses have large gearwheels enclosed in the top of the machine that are not flywheels but are connected to the top of the ram by means of rods attached to eccentric pivots.

Cutting out a shape from a piece of sheet metal on which other operations are then performed is called piercing or punching. Certain presses whose only function is to cut sheet metal with long horizontal blades instead of dies are called shears.

Often more than one function is carried out simultaneously during one stroke of the machine. With a car door, for example, the door may be formed between the dies and blanked out so that a narrow strip of scrap is separated from the perimeter of the door; a hole is then punched out for the door handle. This task is accomplished in a double-acting or triple-acting press; the double-acting press has one ram inside the other, and the triple-acting press has an additional ram below that comes up instead of down. The upper, outside ram is operated by means of a lever or toggle instead of by the crankshaft; such a machine is sometimes called a toggle press.

Presses that make large sheet-metal parts, such as for cars, are called straight-sided presses and are as large as small houses. They are constructed simply by stacking one part of the machine on top of another and held together by huge vertical bolts, which at the lower end, may extend through the floor with the nut tightened on from underneath. Installing the dies in such machines requires large custom-built forklifts and electric traveling overhead cranes. For these reasons, the press room in a large factory is often specially constructed.

By contrast, the open-back inclinable is a common type of press for the manufacture of smaller parts. Its frame is in the shape of a letter C, and it is open at the back so that the finished pieces or the scrap may be ejected through it into storage tubs, often by means of compressed air. It can be inclined on its base for convenience of operation. Such a machine may be only about 8 ft. (2.4 m) high and 4 ft. (1.2 m) wide. For extremely fast production of small parts, such as washers, a dieing press may be used; the punch is pulled down rather than pushed, and it may make several hundred strokes a minute, with mechanical attachments feeding a strip of sheet metal past the lower die.

Large presses are often automated today. A common form of automation in the production of large sheet-metal parts comprises conveyors made of wide rubber belts operated by electric motors and long steel arms with suction cups on the ends that reach into the press and remove the blanked piece, dropping it on the conveyor, which takes it to the next operation. The reaching arms travel on a rack-and-gear device, which is operated automatically by electric limit switches.

The installation of dies in presses can be a complicated operation taking several working shifts to accomplish. Shims (spacers) can be installed behind the dies, and the connecting rods are made of two or more threaded parts so that they are adjustable for length. The clearance between the dies is carefully calculated; a mistake of a fraction of an inch in the wrong direction will result in serious, expensive damage, such as a broken crankshaft or damage to the dies. Springs and pneumatic cushions are used behind dies and parts of dies to adjust the amount of impact during operation of the press.

Safety and maintenance

Safety in the press room is of great importance. The operators of large presses must have both hands on control buttons before the machine will operate, to prevent careless hands from being crushed when the ram comes down. On smaller presses, the operator may have a tough leather strap or wire cable attached to his or her gloves; the other end of the strap is connected, through tubing, to the top of the ram, so if the operator is careless, his or her fingers are jerked away from

◄ When the metal has been drawn to produce the correct shape, the floor pans are clamped in jigs to be spot welded together.

the danger area by the operation of the machine. Smaller automated presses have guards that can be raised and lowered and must be in the down position for the machine to work.

When the press or the dies are being repaired or adjusted, the electric controls are locked out so the machine cannot be accidentally operated, and the repair workers hold the key to the lock. In addition, large wooden beams may be placed vertically between the upper and lower dies.

Maintenance of the presses is important for safety as well as other reasons. The clutch and the brake must be properly adjusted so that the stroke of the ram begins and ends in the right position. Other machine tools can cost more than a press, which is a less complicated machine, but an accident with a press can be more expensive, because a damaged die or a broken crankshaft costs far more to repair or replace than a broken tool in a lathe or a milling machine. It is also interesting to note that, whereas the load on a machine tool is usually continuous, the load on the bearings on a press crankshaft is concentrated at one point in its revolution, namely, the point at which the ram is making contact with the lower die. For these reasons the inspection, adjustment, and proper lubrication of the press are important, as a great deal of machine failure is due to inadequate lubrication to begin with.

Die sinking

Dies are made of expensive, high-quality steel blocks. A large die may be cast to the approximate pattern required before being finished; when the die cavity extends all the way through the block, it may be roughened out by a flame-cutting process or on a jigsaw. Smaller die blocks can be roughed out in a shaper or a band file.

After the block has been roughed out, most die sinking is done on automatic machinery. End-mill cutters of appropriate profile are used in vertical milling machines, with the die block bolted to the table. A device called a pantograph may be used to follow a pattern made of plastic or sheet metal. A tracer attachment to the milling machine may follow, by means of a stylus, a model of the die made of wood or some other soft material. The surface of the die is finished to size and to a high degree of polish by means of hand scrapers, grinding wheels, polishing cloth, and similar tools. Die hobbing is the use of a hardened and polished male plug, pushed into a soft steel block by means of hydraulic pressure. Dies produced in this way are for limited production of simple parts or for production in soft materials.

▲ Robots stamping sheet metal to make automobile body parts. Robots are widely used for dangerous and noisy tasks such as welding and stamping in automobile assembly plants.

SEE ALSO: MACHINE TOOL • METAL CUTTING AND JOINING • METALWORKING

Ship

Boats and ships of one form or another have been in use for many thousands of years: certainly by 2500 B.C.E., the Egyptians were building fairly sophisticated seagoing sailing ships. Sailing ships dominated until the 19th century, when steam engines suitable for marine use were developed, followed later by the diesel engine. Ships can be divided into two broad classes: merchant ships for carrying cargo and passengers, which are considered here; and warships, which have to meet a very different set of requirements.

For many years the majority of seaborne trade was carried in general-purpose dry cargo vessels with a forecastle at the bow, a bridge in the center of the vessel, and a poop at the stern. These superstructures stand clear of the deck and extend to the sides of the vessel. Several holds are provided in the hull for the cargo, access being provided by hatches in the deck, while derricks are normally provided for cargo handling. The ship is subdivided by several watertight bulkheads, which restrict flooding if the hull is damaged as well as supporting the deck and bracing the hull.

A double bottom is incorporated as a safety measure in the event that the outer shell is damaged; it also provides a space for the storage of fuel oil, water ballast, or fresh water. Forward and aft there are peak tanks, which are normally used

▼ Container ships are some of the biggest boats on the ocean. Great care has to be taken when stacking the freight containers to ensure that the ship remains balanced. The largest container ship in the world belongs to the Maersk shipping line and can carry more than 6,000 containers.

for water ballast to give adequate draft when the vessel is unloaded and to adjust the trim in the water if necessary.

The forecastle tween decks ("tween" is short for "between") are used for bosun's stores, the storage of wire ropes and rigging equipment, and paint and lamps. On the forecastle deck, each anchor cable passes from the windlass down through a spurling pipe into the chain locker, where the ends of the cables are connected to the forepeak bulkhead by a cable clench. At the after end, there is a steering-gear compartment where a hydraulic mechanism is used to move the rudder. The control for the steering gear is transmitted from the wheelhouse by a telemotor system. Directly below the steering-gear compartment is the rudder trunk, housing the upper rudder stock that is used to turn the rudder.

The engine room is midship, and the engine is normally a slow-speed diesel with large bore cylinders driving the propeller directly. The propeller shaft passes to the after end through a shaft tunnel; this tunnel protects the shaft from the cargo in the holds, and it provides access for maintenance of the shaft and its bearings.

In addition to the main engine, the engine room contains auxiliary machinery such as diesel generators, oil purifiers, air compressors, ballast

▲ The navigation and communications systems are located on the bridge and are now computerized and situated within easy reach of the officers. The ship is steered from the bridge, but decisions on power requirements have to be rung down to the engine room.

and bilge pumps, cooling water pumps, and many other essential items of equipment. Just forward of the engine room are the settling tanks, oil fuel bunkers, and a deep tank port and starboard, which may be used to carry liquid cargoes or a dry cargo such as grain or sugar.

Accommodation is generally amidships, with the officers berthed on the bridge deck or boat deck. The wheelhouse, chartroom, and radio room are usually together, and the captain may have his dayroom, bedroom, bathroom, and office on the same deck. Galleys, pantries, and recreation rooms are carefully positioned away from sleeping quarters to control the noise level and prevent annoyance to the off-duty crew.

Many of the above features are common to more recent designs, but the configuration has changed significantly with the widespread introduction of specialized types of ships. The general cargo ship has also undergone development, with the bridge superstructure being moved to the stern of the vessel to allow clear deck space for cargo handling. Geared ships often have cranes for cargo handling in addition to derricks, while some vessels have special heavy-lifting gear. The engine room is also moved aft, giving a shorter shaft length and a more generous cargo space.

The size of a ship is expressed in terms of its tonnage, which is actually a measure of volume with one gross ton being equal to 100 ft.³. The gross tonnage is the total volume of the space enclosed within the vessel (including the superstructure), while the net tonnage is the volume of the cargo space. Another measurement used to describe the size of a ship is the displacement tonnage, which is the total weight of the ship and is

normally given as an average of the ship's weight when it is loaded and when it is unloaded. The deadweight tonnage is the difference between the ship's loaded and unloaded weights.

Directional control of a ship is achieved by means of a rudder or rudders fitted to the stern and activated through an electrohydraulic steering engine mounted above it within the hull. The rudder, like an aircraft wing, develops lift when it is turned, developing a turning moment at a point midway along the hull.

For extra maneuverability and to enable the ship to reverse easily, it is often fitted with a pair of "flanking rudders" fitted to each propeller. These rudders are positioned forward of the propeller on either side of the propeller shaft.

To enable maneuvering at low speeds, many ships are fitted with a "bow thruster," a propeller sited in a transverse tunnel close to the bow that can push the bow sideways rather than forward. If another thruster is fitted at the stern, the vessel can be pushed sideways or rotated on its own axis if the two thrusters act in opposite directions.

Braking is achieved by reversing the ship's propellers, producing a backwards thrust. The ship's anchors are deployed to ensure the vessel remains stationary when at rest, although they can be deployed only in relatively shallow waters.

Navigation is achieved using various instruments to find speed, heading, and distance traveled. These instruments include the liquid magnetic compass, usually associated with an azimuth instrument, to take the bearings of visible landmarks. A ship's bearing can also be taken at night or in fog from transmitted radio signals.

Speed is measured using a pitot marine log, which comprises two thin-walled tubes that project from the bottom of the ship and face the

▼ Testing a ship design in a test basin. A variety of conditions can be simulated, from ice to large waves.

CENTERS OF BUOYANCY AND GRAVITY

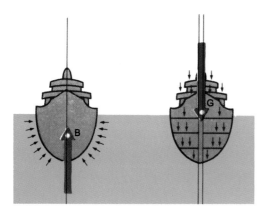

STABLE SHIP

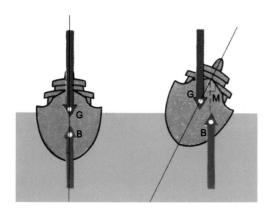

UNSTABLE SHIP

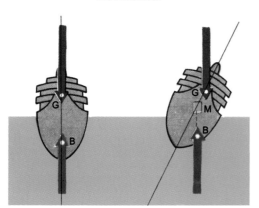

◄ Two forces, gravity (G) and buoyancy (B) act on a ship; their position determines the stability of a vessel. When a ship heels over, the line of action of the buoyancy moves to the side and meets the centerline at the meta center (M). A ship is stable when M is above G (middle picture) and unstable when it is below G (bottom).

► This ferry's bow shell plating opens like a visor to give access to the vehicle decks. The system is operated by a series of hydraulic jacks.

direction of travel. One tube (the dynamic pressure orifice) is open facing forward; the second (the static pressure orifice) has closed ends but has openings at right angles longitudinally. When the ship moves, the dynamic pressure is greater than the static pressure by an amount varying as the square of the ship's speed. Distance can be estimated using the patent log, a vaned rotor towed from the stern. Today an absolute position can also be obtained using the global positioning system, which takes an extremely accurate bearing from orbiting satellites.

Other ships can be detected using radar. The radar transmitter sends out a series of short pulses every degree or so as it rotates. When the pulse hits an object, it is reflected to the radar aerial and thence to the radar receiver. The pulse is then displayed as a bright dot on a cathode-ray tube, with the ship's position at the center of the chart.

Container ships

With general cargo vessels, much time has to be spent in port loading and unloading the loose cargo, which has to be carefully stowed in the hold to prevent damage or shifting due to the ship's movement. Typically such ships have to spend more time in port than at sea, and cargo handling is both labor intensive and expensive. These problems have been overcome by the introduction of container ships, in which the cargo is prepacked into containers that are then handled as single units. The containers also form a complete load for road vehicles or railway freight cars without any further handling. Containers are made to internationally agreed sizes based on an 8 ft. by 8 ft. (2.5 m x 2.5 m) cross section and a 20 ft. (6 m) long module, although many containers are 40 ft. (12 m), double length. Standard corner fittings are provided to take twist-lock lifting grips so that the containers can be lifted by cranes.

In a container ship, the hold length is designed to suit the length and number of containers to be

fitted into the hull and to allow sufficient space for refrigeration coolers and coupling systems for those containers with perishable cargo. All holds have vertical guides to position the containers and to give support, especially to the lowest container, which could distort under the load transmitted down from those above. One advantage of container vessels is that they can carry containers on deck, but the number of tiers depends on the strength of the hatch lids and the necessity of having a clear view from the wheelhouse for the pilot. The stability of a vessel with cargo on the deck must always be checked, as the center of mass will be raised and may cause the ship to loll or even capsize.

The capacity of a container ship is expressed in terms of how many twenty-foot equivalent units (TEU) it can take—large container ships can carry more than 4,000 TEU. Container ships have largely replaced general cargo ships on busy routes, such as across the North Atlantic, and are being increasingly used on less intensive routes as well.

Ro-ro ships

Another development offering rapid cargo handling is the ro-ro (roll-on, roll-off) ship, which has built-in ramps to allow direct loading of wheeled cargo. A common design is the three-quarters stern ramp, which angles down onto the quay when the ship is alongside, though straight stern ramps and side ramps are also used. Internal ramps or lifts provide access to all the decks. In addition to wheeled cargo such as cars, trucks, and container trailers, the ro-ro ship can also carry containers and other cargo. Containers are loaded using trailers pulled by master tug power units, together with other handling equipment such as forklifts, all of which remain on the ship for use as required.

Ferries are generally similar to ro-ro ships. Owing to the need for fast loading and unloading, many ferries have both bow and stern ramps, so traffic can be loaded in both directions. In addition, considerable passenger capacity is usually provided within a large superstructure.

Specialized carriers

Another way loose cargoes can be consolidated into easily handled loads is by the use of barges that allow loading and unloading without special port facilities. Mixed cargoes can be readily handled, and the system allows door-to-door transportation between ports on inland river and canal systems. The LASH (lighter aboard ship) system uses an on-ship gantry crane to lift the lighters out of the water and onto the ship, where they are carried along the deck for stowing in the holds or up to two high on deck.

Each lighter is handled in about 15 minutes, and at present, the LASH vessel is able to carry about 80 lighters, each with a cargo capacity of approximately 400 tons (360 tonnes), a length of

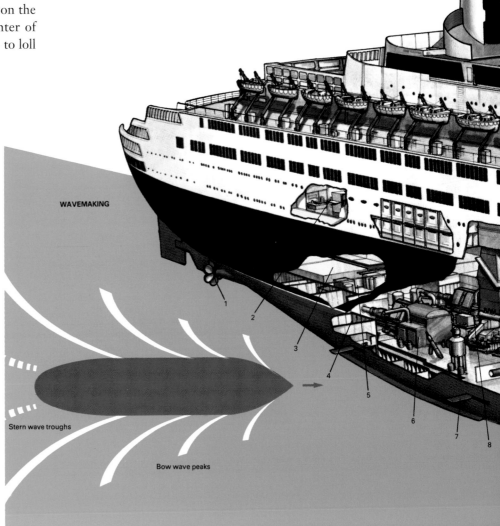

▶ The *Queen Elizabeth II*.
(1) Propeller, (2) safety control room, (3) fresh water tanks—evaporators convert seawater to fresh water, (4) oil fuel tanks, (5) machinery room, (6) steam turbines, (7) stabilizers, (8) steam-turbine control room, (9) main control and computer room, (10) boilers, (11) hospital, (12) swimming pool, (13) refrigerated stores, (14) passenger cabins, (15) bridge and chart room with officers' cabins, (16) bow thrusters for easy berthing.

WAVEMAKING

Stern wave troughs

Bow wave peaks

▲ Inset left: A ship should move through the water as smoothly as possible, as large waves from the prow put an additional strain on the engines.

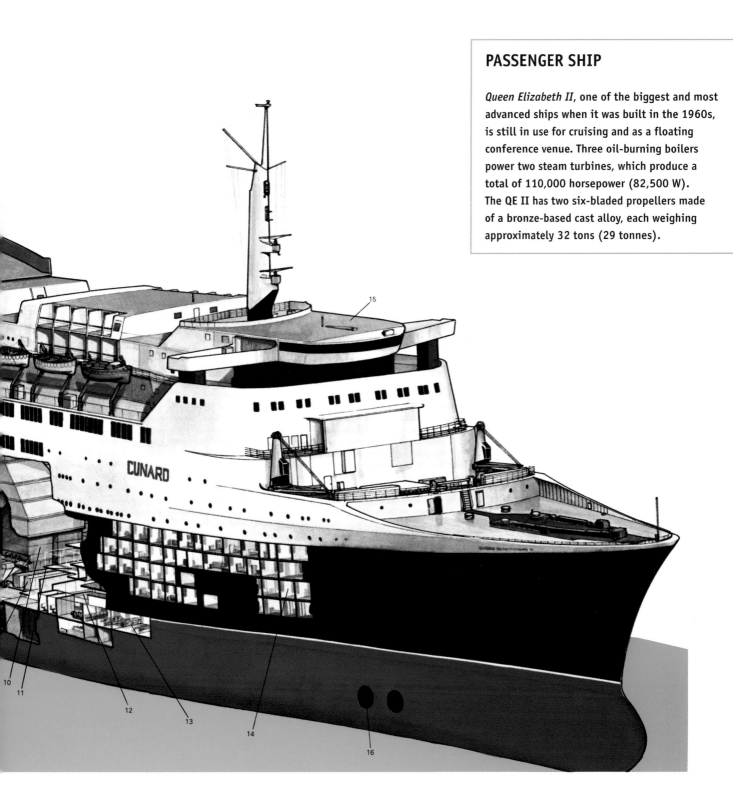

61 ft. 6 in. (18.8 m) and a width of 31 ft. 2 in. (9.5 m).
Larger barges are handled by the Seabee system,
in which they are pushed up over a stern ramp by
a tug. The complete ramp is then lifted to carry
the barge to the appropriate deck, where it is
moved into place on a rail system.

Many other specialist designs have been produced for specific cargoes. Perishable foodstuffs
are carried in reefer (refrigerated transport) ships
with large refrigerated holds. However, many
ordinary container ships have at least one refrigerated hold in addition to the electric sockets for
connecting refrigerated containers. Cars are carried on large transporter ships with a long superstructure containing extra load decks. Loading is
by side and quarter ramps. Large vessels have a
capacity of 6,000 cars.

Bulk carriers

Bulk carriers are usually single-deck, single-screw
vessels that carry large quantities of bulk cargo
such as grain, sugar, bauxite, and iron ore. The
engines are installed at the after end to leave the
better spaces in the hull for cargo, and the accom-

modation is all aft above the engine room so that services and sanitation are concentrated in one region of the vessel. Upper and lower wing tanks extend over the whole length of the cargo holds, and they are also used for water ballast when the ship is in the unloaded or light condition to give sufficient draft to immerse the propeller and give better control over the empty vessel in heavy seas.

The slope of the upper wing tank is designed to restrict the movement of a grain cargo, which could otherwise cause the vessel to become unstable. The double-bottom tank, used for oil fuel or for water ballast, can also be used to make adjustments to the trim of the ship. Some bulk carriers have their own derricks or deck cranes, but many rely entirely on the dockside amenities at the port when they are loading and discharging cargo. The hull construction for these vessels is a combination of two framing systems brought together in order to obtain the maximum strength characteristics from each. In these vessels, the deck, wing tanks, and double bottom are longitudinally framed, and the side shell is transversely framed.

Bulk carriers, like oil tankers, often have to make a return journey empty, and some designs allow the ship to be used for crude oil or container cargo on the return trip. As with oil tankers, bulk carriers offer lower transport cost with increasing size, some vessels having a deadweight of over 200,000 tons (180,000 tonnes).

Passenger vessels

Most modern passenger vessels are used for cruising rather than for traditional port-to-port liner services for passengers and urgent cargo, this function having been taken over by aircraft. Safety remains an important consideration, and stringent regulations are imposed by most maritime countries. Accordingly, such ships are more comprehensively subdivided than other merchant ships so that, if several adjacent compartments are flooded, the ship will remain stable and stay afloat. If asymmetrical flooding occurs, the vessel has cross-flooding fittings that enable the floodwater to be distributed across the ship to reduce the angle of heel. Lifeboats are fitted port and starboard on the boat deck, with sufficient capacity for the total number of passengers that the ship is certified to carry—a regulation that was brought in following the *Titanic* disaster in 1912. Fire control is another important safety aspect, and the vessels are subdivided vertically into fire zones by steel bulkheads. Within these zones, the bulkheads must be capable of preventing the spread of a fire in a 30-minute standard fire test.

A gyroscopically controlled set of stabilizers or fins, a common feature on most passenger vessels, controls the amount of roll and gives a more comfortable crossing. For maneuvering, these vessels are often fitted with bow thrusters, and they usually have twin-screw main propulsion systems, although turbines are also used.

The better cabins are located on the higher decks, and the one-, two-, or three-berth ordinary cabins on the lower decks. Custom-built cruise ships tend to have very large superstructures to give the maximum above-deck cabin space, effectively being floating hotels. One of the most important areas in the accommodation is the foyer with reception desk, purser's office, main

◀ The *Freedom Ship* is one of the grandest design concepts in shipping. Over a mile in length, it will be more like a floating town than a ship if it is built, with its own shopping mall, hospital, recreation areas, and aircraft landing strip. Before it can even be built, a special dock will have to be constructed. Residents will be housed in luxury apartments and will complete a circuit of the globe every two years.

staircase, and lifts. This area is usually centrally placed in order to receive the passengers and enable their immediate needs to be dealt with as soon as they embark. The following public rooms are quite common on most vessels: restaurants, ballrooms, movie theaters, discotheques, shops, cocktail bars, clubrooms, banks, and hairdressers. For recreation, there will be a swimming pool and deck area for games and relaxation and a gymnasium or health center. Young children will have a nursery, and there are playrooms for older children. The officers are berthed near the bridge, and the remaining crew on a lower deck.

Residence ships

At least two giant residence ships are planned, the largest vessels that will ever have sailed the seas. One, called *The World*, was launched at the end of 2001 and is of conventional cruise ship construction. The second, the *Freedom Ship*, is a more speculative venture, and its construction as described will be completely unlike standard seagoing vessels. It will be nearly a mile (1.6 km) long, 750 ft. (225 m) wide, and 25 stories high.

The World, built at the Fosen Mek shipyard in Rissa, Norway, for a Bahamas-based company, will have a set of permanent residents on board in 110 apartments ranging in size from 1,100 to 3,240 sq. ft. (100–290 m²). There will also be 88 guest suites aimed at the luxury cruise market.

The *Freedom Ship* is described by its promoters as essentially a flat bottomed, bolt-up barge with a conventional high rise built on top. Because of its massive size, the ship's maximum speed will be less than 10 knots, and it will take two years to complete its world tour. The top of the ship will be an aircraft landing strip capable of taking small private airplanes. As yet, the idea is still at concept stage, so details of the construction are uncertain.

Other ships include high-propulsion icebreakers, which are built wide to cut a lane through the ice. Their steep-sloped, heavily-plated bows charge the ice and crack it. Industrial ships may process fish into fillets or fish meal; they may act as canners, or as floating hazardous industrial waste incinerators with high smokestacks.

Construction

Steel remains the most common material for ship construction, with the sections being welded together. The way in which a vessel is constructed depends on the type of ship and the facilities of the shipyard, but in most cases, prefabricated sections are assembled in a building dock (so the finished ship can be floated out) or on a slipway. For example, a bulk carrier will usually be constructed

in the following way by most shipyards. First, the bottom shell and longitudinals will be laid on the building berth as a single unit after manufacture in the assembly shed, and then the double-bottom unit will be lowered onto the bottom shell and welded into position. The wing-tank unit is lifted into position, aligned, and welded, and a pair of bulkheads are erected the correct distance apart over the hold length. A side shell panel can then be connected to the lower wing-tank unit and bulkheads to form the sides of the hold. Then the upper wing tank is lowered into place and welded with the remaining deck panel, the amidships structure is finally complete. The ship is also built forward and aft of its midsection simultaneously. This technique, although not adopted by every shipyard, does allow an even spread of the labor force. Working from midships gives a good reference structure for taking dimensions during the building of the vessel. When each heavy unit is lifted onto the berth, the bottom of the vessel is checked for alignment by an optical system; otherwise distortion can occur.

▲ Top: The SS *Canberra* was converted into a troopship during the Falklands War in 1982. The conversion work involved building two helicopter pads, removing breakable and inflammable material, and converting cabins for use by soldiers. Bottom: The Russian icebreaker *Lenin* is powered by two pressurized, water-cooled nuclear reactors, which enable the ship to remain at sea for many months without refueling.

SEE ALSO: BOAT BUILDING • FREIGHT HANDLING • MARINE PROPULSION • PROPELLER • RUDDER • TANKER • WARSHIP

Shutter

A camera shutter controls the time during which light is allowed to fall on light-sensitive film in a camera. Together with the aperture, the shutter controls the amount of exposure of that film.

In the early days of photography, film had so little sensitivity to light that exposure could be adequately controlled by removing the lens cap, counting the appropriate number of seconds, and then replacing the cap. Sometimes, metal flaps were mounted on the lens; these flaps resembled window shutters, and thus, the word *shutter* came to be used for descendants of such devices.

When dry plates were introduced in 1880, their greater sensitivity created a need for faster and more accurate shutter times than ever before. This requirement led to the development of the mechanical shutter. Since then, each successive improvement in film sensitivity has necessitated a corresponding increase in shutter speeds.

Many of the early shutter designs were highly ingenious. The simplest was the guillotine, or drop shutter, which consisted of a rectangular plate with a slot that passed in front of the lens. Variations of this system used two metal plates that moved in opposite directions or slotted disks that rotated to allow a brief exposure.

Whereas most early shutters were placed near the lens—a position established with manual shutters—an alternative approach is to have the shutter near the film, in the plane on which the lens focuses light. These shutters, called focal-plane shutters, generally resemble a roller blind with a slot that moves across the film.

▶ Interlens, or leaf, shutters sit in or near the lens. Exposure is governed by a complex mechanism of springs and gears.

Interlens shutters

If a shutter is placed just behind or in front of a lens, it will be very slightly in focus, and the image will not be evenly illuminated. When the shutter is positioned between the lens components (most lenses have more than one element), the shutter will be completely unfocused. Such a design is called an interlens shutter and is popular for cameras that use a single lens without interchanges. The most simple interlens shutter has a single moving disk driven by a spring so that an oval

▼ Leaf shutters have several fine blades that spring open and then close again in the sequence 1 through 6 below. The flash is timed to reach peak intensity when the shutter is fully open (4), ensuring even exposure across the whole of the film.

hole in the disk passes in front of the lens to admit light. A capping plate covers the lens while the disk is moved back to its original position ready for the shutter to be fired again.

This type of shutter has three speed settings— I, B, and T. I is the instantaneous setting—that where the hole passes straight over the film. The speed of the I setting has increased from an exposure time of ½ second to around ⅙₅ second over the years. B stands for "bulb," which refers to the

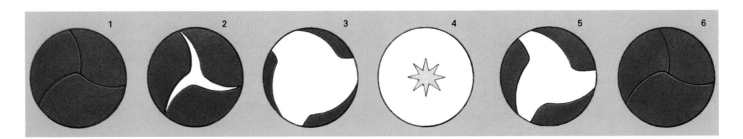

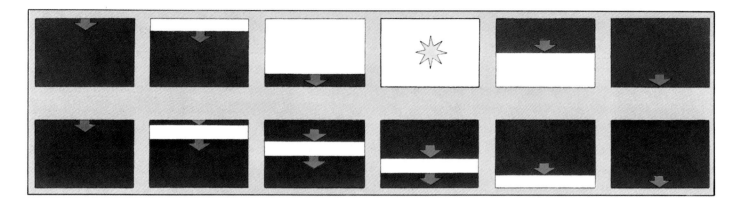

original actuation mechanism—a rubber bulb and tube that held the shutter open while the bulb was squeezed. The B setting holds the shutter open as long as the shutter release is pressed. T is for "time"; in this setting, the shutter opens when the lever is pressed and released and stays open until the lever is pressed a second time.

A more sophisticated early interlens shutter was the Compound, introduced by the German firm Deckel in 1902. The Compound had settings for several speeds and a separate lever to tension the spring. In 1912, the Compound was modified and relaunched under the name Compur.

Focal-plane shutters

Most focal-plane (fp) shutters have two blinds; one closes across the film at a precise interval after the other has opened. A widely used blind material is black silk sprayed with plastic. In the majority of focal-plane shutters, the blinds move along the longer axis of the negative, which is commonly 1 to 1½ in. (25–38 mm); the Contax shutter had metal blinds that traveled along the shorter axis. The Japanese Copal Square is a more modern shutter that also has metals blinds that travel across the shorter axis of the frame.

Shutter speeds

Normal shutter speeds range from 1 to $\frac{1}{500}$ second for interlens shutters and 1 to $\frac{1}{1000}$ second for focal-plane types. The exposure times of older shutters followed the series $\frac{1}{25}$, $\frac{1}{50}$, $\frac{1}{100}$ second, and so on; modern shutters follow the series $\frac{1}{30}$, $\frac{1}{60}$, $\frac{1}{125}$ second. Some focal-plane shutters have faster speeds, such as $\frac{1}{2000}$ second; some older models, such as the Exakta, used gear-train mechanisms to give exposure times as long as 12 seconds.

Electronic shutters

Strictly speaking, electronic shutters are spring-operated shutters controlled by electronic timing circuits. An electrical charge, stored in a capacitor, discharges through an electromagnet that holds the shutter open against the springs. Exposure time depends on the amount of charge in the capacitor, thus allowing the integration of shutter and exposure-metering systems for automatic exposure control. Instead of the camera's built-in exposure meter indicating a shutter speed to be set on the dial, the electric energy from a battery passing through the meter cell is used to control capacitor charge and hence exposure.

Synchronization

All shutters—even simple ones—now have provision for being used with flash guns or bulbs. Older cameras used flash bulbs or cubes at $\frac{1}{30}$ seconds exposure time; modern cameras use electronic flash bulbs. Interlens shutters can be synchronized for electronic flash—the X setting—at any speed; focal-plane shutters must operate at less than $\frac{1}{60}$ second, otherwise the blinds might be only partially open at the time of the flash, causing uneven exposure of the frame. So-called M synchronization of small bulbs or cubes makes contact in the bulb circuit around 16 milliseconds before the shutter opens fully, so the bulb is burning brightly. Focal-plane shutters often have F synchronization for bulbs that have long flash times, which allow fast shutter speeds.

Unusual shutters

One offbeat shutter, produced around 1945, had a gravity-assisted shutter. The speed of this shutter was around $\frac{1}{100}$ second when the camera was used one way up, around $\frac{1}{25}$ second when turned through 180 degrees, and intermediate speeds when tilted sideways to make an exposure.

For high-speed photography, disk shutters are used that have blades that rotate continuously instead of intermittently, so they can move faster. Also, movie cameras for ultrafast recording can have rotating glass prisms or cubes to interrupt the light beam and provide successive fast exposures. Pneumatic shutters, operated by air pressure, have also been used occasionally.

▲ Focal-plane shutters have two blinds that open and close across the film from opposite sides. At slow speeds (top), of $\frac{1}{125}$ seconds or more, one blind opens completely before the other closes. The flash, if used, is synchronized to the instant when both blinds are open. At faster speeds, one blind starts to close before the other is fully open, so the frame is never fully exposed.

| SEE ALSO: | CAMERA • MOVIE CAMERA • PHOTOGRAPHIC FILM AND PROCESSING |

Silicon

The element silicon (symbol Si) accounts for about 25 percent of Earth's crust by weight; it is second only to oxygen in abundance. Its name is derived from the Latin *silex*, which means "flint." The silicates, compounds containing silicon and oxygen, are the main components of more than 95 percent of the rocks found on Earth.

Although very common, silicon does not occur naturally in the pure form, and it was not until relatively recently in history that the element was isolated. An early stumbling block was the well-known inertness of the compound silica, silicon oxide (SiO_2), which occurs naturally as quartz or sand and which also forms minerals such as agate, opal, and jasper. The first investigators thought that silica was itself an element and did not therefore make any attempt to determine its atomic composition. In 1787, the French chemist Antoine Lavoisier suggested that silica might be the oxide of an undiscovered element, but it was not until 1823 that the Swedish chemist J. J. Berzelius confirmed this hypothesis by preparing an impure sample of elemental silicon for the first time. Pure, crystalline silicon was first prepared in 1854 by the method developed by the French chemist H. Sainte-Claire Deville.

Pure silicon is a dark gray solid with a diamond crystal lattice that melts at 2577°F (1414°C). Silicon has four electrons in its outer shell and so belongs to the fourth group of the periodic table, where it is positioned below carbon in the third period.

Production

On a commercial scale silicon is prepared by reducing silica with carbon in an electric furnace:

$$SiO_2 + 2C \rightarrow Si + 2CO$$

silica   carbon   silicon   carbon monoxide

The resulting silicon is about 98 percent pure, and while this is suitable for many purposes, it is not sufficiently pure for making semiconductors, which today is one of the most important uses of silicon. For this application, the silicon is converted into trichlorosilane ($SiHCl_3$), a volatile compound that can easily be purified by fractional distillation. The purified trichlorosilane is then decomposed onto a silicon rod in the presence of highly purified hydrogen gas at a temperature of about 1832°F (1000°C):

$$SiHCl_3 + H_2 \rightarrow Si + 3HCl$$

trichlorosilane   hydrogen   silicon hydrogen chloride

Quartz crystals embedded in dolomite crystals. Quartz is a silicon dioxide crystal.

Muscovite, a type of mica containing silicon, is found in igneous and metamorphic rocks and has a platelike crystal structure that allows it to be cleaved easily into sheets.

These rods may be up to 3 ft. (0.91 m) long with a final diameter of around 6 in. (15 cm), the silicon deposit being in a polycrystalline form. Typically the silicon produced this way will have the impurities reduced to a level of about 1 in 10^9 and is suitable for making semiconductor devices such as transistors and rectifiers. In addition, the silicon used to make silicon chips usually has to be in the form of single crystals, and such crystals are grown from the pure polycrystaline silicon. The orientation of the crystal structure also affects the properties of the chip, so this too must be accurately controlled.

Float zoning is one of the techniques used for growing crystals and can also be used to further purify the silicon. The rod to be treated is mounted vertically inside a water-cooled furnace tube of fused silica (SiO_2). Outside the silica tube there is a copper heating coil carrying a high-frequency current. The magnetic field produced by the coil induces eddy currents within the silicon rod, causing local heating that melts the rod. Since the silica of the furnace tube is nonconducting, it does not become heated during the process.

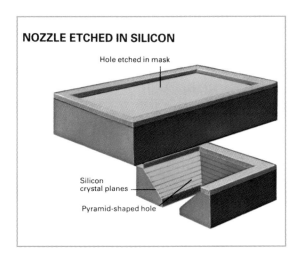

NOZZLE ETCHED IN SILICON

Hole etched in mask

Silicon crystal planes

Pyramid-shaped hole

◀ Silicon can be etched very cheaply and efficiently to make simple micromechanical devices, such as nozzles for ink-jet printers.

The coil is comparatively short and is slowly moved up the furnace tube so that the molten region moves up the silicon rod with the silicon solidifying behind the heated zone. Any impurities in the silicon tend to be carried along in the molten region and finish up at the end of the rod, which can be cut off. Only a small section of the rod is in the molten state at any time, and surface tension effects retain it in place between the solid sections of the rod. Silicon is highly reactive at its melting point, so it is important to make sure that the rod is supported completely clear of the silica furnace tube. In addition, the tube is usually filled with hydrogen gas to give a reducing atmosphere during refining.

Single crystals

Production of single crystals is carried out in the same manner, but the rod is mounted over a seed crystal, which is a single crystal of silicon that has been cut to give the required alignment to the crystal structure. The heating coil is arranged so that it first melts the top of the seed. Then it is moved slowly upward so that the molten silicon crystalizes on top of the seed, extending the single-crystal structure with the same orientation. Rotation of the silicon rod and seed crystal during the process ensures even heating and gives a uniform structure. This process continues until the entire rod is converted into a single crystal. Such crystals are usually around 4 in. (10 cm) in diameter and several feet long. An inert helium or argon atmosphere is generally used in the furnace. Another method used to grow single crystals from the purified silicon is the Czochralski Pulling Technique. Here the purified silicon is melted in a quartz-lined graphite crucible, and a seed crystal is dipped into the molten silicon. This seed is then slowly moved upward so that the molten silicon is pulled up out of the crucible and crystallizes on the seed, taking up the single-crystal structure and orientation. The seed puller may also be rotated while it is being withdrawn to ensure a uniform structure in the single crystal produced. Induction heating is used to melt the silicon on the crucible, and a silica furnace tube is used to enclose the crucible and growing crystal with an inert atmosphere to maintain purity.

For some applications, the silicon crystal has to be uniformly doped with precise levels of specific impurities such as boron, which are added to the molten silicon before the crystals are produced.

Silicon compounds

The most common silicon compound is silica, which finds application in the ceramics industry, in the manufacture of glass, as a refractory heat-resistant lining for furnaces, and (in the form of quartz) in piezoelectric crystals and crystals for controlling the frequency of radio oscillators.

Silicones, an important compound of silicon, are formed from polymers of alternating silicon and oxygen atoms. These polymers possess a diverse range of useful properties and may be formed into elastomers, gels, or fluids.

Silicate minerals are widely distributed in Earth's crust, and many of them are of commercial importance. Clay, for example, is a hydrated (water-containing) aluminum silicate; asbestos is a calcium magnesium silicate; and mica, used in the manufacture of capacitors and other electric components, is the name given to a group of silicate minerals containing potassium, aluminum, and sometimes magnesium. Although some silicates can be written as a chemical formula—for example, muscovite (a type of mica) is $H_2KAl_3(SiO_4)_3$—many have extremely complex structures and cannot be accurately represented in this way.

▶ Making silicone rubber tubing for medical use. Silicone has found a wide variety of uses because of its ability to polymerize.

SEE ALSO: CERAMICS • ELEMENT, CHEMICAL • GLASS • INTEGRATED CIRCUIT • SEMICONDUCTOR • SILICONE

Silicone

One of the most common silicones is polydimethylsiloxane (PDMS), which has the formula already given with both R and R′ representing methyl groups. It is prepared by first reacting silicon with methylchloride, CH_3Cl, in the presence of a catalyst containing copper and copper oxide to produce a mixture of compounds, the most important being dichlorodimethylsilane, $(CH_3)_2SiCl_2$:

$$2CH_3Cl \; + \; Si \; \rightarrow \; (CH_3)_2SiCl_2$$
methylchloride   silicon   dichlorodimethylsilane

This compound is separated from the other products by distillation and then polymerized by a carefully controlled hydrolysis reaction:

$$n(CH_3)_2SiCl_2 \; + \; nH_2O \; \rightarrow \; \left[\begin{array}{c} CH_3 \\ | \\ -Si-O- \\ | \\ CH_3 \end{array} \right]_n + 2n \; HCl$$

dichlorodimethyl   water   polydimethyl   hydrogen
silane   siloxane   chloride

The letter n simply denotes a large number whose exact value will depend on the conditions under which the reaction is carried out.

Silicone polymers may be joined together using organic groups, and the type and number of these bonds may be varied to create different properties. Elastomers, for example, owe their elasticity to the many cross-links between the silicone polymers, reducing the amount of free PDMS and preventing the levels of movement found in gels or fluids. Gels have fewer cross-links and more free PDMS, while fluids have the fewest cross-links and usually consist of only linear chains of silicone.

Because silicones do not conduct electricity, they are often used in the electronics industry as insulators. Fluid silicones may be used as lubricants, especially where tolerance to extreme temperatures is necessary. Silicones are also able to take different pigmentations, making them useful as paints. In addition, the ability to allow the passage of water vapor while preventing penetration by water and other liquids makes silicones suitable as sealants and as protective coatings for certain materials, such as concrete.

The name silicone, or more correctly, polysiloxane, refers to a wide variety of polymers made from chains of alternating silicon and oxygen atoms that may be formed into elastomers, gels, or fluids. Because the backbones of silicones lack carbon atoms, they are classed as inorganic compounds. Attached to each silicon atom, however, are pairs of organic groups, which give silicone polymers partially organic characteristics. The general formula for silicones may be written as

$$\begin{array}{ccccc} R & & R & & R \\ | & & | & & | \\ -Si & -O- & Si & -O- & Si-O- \\ | & & | & & | \\ R' & & R' & & R' \end{array}$$

where R and R′ represent the organic groups—most commonly methyl.

In silicone, the bonds between the silicon and oxygen atoms are strong single bonds that allow the atoms to freely rotate, and therefore, any functional groups attached to the silicon are also able to rotate around the silicon–oxygen chain. The bonds in the silicone chain are also able to bend through large angles, and it is the combination of the ability to bend and rotate that give silicones their flexibility. In addition, silicones are resistant to high and low temperatures, and they are unaffected by oxygen, ozone, and ultraviolet light. These combined qualities make silicones suitable for a broad range of commercial applications.

▲ Silicone gels may be used for breast implants, though potential health risks have now curtailed their use.

SEE ALSO: ADHESIVE AND SEALANT • CHEMISTRY, INORGANIC • CHEMISTRY, ORGANIC • LUBRICATION • PLASTIC SURGERY • POLYMER AND POLYMERIZATION • SILICON • SURGERY • TRANSPLANT

Silver

Silver is the whitest of all metals. This property, combined with its high reflectivity, was responsible for its Latin name *argentum* (meaning "white and shining"), from which the chemical symbol for silver, Ag, is derived.

Because it does not readily oxidize, silver can be found in its native state—in metallic form rather than as a compound—and can therefore be assumed to have been one of the first metals discovered by humans. It has been found in tombs dating from 4000 B.C.E. and it was probably used as money by 800 B.C.E. in the countries between the Indus and the Nile Rivers.

Extraction

Silver is a comparatively rare metal, constituting just 0.05 parts per million of Earth's crust, but is widely distributed throughout the world. The amounts of silver collected in the native (metallic) state are no longer commercially significant, although some ores containing the mineral argentite (silver sulfide, Ag_2S) are still mined. However, the majority of silver is obtained as a by-product of the extraction of lead, copper, and zinc. Another major source of silver is from the recycling of scrap, notably from the photographic, jewelry, and electrical industries.

Silver has a melting point of 1861.4°F (960.8°C) and a boiling point of 4014°F (2212°C). Its specific gravity is 10.5 at 20°C. It is separated from smelted lead bullion by the Parkes process, wherein zinc is added to the molten bullion, which has been heated to above the melting point of zinc. When the zinc has dissolved, the mixture is cooled, and a crust of zinc–silver alloy forms on the surface, because the silver combines more readily with the zinc than with the lead. The crust is removed, pressed to remove excess lead, and then processed in a retort to recover the zinc for reuse, leaving a residue of silver–lead bullion that has a high silver content.

Further refining of the bullion is carried out in a cupellation furnace, in which air is blown across the surface of the molten metal to oxidize the lead and other impurities to a slag, leaving the silver, which is cast into anode blocks. Final purification of the silver is by an electrolytic process.

Straightforward silver ores can be treated in a number of ways, the main methods being amalgamation and cyanidation. The patio process was introduced in Mexico early in the 16th century and involved mixing the powdered ore, salt, and copper sulfate with water to form a mud. Chemical reactions in the mud resulted in the

◀ A silver-containing paste is being deposited on a resin base. Silver is widely used in industry because of its high electric conductivity.

production of silver chloride, which was then extracted by the addition of mercury and thorough mixing to give an amalgam (a solution of silver in mercury). The amalgam was then removed and retorted to separate the silver from the mercury. This was a comparatively inefficient process with high mercury losses, but it persisted in some areas up to the start of the 20th century, although it had been generally superseded by more efficient methods, such as the von Patera process. In this process, silver chloride was made by heating the ore with 70 percent rock salt and then leached out with sodium hyposulfite solution (a similar reaction to that used to fix photographic materials).

The method of extracting silver by cyanidation, the method that subsequently replaced the von Patera process, is essentially the same as that used for gold. The silver ore is dissolved by a dilute solution of sodium cyanide in the presence of air, the solution filtered and the metal reprecipitated by the addition of zinc dust.

When molten, silver can dissolve up to 22 times its volume of oxygen. When it solidifies

silver plates so that two pressure welds were formed. The complete sandwich could then be rolled down to any thickness, the product being known as Sheffield plate.

Silver tarnishes by the formation of a thin surface layer of silver sulfide as the metal reacts with small quantities of sulfur pollutants in the atmosphere. Tarnish can be removed with a suitable metal polish, by an electrolytic technique, or by dipping the article in a dilute solution of tin chloride. On the other hand, it can be prevented by thinly electroplating the silver with rhodium.

Another application, which utilizes the high reflectivity of silver, is in the coating of mirrors, although a cheaper metal, aluminum, has largely replaced silver for this purpose. The surface to be treated is immersed in a mixed solution of silver nitrate, $AgNO_3$, and ammonium hydroxide, NH_4OH, and the silver is precipitated out onto the glass by adding a suitable reducing agent.

Silver solder is an alloy of 30 percent copper and 10 percent zinc in silver. It has a high melting point (for a solder) of 1418°F (770°C) and very great strength. It is used in high-quality engineering work and in the jewelry industry. Historically, one of its major uses was as money, either as reserves of silver bullion or as coins.

Dentists' amalgam used for filling teeth consists of an alloy of silver (70 percent) and tin with small amounts of copper and zinc dissolved in mercury (with roughly equal proportions of mercury and alloy). When mixed, it is plastic, but shortly after—when the filling is in place—a reaction occurs to give a hard silver–tin–mercury compound, which should last for many years.

Photography

The most important user of silver compounds is the photographic industry, which consumes thousands of tons annually as chloride and bromide salts, AgCl and AgBr, respectively. A photographic image is made up of myriads of minute crystals of silver. They are precipitated from the halide salt during development to an extent dependent on the amount of light to which the salt has been previously exposed. Development is a reduction reaction, and the acid hydrogen bromide that is formed in this reaction is immediately neutralized by an alkali such as sodium carbonate, Na_2CO_3, present in the developer solution. After development the image must be fixed by removing the excess silver bromide that was not activated by light during exposure.

again, most of the oxygen is expelled—a process known as the spitting of silver. It is possible to control this process by adding a deoxidant, for instance, charcoal, while the silver is molten. The metal can be superficially oxidized by applying moist ozone, although moist air and dry oxygen will not oxidize it.

Properties and uses

Silver combines the highest thermal conductivity of any metal with the highest electric conductivity, and thus, it is particularly useful in some special circumstances, for example, for coating wires carrying high-frequency currents that flow only in the surface layers. It is also used in making printed electrical circuits and as an alloy with nickel or palladium in electrical contacts. It is also vapor-deposited as a coating for electronic conductors.

Solid silver, as used for cutlery and ornaments, is never completely pure because it would be too soft—it is usually mixed with 5 percent copper to form the alloy known as sterling silver. In jewelry the copper content can be as high as 20 percent. Base metals can be electroplated with silver, as in EPNS (electroplated nickel silver) ware, in which an alloy of copper and nickel called nickel silver is plated with a thin layer of silver. Before the advent of the electroplating technique in 1840, an alternative method of plating was used in which a copper block was heated and pressed between two

▲ These implements are made of sterling silver, which is an alloy of silver with 5 percent copper; the copper adds strength to the silver, which is too soft in its pure state to be used for cutlery or ornaments. Despite its softness, silver has been one of the most sought-after metals through history, and the possession of articles made from the metal has almost everywhere been a sign of status and wealth.

SEE ALSO: METAL • MIRROR • PHOTOGRAPHIC FILM AND PROCESSING • SURFACE TREATMENTS

Sine Wave

The sine wave is a very important mathematical function used extensively by both scientists and engineers. It is the wave shape described in the simple harmonic motion executed by such devices as pendulums and oscillators. Also, it is closely associated with the properties of a circle and right-angled triangles within a circle.

A quality or property of something that alternates in the manner of a sine wave is said to be sinusoidal. The prongs of a tuning fork oscillate with sinusoidal motion, and the voltage waveform of the alternating current used in household electricity supplies is sinusoidal.

From circular to linear motion

The piston on a steam locomotive moves backward and forward with near-sinusoidal motion because the piston is linked to the perimeter of the drive wheel. With a train traveling at constant speed, the piston undergoes reciprocal motion—speeding toward its central position, overshooting and slowing down as it reaches the end, reversing and speeding back toward the center again, and so on.

Consider a wheel-and-piston arrangement with a pen attached to the piston and touching a roll of paper that moves, via gears, according to the motion of the wheel. The shape produced on the paper is a sinusoid. When the pivot point on the wheel is positioned horizontally to the right of the wheel axis, there is no vertical displacement of the pivot, and the pen is at the center of the paper. Turning the wheel counterclockwise moves the pivot upward and to the left. The pivot and the pen are now displaced above their central positions. The pen recording is therefore a plot of vertical displacement against the angle of turn of the wheel (or distance along the paper). For the first 180 degrees, the displacement is above the

◀ Electric power and the light waves it generates, as illustrated by these streetlights, are sinusoidal waveforms.

▼ A device to demonstrate the relation between circular and periodic motion. Angles swept out by the wheel are traced out by a pen recorder onto paper, which advances to depict a sine wave.

central line and labeled positive displacement; from 180 degrees to 360 degrees (completing the circular motion of the wheel) the pivot is below the line and labeled negative.

After a 360-degree turn, the pivot (and the pen) is back where it started, and as the wheel continues to turn, the pen-recorded waveform is repeated—that is, the basic sine wave shape is repeated. The sine wave is therefore said to be a periodic function; the length of one complete sine wave, from crest to crest, is the wavelength.

If the wheel is set spinning at constant speed, the pen is said to be moving with simple harmonic motion. If the wheel is spinning at 10 revolutions per second (10 rps), then there are 10 repetitions of the basic sine wave shape per second. The frequency of oscillation of the pen is then 10 cycles per second—usually written as 10 hertz (10 Hz).

Sine and cosine functions

Mathematicians have given the sine wave its own function, which labels and describes its shape—this is the sine function, which is abbreviated as sin. If the pivot on the wheel is displaced by θ degrees from its original (zero displacement) position, then its vertical displacement is $\sin \theta$ (assuming that the wheel has unit radius—for example, one foot).

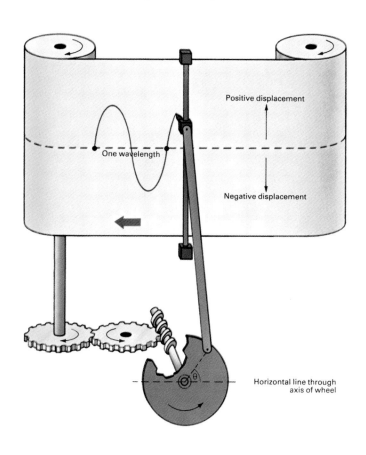

One wavelength

Positive displacement

Negative displacement

Horizontal line through axis of wheel

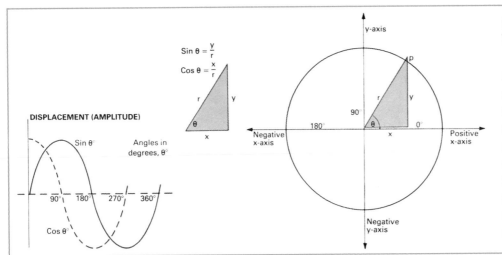

COSINE AND SINE WAVE CONSTRUCTION

A sine wave is related to a cosine wave by a shift in phase. To construct a sine wave (left), angles are measured clockwise from the positive *y* axis. A complete sine or cosine wave is plotted (far left) from 0 degrees to 360 degrees in steps of 90 degrees. For example, sine of 90 degrees equals 1, but cosine of 90 degrees is 0.

Plotting sin θ on the vertical axis of a graph against increasing values of θ degrees (horizontally) produces a sine wave. Plotting the cosine for increasing values of θ degrees produces an identical shape when plotted on a graph, but it is shifted to the left by 90 degrees; sin θ and cos θ are thus complementary functions.

◀ The pistons and connecting rods on a steam train drive the wheels with a motion that is nearly sinusoidal.

Trigonometry

The relationships between sine and cosine functions can be more easily seen from the properties of a right-angled triangle—which is where such functions are usually first encountered. These functions form an important part of the branch of mathematics known as trigonometry.

The full significance of these functions is best demonstrated by placing a right-angled triangle inside a circle such that the hypotenuse (*r*) is a radius of the circle. Then *x* represents a horizontal displacement from the center of the circle and *y* the vertical displacement.

Clearly when θ degrees = 0, then *y* = 0 and sin 0 degrees = 0, but at this same moment, *x* = *r* and cos 0 degrees = 1. When θ = 90 degrees, *y* = *r*; so sin 90 degrees = 1, but *x* = 0, so cos 90 degrees = 0. By suitable labeling of the axes as positive in one direction and negative in the opposite direction, sin θ and cos θ can be described for angles up to 360 degrees. So, sin 180 degrees = 0 and cos 180 degrees = –1, sin 270 degrees = –1 and cos 270 degrees = 0, and finally sin 360 degrees = sin 0 degrees = 0 and cos 360 degrees = cos 0 degrees = 1. All values in between correspond to the shape of the sine wave.

From Pythagoras's theorem, the sides of a right-angled triangle are related by the expression $r^2 = x^2 + y^2$. Dividing both left- and right-hand sides of this expression by r^2 gives

$$1 = \left(\frac{x}{r}\right)^2 + \left(\frac{y}{r}\right)^2. \text{ But } \frac{x}{r} = \cos \theta \text{ and } \frac{y}{r} = \sin \theta,$$

and so $1 = (\cos \theta)^2 + (\sin \theta)^2$. This expression, therefore, completely relates the sine and cosine values of an angle θ degrees.

SEE ALSO: Electricity • Mathematics • Oscillator • Wave motion

Siphon

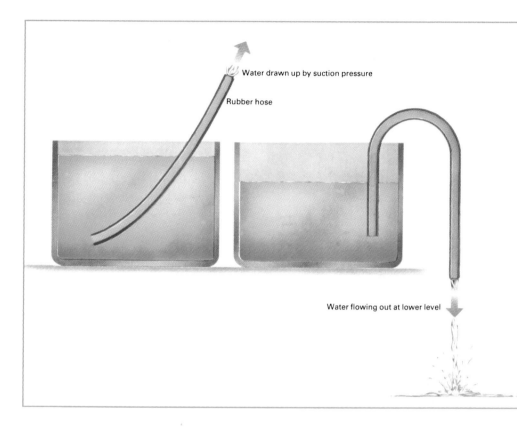

Water drawn up by suction pressure

Rubber hose

Water flowing out at lower level

The word *siphon* is of Greek origin, and it was almost certainly the Greeks who first made use of the siphon principle for conveying water over long distances. This method avoided using open aqueducts, which had to follow the contours of the countryside or be routed across valleys by means of channels supported on stone arches.

The siphon consists of a tube that is bent to form two legs of unequal length, and can be used to convey liquid over the edge of a vessel and deliver it to a vessel at a lower level. In the case of the Greek water-supply siphons, water was transferred over any hump or ridge between the source and the point of required delivery. The small decanting siphon is used by filling the tube with the liquid to be decanted and plunging the shorter leg into the liquid to be drawn. The action of the siphon depends on the difference in pressure in the liquid at the extremities of the tube. The flow is toward the lower level, and it ceases when the levels within the source and the delivery vessels coincide.

A simpler way of understanding how the device operates is to consider the pressure in the liquid at each side of the bend at the highest point of the siphon. On the side with the shorter leg, the pressure will be atmospheric minus a pressure equivalent to the height of the column of liquid in that leg. On the other side of the bend, the same principle applies, but the height of the column of liquid is greater (and the resulting pressure lower), and flow must take place from the higher to the lower pressure. The shorter leg length must not be greater than the height of liquid that atmospheric pressure can support (approximately 30 ft., or 9 m, for water)—there is no way that the liquid can be made to rise higher without pumping.

Siphons can be of any physical size, from the glass laboratory device up to water-supply pipes 20 in. (0.5 m) diameter or more. The large varieties must, however, have a vent or stop cock at the highest point in order to bleed out trapped air. A pipeline that crosses several ridges and valleys can have very large differences between the pressure of the liquid at the highest and lowest points and so must be built with much thicker sections in the valleys.

A good example of the application of the siphon principle is in the flush tank. The handle is linked to a piston inside the short leg of a siphon, and as the piston is pulled up, it fills this leg with water. Once the level of water reaches the high point and starts flowing down the long leg, the siphon is complete. Water continues to flow until the tank is empty, and at this point, the short leg draws air and destroys the effect.

SEE ALSO: ENERGY STORAGE • HYDRODYNAMICS • PLUMBING • PRESSURE • TOILET • WATER SUPPLY

Ski and Snowboard

Skiing developed in northern Europe as a means of traversing snow more rapidly than on foot. Traditional skis for cross-country skiing were made of solid wood and were up to 8 ft. (2.4 m) in length—much longer than those of today. They were best suited to straight running over uncrowded, mainly soft snow. Such skis had wooden soles that would be waxed daily with a hot iron. If they had metal edges at all, they were limited to the most wearing parts; even after World War II, steel edges were bought separately in strips and screwed to the wooden skis.

The decade after World War II saw a revolution in Alpine (downhill) skiing not only in the numbers participating but also in technique. In particular, the craze for constant turning led to the creation of pistes (tracks) and bumps (now called moguls) on the steeper slopes. Traditional wooden skis were too flexible for the changed

▲ Snowboarding has gradually grown in popularity since the 1970s. As with a ski, the midlength waist of the board is its narrowest point. The shovel is the widest point, and the heel is almost as wide.

practices, and solid wood gave way first to wooden laminations, then to metal, and in the early 1960s, to polymeric materials. Longer wooden skis continue to be popular for cross-country rather than for fast downhill skiing.

Snowboarding—a hybrid between surfing and skiing—originated in the 1970s. Snowboarders use a wide single board rather than slender twin skis, and they stand sideways to the direction of motion. Nevertheless, the designs of skis and snowboards have much in common.

Design

Skis and snowboards have approximate hourglass profiles viewed from above; the following description of a ski applies to snowboards, but a snowboard is considerably wider. From the tip, the body of a ski curves down and broadens to a shoulder before tapering back gradually to the waist—the narrowest part and the approximate midpoint of the length. The part of the ski between the tip and the waist is called the fore-body, and it resembles a rounded shovel. Behind the waist, the afterbody widens out to the heel—the second widest point after the shoulder. The tail curves up from the heel and tapers back.

Side cut. The side cut, or side camber, is the curve of the ski side between the shovel, waist, and heel. During a turn, the skier leans into the turn, and the tip and heel rise toward the skier, forming a curved trace in the snow. The side cut ensures that the ski digs evenly into the snow during this maneuver, so the profile of the side cut is a determining factor in turning performance.

Camber. The camber, or arch, of a ski is the downward curve of the tip and heel from the waist; it can be clearly seen when the running surfaces of two skis are put together. The purpose of the camber is to spread the skier's weight along the length of the ski, since that weight would be concentrated at the waist of a camberless ski. The camber also provides a springboard effect to assist in unweighting (lifting) the skis for turning. Too much camber makes turning hard work; too little will lead to adhesion loss at the tip and heel.

Flex pattern. The thickest and least flexible part of a ski is the waist; thickness diminishes toward the tip to provide fore flex and to the heel to provide aft flex. The combination of fore flex and aft flex of a given ski design is called its flex pattern. A ski may be flexible or stiff overall, or it may be soft in front and stiff behind, for example. Softer skis are easier to turn and better for light skiers; stiffer skis are better for straight running

SKI CONSTRUCTION

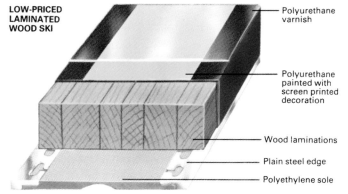

LOW-PRICED LAMINATED WOOD SKI
- Polyurethane varnish
- Polyurethane painted with screen printed decoration
- Wood laminations
- Plain steel edge
- Polyethylene sole

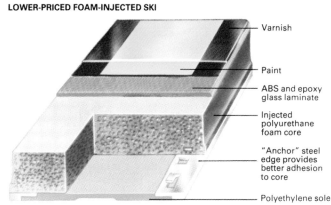

LOWER-PRICED FOAM-INJECTED SKI
- Varnish
- Paint
- ABS and epoxy glass laminate
- Injected polyurethane foam core
- "Anchor" steel edge provides better adhesion to core
- Polyethylene sole

HIGH-QUALITY GLASS FIBER SANDWICH SKI WITH PREMOLDED FOAM CORE
- Varnish
- Protective aluminum top edge
- Paint
- ABS top surface
- 2 layers of epoxy glass laminate
- Polyethylene sidewall (other makers use phenolic)
- Steel edge in sections for greater flexibility

Polyurethane foam core — Polyethylene inner sole — Extra low friction outer sole — 2 layers of epoxy glass laminate

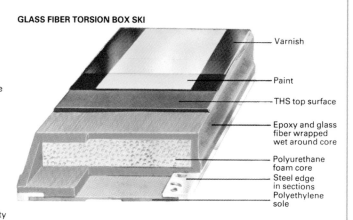

GLASS FIBER TORSION BOX SKI
- Varnish
- Paint
- THS top surface
- Epoxy and glass fiber wrapped wet around core
- Polyurethane foam core
- Steel edge in sections
- Polyethylene sole

Most skis have a polyethylene running sole, which requires little waxing, and an ABS upper surface. The edges are almost invariably steel strips of an L-shaped cross section, and they may be continuous or segmented for greater flexibility.

The simplest skis have laminations of wood that are glued together, shaped by heating and clamping, and fitted with the running sole, edges, and top surface. More elaborate designs have alternate wood and metal laminations, whose multiple layers give the required strength and flexibility.

In sandwich construction, layers of glass fiber or metal surround a core of wood—by preference hickory or okoumé, a Gabonese mahogany. The lamination strips are bonded vertically for torsional rigidity.

Foam cores may be premolded and have the sandwich materials added, or the foam may be injected into a mold in which the sandwich sheets are already in place. Better bonding can be effected by the first method, but two separately shaped molds

are necessary, so the process is expensive. Sometimes, metal cores are molded into foam cores for increased rigidity.

It is more difficult to bond to foam than wood. The strongest epoxy adhesives are used, and often a thin rubber sheet is inserted between the sandwich sheets and the core to allow for the differential expansion of the materials.

Metal sandwich sheets are made of aluminum or Zicral, a strong lightweight alloy used extensively in aeronautics. Glass fiber, in the form of unidirectional woven fabric, is applied to the mold either soaked in epoxy resin—a messy operation known as wet layup—or in semiprecured sheets, known as prepreg. The wet method gives a better bond with the core; prepreg is commonly used for foam-injected skis.

Glass fiber usually provides greater sensitivity and "liveliness" in a ski than metal, at the expense of some durability. Skis of a compound construction of glass fiber and metal provide a compromise.

▲ These four ski formats give different combinations of cost and quality. Cost is determined by the costs of raw materials and the complexity of the manufacturing process.

The other main method of construction used extensively is the torsion box. A premolded wood or foam core has wet glass fiber wrapped completely around it to form a longitudinal box. This construction, though slow and costly, ensures high torsional rigidity, imperviousness, and durability. Torsion can be varied at any point along the length of the ski by altering the thickness of the box. A sandwich ski has an equal torsion along its whole length.

Flexible steel edges can be an integral part of a sandwich construction, or they can be laid in the mold for subsequent injection molding of foam. Once all the components are in place, the rough ski is pressed in a mold, sometimes with heating, for 10 minutes to an hour to ensure that all the components hold together.

(tracking) and for heavier skiers. The composite materials currently in use allow great variations in flex patterns and associated performance.

Torsion. Torsion is the ease with which a ski will twist along its length. A low resistance to twisting makes for poor hold on icy slopes but is more forgiving for novice skiers. High torsion resistance is good for slalom skiing, but too much torsional stiffness can lead to vibration and loss of contact with the snow during turns.

Dimensions. The choice of ski length depends first and foremost on the height of the skier. Short skis, which reach the nose or forehead of the skier when held upright, are lighter and less tiring than longer skis, easier to turn, and slower and less alarming for novices. They are also safer, since they exert less leverage in a fall. They are less stable at high speed than long skis, however.

A typical Alpine ski might be 5 ft. 10 in. (177 cm) in length and 4.4 in. (11.2 cm) wide at the shoulder. The waist might be 3.2 in. (8.1 cm) wide, and the heel 4.1 in. (10.4 cm) wide. Such sidecut dimensions correspond to a turning radius of around 25 yds. (23 m) for smooth turning.

Cross-country skis are narrower and lighter than Alpine skis and have a more pronounced camber and tip curve. Often, they have parallel sides, though some designs have side cuts to help turning. Jumping skis are generally longer and heavier and may have several running grooves to give straight-line stability down the jump.

A typical snowboard might be 5 ft. (150 cm) long and 10 in. (25 cm) wide at the shovel. As with skis, the turning radius of a snowboard is determined by the depth of the side cut.

Turns

The characteristics of a ski or snowboard are determined by the complex interplay between side cut, camber, flex pattern, and torsion. The performance in practice also depends largely on the techniques and skill of the skier or snowboarder, and this ability is most evident in turns.

In smooth turns, the pressure of the skier's weight causes the ski to flex and cut an arced trace in the snow as already described. In skidded turns, the skier forces the tip of the ski harder into the snow, making the shovel act as a moving pivot, and the ski skids around this pivot to make a tighter turn than would be possible by smooth turning.

Straight running

While skiing across a slope, gravity acts at an angle to the desired course of the skier or snowboarder. One device that improves the ability to stay on course is a running groove cut lengthwise down the center of the underside. A deep

groove would be excellent for tracking (holding course) but would resist turning, so a compromise has to be made. A shallow, rounded groove sacrifices some stability for easy turning and is good for novices. A square-cut one favors the faster skier.

Bindings

When skiing, a skier's ankle acts as a pivot that allows the ski to conform to the snow surface. The torque exerted by a ski can put the ankle under great stress, however, particularly in a fall. The risk of serious injury is reduced by a combination of boots with strong ankle supports and bindings that release the boot before the torque on the ankle becomes sufficient to injure.

The front binding has a flange that fits into a matching slot in the toe of a ski boot. This flange is mounted on a pivoted support that holds the boot in place under normal conditions but can turn to release the toe when sideways torque becomes excessive. When placed in the binding, the heel of the boot presses on a pedal in the rear binding. As the pedal is pushed down, it pulls a spring-loaded upper flange into contact with the top of the boot's heel; the heel of the boot is then firmly held between the pedal and the upper flange. If a fall causes excessive vertical torque, the spring-loaded clasp releases the heel. To remove the boot, the skier uses a ski pole to press on a release lever that simultaneously retracts the upper flange and raises the pedal. For snowboards, the bindings are mounted across the board rather than along it, and it is more usual to have a safety strap between board and boot that prevents the board from slipping away.

Poles

Ski poles provide support and balance. They have a handgrip at one end, and at the other end is a tip whose multiple points give grip in snow and ice. A broad collar, called a basket, a short way along the shaft from the tip prevents the pole from sinking deep into soft snow. Poles for downhill racing tend to fit around the skier for streamlining.

▲ This picture shows the instant after the front binding has released the right boot during a fall. The clasping slot in the toe of the boot is clearly visible.

SEE ALSO: FRICTION • GLASS FIBER • PRESSURE • SAILBOARD • SPORTS EQUIPMENT

Skin

Skin is the barrier between the living body and the outside world. It is the body's largest organ, covering about 18 sq. ft. (1.7 m²) and weighing approximately 6.6 lbs. (3 kg) in humans. It keeps body fluids in and foreign agents out. It also regulates body temperature and acts as a shield against harmful rays from the Sun. It contains dense clusters of nerve endings that convey the sense of touch and pain, and it renews itself constantly—although it does lose elasticity with age.

Skin is divided into two layers: the dermis and the epidermis. The paper-thin outer layer is the epidermis, whose outer cells are dead. When dermis and epidermis are temporarily parted by the formation of a blister, the transparent outer epidermis can be cut off because it has no blood supply. Millions of living epidermal cells, called keratinocytes, are created daily on the inside of the epidermis, but as they work outward, they produce a horny substance called keratin. By the time they reach the surface, they are completely dead. This outer layer of keratin, a defense for the body, is constantly flaking away or being scratched or washed away to be replaced from within.

The dermis

The dermis, which lies beneath the epidermis, is a tough, elastic layer that holds some of the vessels and the fatty tissues of the body in place. It is a network of collagen fibers with interweaving blood and lymph vessels, sweat glands, sebaceous glands, hair follicles, and nerve endings. The presence of blood vessels and nerve endings means that a cut in the dermis produces both pain and blood. It is extraordinarily sensitive—the human dermis contains hundreds of nerve endings and 12 ft. (3.7 m) of nerves to each 0.15 sq. in. (1 cm²) of surface area on average. This network can detect pain, pressure, heat, cold, and vibration.

There are about 10 hair follicles to each 0.15 sq. in. (1 cm²) of human skin. This number does not vary between men and women and is not markedly smaller than the number of follicles in the skin of hairier primates. The follicle is a tube with a core of keratinized, dead cells that are pushed upward as new cells are produced to form a hair. Human hair is usually finer and more lightly colored, so it forms a less dense and less apparent covering than is seen on other primates.

Temperature regulation

Hair plays a key part in the skin's essential function of regulating temperature. Humans need to maintain a constant body temperature of 98.6°F (37°C). If the body begins to overheat, the control center in the brain causes an increased blood flow, and the dilated blood vessels in the dermis will give a flush to the skin in order to lose heat by radiating it to the outside. At the same time, the sweat glands become more active, and the evaporation of sweat from the surface of the epidermis has a cooling effect. To combat cold, the surface blood vessels constrict, sweating stops, and the erector muscle at the base of each hair contracts, causing the hairs to stand on end and trap air.

The same thing applies to the sebaceous glands near the hair follicles, which produce a fatty substance called sebum that oils the hair and surrounding skin. Sebum helps hair to become waterproof and enhances its capacity to retain heat.

Skin also helps shield against the harmful ultraviolet rays of the Sun. There are millions of cells called melanocytes in the dermis, producing a pigment called melanin. When exposed to sunlight, these pigment granules rise from the lower epidermis to the surface, giving a tan that screens out ultraviolet. Skin color depends on the degree of melanin. All races have the same number of melanocytes, but genetic factors control the amount of melanin found in the epidermal cells.

With age, skin tends to become thinner and more transparent. Fat in the subcutaneous layer below the skin diminishes so that wrinkles form, and skin fibers become less elastic so that the skin hangs more loosely.

Artificial skin

The commonest way for very large areas of skin to be lost is through burn wounds. The quick replacement of some sort of protection for the body surface exposed by the wound becomes vital once a certain percentage of body area (over 75 percent in young people and over 23 percent in the aged) loses its dermal and epidermal layer. In such a critical situation, the wound dressing needs to possess certain qualities in common with the skin it is replacing. A number of substances have been developed to serve as artificial skin in the clinical management of large areas of skin loss.

Without its protective layer of skin, the body faces two immediate dangers: rapid loss of body fluids out through the wound and infection. Two

SKIN TISSUE

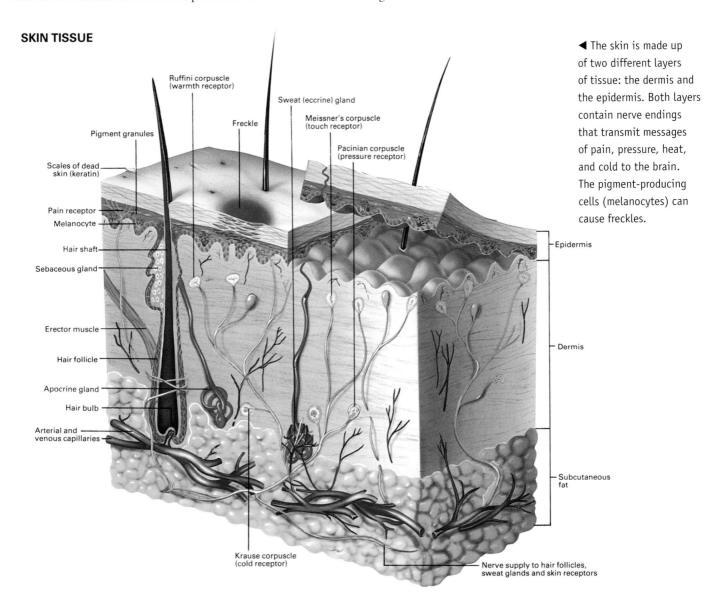

◀ The skin is made up of two different layers of tissue: the dermis and the epidermis. Both layers contain nerve endings that transmit messages of pain, pressure, heat, and cold to the brain. The pigment-producing cells (melanocytes) can cause freckles.

Ruffini corpuscle (warmth receptor)

Sweat (eccrine) gland

Freckle

Meissner's corpuscle (touch receptor)

Pacinian corpuscle (pressure receptor)

Pigment granules

Scales of dead skin (keratin)

Pain receptor

Melanocyte

Hair shaft

Sebaceous gland

Erector muscle

Hair follicle

Apocrine gland

Hair bulb

Arterial and venous capillaries

Epidermis

Dermis

Subcutaneous fat

Krause corpuscle (cold receptor)

Nerve supply to hair follicles, sweat glands and skin receptors more undesirable effects occur as the healing process gets under way and skin regrows over the wound: the skin contracts and scarring takes place. Contraction can be so severe that a patient is no longer able to extend a joint fully. Scarring takes place because fibrous tissue multiplies far faster than the natural epithelial cells and prevents them from growing over the wound.

Two-layer membrane

To combat these harmful processes, a number of synthetic materials—usually constructed from polymers—have been designed as temporary or semipermanent dressings. One means of managing the first stage of wound closure (keeping fluids in and infections out) is a two-layer membrane consisting of an artificial silicone polymer on the outside and a mixture of collagen fibers (taken from animal skins) and a polysaccharide (obtained from the cartilage of sharks) on the inside. The silicone keeps harmful bacteria out and body fluid in—although it has to let some fluid out or it would build up between the wound and the dressing—and the inner layer has properties that encourage the healing process.

The silicone outer layer is performing the barrier role played by the epidermis of natural skin. The inner layer has been carefully treated so that it is not an irritant nor likely to be rejected by the body's immune system. The entire dressing is flexible and adhesive enough to drape over the wound so that no air pockets form between wound surface and dressing. If the wound surface is surgically cleaned before the artificial skin is applied, a strong bond results.

The inner layer of the dressing provides nutrients that encourage cells to build a new natural dermal skin layer and migrate into it. As the new skin cells populate the inner layer of the dressing, its constituent fibers begin to break up and are cleared away by the phagocyte blood cells that perform the task of clearing away debris in the body. After 20 days, the synthetic skin has vanished and been replaced by a naturally grown inner, or dermal, layer of skin. The remaining silicone layer is removed, and epidermal cells will either grow in from the edges of the wound or be grafted onto it.

Scientists can also now culture a patient's natural skin in the laboratory so that a small graft can produce hundreds of times its surface area within a few days. However, this type of artificial skin has already been overtaken by a version that encourages the regrowth of both dermis and epidermis. Although structurally the same, it has an addition of basal cells isolated from a graft of the patient's skin. The whole process is very swift—the graft is taken, and the basal cells are isolated and spun into the polymer network in a centrifuge within four hours, enabling a dressing to be applied quickly enough to prevent a deadly loss of body fluid.

Once this dressing is seeded with basal cells and stitched into place, the same process of growing a new dermis occurs. At the same time the basal cells proliferate to form a new epidermis. Within 14 days the epidermis is complete enough for the silicone layer to be removed, and within 30 days the skin seems almost intact again.

However, the reestablished dermis has no hair follicles or sweat glands, and there is still the possibility of some scarring. Nevertheless, the artificial skin does provide a lifesaving barrier, and the skin contracts much less than it would if left completely unprotected.

Skin diseases

There are a number of common skin diseases, the commonest being eczema, or dermatitis, a skin inflammation of the upper dermis and epidermis. The keratinocytes in the epidermis swell and fluid accumulates between them. Less common is psoriasis, which is a faster than normal growth of keratinocytes and forms raised, scaly areas, notably around the knees, elbows, buttocks, and knuckles. Skin cancer is one of the commonest types of cancer in humans, and although it can be seen and recognized early, significant mortality results.

◀ Differences in skin color arise from pigments in the upper layer called melanocytes. Melanin pigment produces brown shades, while yellow tones are carotene.

SEE ALSO: Bioengineering • Cancer treatment • Cell biology • Microsurgery • Muscle • Operating room • Phototherapy • Plastic surgery • Silicone • Surgery • Transplant

Skyscraper

The term *skyscraper* was coined in the 1880s to describe the multistoried buildings that were starting to transform the skylines of the business districts of major U.S. cities, notably Chicago and New York. At that time, buildings of more than five or six stories were considered remarkable; now, only buildings that have 50 or more stories are considered to be skyscrapers.

Why build higher?

The disadvantages of skyscrapers are numerous. The complexity—and therefore cost per unit floor area—of construction increases rapidly with increasing height, since the load-bearing structures of each story must carry the weight of all the overlying stories. Furthermore, the proportion of useful floor space decreases as more elevator shafts are included to service upper floors. An additional setback is the time spent in reaching and returning from upper floors by elevator.

Despite these disadvantages, skyscrapers are economically viable where land is so expensive that it is cheaper to build many stories on a small plot than to accommodate the same floor space in

▲ On their completion in 1998, the Petronas Twin Towers in Kuala Lumpur, Malaysia, became the tallest in the world at 1,483 ft. (452 m). The towers are unlikely to keep their record for long—there are already plans to build much taller structures in Shanghai, China, and Katangi, India.

low-rise buildings. Thus, skyscrapers are almost always located in the business districts of major financial centers, such as Manhattan, Hong Kong, and Singapore. In these districts, fierce competition for limited ground area drives land costs to phenomenally high values.

A less logical driving force for building skyscrapers—a powerful one, nevertheless—is the desire for the prestige conferred by having office space in an imposing skyscraper. The ability to pay for such office space implies success and attracts the interest and respect of customers and associates. Furthermore, when a notable or even record-breaking skyscraper carries the name of its owner, it is a source of valuable publicity. Hence, the progression to ever taller and more striking buildings is fueled by pride as well as by thrift.

Early skyscrapers

It is arguable that the skyscraper became a viable proposition in 1857, when the U.S. inventor Elisha Otis launched the first passenger safety elevator. Without rapid and safe elevators, the construction of buildings with 10 or more floors for public use would be impractical.

The construction of skyscrapers required a departure from traditional construction materials and from conventional approaches to structural design. Around the mid-19th century, bricks and stone were almost universally used to build tall buildings; these materials were strong enough to support approximately five stories whose weight was distributed across load-bearing walls. Additional stories would have exceeded the weight that could be carried by load-bearing walls of acceptable thicknesses, however.

The first great break from then-current building methods was made by the U.S. architect William Le Baron Jenney in his design for the 10-story Home Insurance Company Building, built in Chicago, Illinois, between 1884 and 1885. Jenney rejected masonry walls in favor of a metal frame for carrying the weight of the building; the frame was clad in bricks and tiles to prevent the metal from softening by heat in the event of a fire.

Jenney's original design specified cast-iron columns as the upright members of the frame and wrought-iron beams as the horizontal members. These materials were chosen because they are stronger than the equivalent weights of stone and brickwork. Hence, an iron structure can reach a much greater height than a masonry structure before the weight of upper stories exceeds the load that lower stories can carry.

The construction of the Home Insurance Company Building witnessed yet another change in materials—this time in favor of steel. Jenney had intended to use hard-but-brittle cast iron to carry vertical compressive loads in the columns while using softer wrought iron in the beams, where shear (transverse) forces could cause cast-iron beams to snap. Steel, like cast iron, is an alloy of iron with carbon. In both cases, the presence of carbon adds hardness, but the lower carbon content of steel keeps it flexible. Hence, steel can be used for horizontal and vertical frame elements.

Jenney used a steel frame for two floors of the Home Insurance Company Building. The first fully steel-framed skyscraper was the Ludington Building of 1891, also designed by Jenney, which was built to house the American Book Company. Whereas the Home Insurance Company Building was demolished in 1931, the terra-cotta-clad Ludington Building still stands at 1104 South Wabash Avenue in the South Loop of Chicago.

William Le Baron Jenney was the leading figure of the Chicago school—an informal group of skyscraper architects of the late 19th century. The work of these architects was characterized by steel frames and lightweight "curtain walls" that consisted of masonry frame cladding interspersed by large areas of glass—a weight-saving measure. These traits are still seen in modern skyscrapers, although materials and dimensions have changed.

Substructure

In addition to setting the format for the visible structures of skyscrapers, the architects of the Chicago school also established methods for building adequate foundations for high-rise buildings. This part of the structure, called the substructure, starts below ground—often below one or more basement stories.

With the framework structure, the weight of a building is carried by vertical steel girders whose cross-sectional area is small. Since pressure is force (in this case, weight) divided by area, the pressure at the bottom end of such a girder is immense—easily capable of cutting through soft clay. For low-rise buildings, the pressure can be reduced to a bearable value by resting the vertical girders on pyramids of stacked steel girders, called spread footings, so the weight of the building spreads over a wide area.

For high-rise buildings, the pressure at the bases of spread footings would be too great to find support in soft clay, and some direct connection with solid bedrock must be made. In the 1890s, the German-born U.S. architect Dankmar Adler adapted the caisson method used in bridge construction to dig through to the bedrock. Manual laborers worked inside cylindrical shields, called caissons, that held back the surrounding clay as they dug. Once the bedrock was reached, concrete would be poured into the shaft and left to set, forming a rigid support for the building.

An additional complication encountered with high buildings is their tendency to sway in the wind. While some amount of sway is tolerable—and even desirable in the event of an earthquake—excessive sway would create an effect similar to seasickness in a building's occupants. For this reason, the Chicago school introduced wind bracing to keep sway under control.

◀ Illuminated skyscrapers form a dramatic skyline on this misty night on Manhattan Island.

◀ Originally called the Fuller Building after its constructor, the Flatiron Building, New York City, gained its name for its distinctive triangular footprint. Located at the junction of 23rd Street, Broadway, and Fifth Avenue, and completed in 1902, the Flatiron Building is the oldest standing skyscraper in New York City.

In the simplest form of wind bracing, each of the joints in the support frame is fixed at top and bottom to keep the frame rigid. For taller structures, plates or diagonal struts hold key parts of the frame square, just as the back panel or diagonal safety struts brace a freestanding bookcase.

Early 20th century

Using the techniques established by the Chicago school, skyscraper projects of the early 20th century grew rapidly in scale and spread beyond the limits of the school's home city. In 1909, the Metropolitan Life Building was erected in Madison Square, New York City, its 50 stories reaching 700 ft. (213 m). Four years later, the 57-story Woolworth Building reached 792 ft. (241 m). By 1929, the 71-story Bank of Manhattan Building set a new record at 927 ft. (283 m).

The design approach to these buildings makes up a catalog of architectural fantasy: the Woolworth Building and the Chicago Tribune Tower are both Gothic in style, while other skyscrapers included classical elements and Renaissance domes. The advent of lightweight building materials not only reduced the load to be carried by the structural frame but also freed designers from the stylistic restrictions of the past.

The era culminated in a race between two U.S. business magnates to build the world's tallest building in New York City. The first was Walter Chrysler, founder of the automobile Chrysler Corporation. In 1928, Chrysler started construction of the Chrysler Building at 405 Lexington Avenue. The project was cloaked in mystery, the

▼ The waterfront of Hong Kong's business district is dominated by skyscrapers. Small countries such as Hong Kong and Singapore have had to build upward rather than outward because of the pressures of space.

intended height a complete secret until the very end. When 70 stories of conventional construction were complete, work started on seven more stories concealed within the building. Clad in stainless steel to mimic chrome-plated automobile parts, the gleaming pinnacle was winched into place and affixed within one and a half hours one day in 1930, making it the tallest building at 1,048 ft. (319 m).

The glory of the Chrysler Building was soon to be outshone, however. On March 17, 1930—before the Chrysler Building was even complete—John Jakob Raskin, a former vice president of General Motors, started construction of the Empire State Building at 350 Fifth Avenue, New York City. Not knowing how tall the Chrysler Building would be, Raskin simply instructed his architects to build as tall as possible. The original plan included 80 stories; then, when the Chrysler Building passed that mark, construction continued to 86 stories—the top of the masonry-clad edifice—and 1,050 ft. (320 m).

To guarantee the record of tallest building would hold, Raskin then requested the addition of a metal tower to 102 stories and 1,224 ft. (373 m), topped off by a 230 ft. (70 m) lightning conductor and mooring mast for airships. The mooring mast was never equipped for receiving passengers, since a trial mooring in September 1931 showed wind conditions at 1,454 ft. (443 m) to be too extreme for airships to moor in safety. The tower now carries a multitude of antennas.

The Empire State Building held the tallest-building record until the completion of the World Trade Center in 1972. The speed and efficiency with which it was built is yet to be bettered: 17 months for design and construction, with a total

STRUCTURAL FORMATS

In the second half of the 20th century, the introduction of new materials for skyscraper construction opened up the range of possible construction formats and techniques. Steel and reinforced concrete are the principal structural materials, while plate glass has become the dominant cladding material.

In unit slab construction, steel or reinforced concrete columns form the vertical structural members. The floors are monolithic concrete slabs that are cast in situ and then winched into place. The integrity of the slab floors removes the need for separate horizontal beams. Lightweight glass cladding requires little support to hold it in place.

In cantilevered slab construction, a tubular central core takes the place of the vertical columns of a conventional frame structure and acts as a conduit for elevators and other service equipment. Symmetrical concrete slab floors are hung on the core, their weight balanced at the center of the core.

In tubular frame construction, the structural frame forms the outside of the building, and the floors and cladding are hung on that frame. In another method (lower far right), floors hang on an internal frame of reinforced concrete, and cladding hangs from the floors.

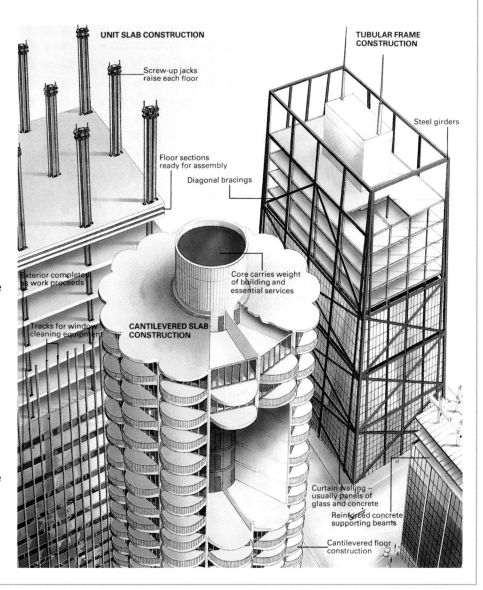

UNIT SLAB CONSTRUCTION

Screw-up jacks raise each floor

Floor sections ready for assembly

Diagonal bracings

Exterior completed as work proceeds

Tracks for window cleaning equipment

CANTILEVERED SLAB CONSTRUCTION

Core carries weight of building and essential services

TUBULAR FRAME CONSTRUCTION

Steel girders

Curtain walling – usually panels of glass and concrete

Reinforced concrete supporting beams

Cantilevered floor construction

---

time of only 1 year and 45 days to put around 365,000 tons (331,000 tonnes) of material into place, including more than 57,000 tons (52,000 tonnes) of structural steel.

Modernism

The economic depression of the 1930s, followed by World War II and its aftermath, slowed skyscraper construction to a near halt for the 1930s and 1940s. By the time the economy recovered sufficiently for skyscrapers to be built, fashions in construction had changed: the ornate forms of 1920s and 1930s Art Deco styling had given way to the clean lines of the International Style.

The 1950s invention of the float-glass process facilitated the fabrication of large sheets of perfectly flat glass. The availability of this material made it possible to apply the principles of the International Style to skyscrapers, and the stone cladding of the Empire State Building and its contemporaries was replaced in newer buildings by a sleek covering of weatherproof smoked glass that concealed or camouflaged all traces of the structural framework of the building.

The prototypical constructions of this type were two 26-story apartment blocks, locally known as the "glass houses," designed by the German-born U.S. architect Ludwig Mies van der Rohe and built between 1949 and 1951 on Lake Shore Drive in Chicago. These blocks were supported by a rectangular frame in the external walls on which the the floors rested and flush glass cladding was hung. While not being skyscrapers themselves, these blocks were the forerunners of many modernist skyscrapers, including the 110-story Sears Tower in Chicago.

Whereas each block of the Lake Shore Drive development was based on a single frame of rectangular floor plan, the Sears Tower consists of nine "tubes"—square frames with 75 ft. (23 m) sides within which there are no supporting columns. The tubes are clustered in a three-by-three square block, clad in bronze-tinted glass and black anodized aluminum. The nine tubes rise together to the 49th story in a massive square block; then successive tubes top out, leaving the central tube and a central side tube to rise to a height of 1,454 ft. (443 m) at the 110th story.

After modernism

From the 1980s on, the elegant but austere forms of the modernist block skyscrapers fell out of favor with architects. The first departures from modernist discipline gained the sobriquet postmodernist, and were mostly rectilinear blocks crowned with decorative structures.

Late 20th-century skyscrapers have more complex forms, including curves, stars, and other geometric shapes in their floor plans and vertical profiles. In many cases, these buildings were made possible by the core construction technique, whereby the principal structural element is a rigid tube that runs vertically through the whole height of the building. Concrete slab floors project out from the core to make up the building's profile, which is then clad in glass or masonry.

As of 2001, the world's tallest buildings were the conjoined edifices of the Petronas Twin Towers in Kuala Lumpur, Malaysia. They have floor plans based on eight-pointed stars, and their 88 stories taper in stages to pinnacles at 1,483 ft. (452 m) above street level.

Environmental issues

The scale of skyscrapers sets them apart from low-rise buildings both in the effect they have on their environment and in their sensitivity to the environment. Wind can create very unusual and disturbing conditions around high buildings, for example, particularly on confined sites or where the building is a tall slab rather than a tower. One of the first times this effect was noticed was in 1902, when the Flatiron Building was completed in New York City. The presence of the building channeled wind down 23rd Street, producing powerful drafts

▼ The John Hancock Center, Chicago, during construction. The frame that supports the weight of the building is clearly visible, as are the diagonal braces that help prevent movement in strong wind. Completed in 1969, the edifice has 100 stories and its roof stands at 1,127 ft. (344 m) above street level.

that threatened to raise the long skirts that were popular at the time. The sensitivity of skyscrapers to the elements was noticeable at the slablike United Nations Headquarters in New York City: great difficulties were experienced shortly after completion in 1952, when wind-blown rain penetrated the protective joints in the light-weight curtain walling. The problem was resolved using redesigned seals, but it highlighted the vulnerability of the joints in lightweight cladding, whether curtain walling, sheeting, or panels. The development of neoprene rubber and the invention of more effective synthetic sealing mastics has gone a long way toward eliminating seal problems.

As more skyscrapers were built, another environmental problem was noted: the exclusion of light from street level, leading to the zoning laws of 1916, which limited the height of buildings at the street boundary in relation to street width. The familiar stepped building outline of skyscrapers—typified by the Empire State Building—is a result of this early planning control.

Later planning regulations addressed another problem of skyscrapers: the road and subway congestion caused by the dense concentration of office space in skyscrapers. The solution was to limit the total amount of floor space in proportion to the site area. An outstanding example of a complex of high-rise commercial buildings that conformed to these requirements is Rockefeller Center on New York's Fifth Avenue. Fourteen buildings were built on a site of 12.5 acres (5 hectares) between 1931 and 1940, and several more buildings were added after World War II. The complex, which includes the 70-story RCA Building, is planned around a concourse and sunken plaza. Despite its huge scale, Rockefeller Center provides a tranquil pedestrian oasis in congested midtown Manhattan.

Fittings and services

The provision of comfortable and functional environments within skyscrapers calls for extensive service systems. The basic utilities—power and water—are provided through networks of pipes and cables. There is seldom a widespread gas supply, partly because of the risk of explosion, partly because cooking and heating facilities tend to be centralized. The pipes and cables for each floor radiate through the spaces above false ceilings, and the vertical components of the networks pass through a service shaft, which usually occupies the structural core in core-construction skyscrapers.

The underfloor spaces and service shafts are also occupied by drainage pipes from washrooms and coffee-making areas, by air-conditioning ducts, and by cables for telephone and computer networks. Hatches in the service shaft lead to vertical refuse shafts and sometimes mail shafts.

Modern skyscrapers tend to be divided into vertical zones, catered for by individual service zones that house water tanks, electrical switch gear, backup generators, an air-conditioning plant, and sometimes elevator machinery for that zone. Thus, any system failure affects a limited area of the whole building; the local distribution and collection networks require smaller and more economical duct and pipe sizes; and accessibility, maintenance, and replacement are much easier compared with other building systems.

Window cleaning is now highly automated, and a number of skyscrapers, such as the National Westminster Bank Building, were built with channels in their external surfaces to guide automatic window-cleaning cradles. The future may see robotic window cleaners that move across the glass surfaces on suction cups and use sensors to "feel" their way around a building.

Elevators

Elevators are a vital service, and they also have an influence on the forms of skyscrapers. The Empire State Building has 73 elevators—of which 6 carry freight—that can travel at up to 1,400 ft. (427 m) per minute. The elevators are in seven banks, each of which serves a narrow band of floors to minimize loading and unloading times. In such an arrangement, the elevator machinery often sits in the floor above the top floor served by a given shaft, and the walls of floor above can then taper in without losing floor space.

The Sears building uses a different approach: double-deck express elevators carry passengers between the ground-floor lobby and two sky lobbies. Local elevators operate between these sky lobbies and the nearby floors. This type of system, sometimes called a metro system, is likely to be used in taller skyscrapers of the future. One of its advantages is that several local elevators can share a single shaft, split into zones, with independent elevator machinery for each zone.

◄ Exterior channels on the National Westminster Building, London, simplify the task of cleaning windows by guiding the window-cleaning cradle up the face of the building.

Fire protection

Fire protection is a crucial consideration in skyscrapers, since it is impractical to count on the population of a skyscraper being able to escape quickly down stairs. The first principle is containment: the provision of fire doors and other fireproof barriers that prevent the spread of small-scale fires long enough for them to be extinguished by automatic sprinkler or drencher systems or by manual firefighting equipment. Portable extinguishers and fire blankets are augmented by hoses connected to hydrants and riser ducts that deliver water and firefighting foams.

As was revealed by the tragic collapse of the World Trade Center Twin Towers in New York City on September 11, 2001, a weak point of many skyscrapers is that their structural steel can soften in the prolonged intense heat of a major fire. Some buildings minimize this vulnerability by having the steel frame outside the cladding; others have tubular steel frames filled with cooling water. Reinforced-concrete frames, in which the concrete insulates the reinforcing bars from heat, remain the safest option in this respect.

Future developments

The future construction of skyscrapers remains an open question. Changes in working practices, with more emphasis on working at home and e-mails, has reduced the pressure for corporations to centralize their administration but not the prestige of owning a tall building. In the distant future, skyscrapers may suddenly soar to new heights with the introduction of new structural materials, such as lightweight materials based on carbon nanotubes that would be much stronger than the steel and concrete in current use.

 SEE ALSO: Building techniques • Concrete • Elevator • Glass

Slaughterhouse

◄ Following stunning and bleeding, animals in large slaughterhouses are processed on a production line. Some slaughterhouses can process several hundred head of cattle in a single hour—taking the animal from live to halving in just 10 minutes.

The origins of animal slaughter are lost in the unrecorded past when humans, in their evolutionary development, became hunters. Only in comparatively recent times, perhaps 20,000 years ago, did we achieve one of our greatest advances—the domestication of animals for food. After that the slaughtering process ceased to be the culmination of a thrilling chase and became a calculated operation.

By medieval times, slaughtering was becoming an organized industry in many parts of the world, but up to the 19th century, it was conducted on a local basis, the animals being driven on foot from their pastures to the area of consumption.

Large-scale slaughterhouses first developed in the United States (chiefly Cincinnati and Chicago) and were operated most intensively in the cool autumn and winter months. If the meat had to be shipped any distance, it was first heavily salted, smoked, or dried. Between 1860 and 1880, effective mechanical refrigeration was developed, and it enabled fresh-frozen meat to be transported to any part of the world from slaughterhouses in the producing areas.

The slaughtering industry was probably the first to adopt production line methods, and it is said that Henry Ford was inspired by the Chicago packinghouses to apply the technique to his motor factories in Detroit. Certainly the slaughtering industry today is very large in scale, with about four billion animals being processed in the United States every year.

Preslaughter treatment

It is important to the quality of the meat that animals should not be unduly stressed or fatigued prior to slaughter; otherwise the glycogen, or muscle sugar, is depleted, resulting in lack of acidity in the chilled carcass, a state that favors more rapid bacterial growth and can adversely affect the flavor of the meat. Care is therefore taken not to excite or abuse the animals during transportation to the slaughterhouse. Sometimes large establishments retain a Judas sheep, which is trained to lead reluctant flocks more easily into the slaughterhouse; the Judas sheep is not itself killed.

A period of rest is desirable between transportation and slaughter, during which the livestock are watered and, if necessary, fed. The feeding in the case of pigs can be with a sugar solution that aids rapid replenishment of the glycogen. Another advantage is that livestock so treated are less prone to restlessness or fighting during the preslaughter period.

Stunning

Virtually all developed countries now have legislation requiring livestock to be anesthetized before being killed; methods vary according to the type of animal, the size of the slaughterhouse, and the scale of its operations.

Cattle, which were formerly roped round the neck and dragged to a ring fixed in the floor, are now led to a knocking pen where they are closely confined and can be stunned without danger to the slaughterhouse worker. For pigs and sheep, a restrainer, a type of conveyor that carries them along without their feet touching the ground, may be employed. The old pole axe has now been replaced by the captive bolt pistol, which is held against the front of the animal's skull and fires a pointed bolt that penetrates to a depth of about 2 in. (51 mm); the bolt is subsequently withdrawn. After the cattle are stunned, they are usually pithed by inserting a long rod through the aperture made by the bolt, destroying the brain and enabling subsequent operations to proceed without the danger of reflex muscular action.

Electric stunners are also used for cattle in some countries, but this technique is more commonly used when dealing with large numbers of sheep (including lambs) and pigs. In this method, electrodes at the end of tongs grip each side of the head, and a current of about 80 volts and not less

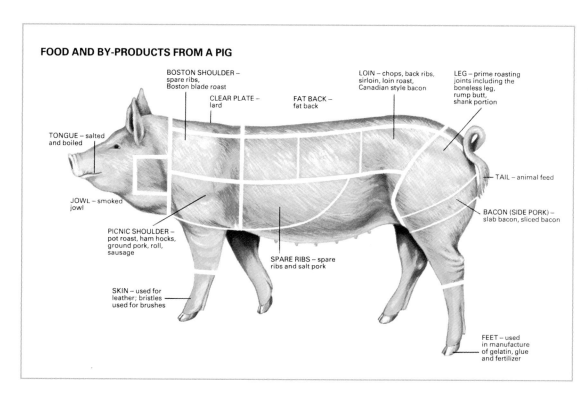

FOOD AND BY-PRODUCTS FROM A PIG

BOSTON SHOULDER – spare ribs, Boston blade roast

CLEAR PLATE – lard

FAT BACK – fat back

LOIN – chops, back ribs, sirloin, loin roast, Canadian style bacon

LEG – prime roasting joints including the boneless leg, rump butt, shank portion

TONGUE – salted and boiled

TAIL – animal feed

JOWL – smoked jowl

BACON (SIDE PORK) – slab bacon, sliced bacon

PICNIC SHOULDER – pot roast, ham hocks, ground pork, roll, sausage

SPARE RIBS – spare ribs and salt pork

SKIN – used for leather; bristles used for brushes

FEET – used in manufacture of gelatin, glue and fertilizer

◀ Slaughterhouses try not to waste any part of an animal. In this diagram, you can see that the entire pig is used, even the tail and hooves.

than 250 milliamperes is passed through the brain, causing temporary loss of consciousness without distress. Another technique widely used for pigs and sheep involves the use of chambers or tunnels with an atmosphere containing 70 percent of carbon dioxide, which rapidly and painlessly produces temporary unconsciousness.

Killing and dressing

Whatever method of stunning is employed, the next stage is to bleed the animal as quickly and completely as possible by shackling a hind leg, hoisting the animal to a hanging position, and sticking it with a very sharp knife so as to sever the main blood vessels of the neck. If the blood is to be used for edible products, it may be caught in containers or drawn off from the sticking hole through a hollow knife and a system of vacuum tubes. The blood must be retained in separate batches until all carcasses have been passed fit for human consumption.

From the moment an animal dies, its natural defenses against the bacteria inhabiting its digestive tract cease to function, so speed is essential in completing the dressing and cooling of the carcass before these bacteria invade the muscular tissue and begin to multiply rapidly. Because some cattle slaughter lines handle several hundred head per hour and pigs can be killed at over 1,000 per hour, full production line methods are usually employed. The carcass is carried by an overhead conveyor system, and each worker performs one particular job as the carcass passes by. Power tools such as saws are used where appropriate, but much of the work is still done with knives. The

▶ Animal carcasses are carried through the slaughterhouse on an overhead conveyor belt. Workers use power tools, such as large saws, to halve the carcasses as they pass by.

use of a conveyor system also helps maintain high standards of hygiene by keeping the carcasses away from sources of contamination.

Following killing and sticking, the first process in dressing the carcass is flaying (skinning) and the removal of horns and feet.

Pigs are seldom skinned but are passed through a scalding tank of water at 140°F (60°C) to loosen their hair and then through a mechanical dehairer. Those carcasses destined for bacon production are then singed for about 15 seconds in a vertical furnace to tenderize and sterilize the rind, after which they are showered and scraped by a scraping machine with spring-steel fingers to remove the outer skin.

Once the hide, fleece, or hair has been removed, the abdominal cavity is opened with a long incision, and the viscera (stomach and intes-

tines) are removed. Then the chest cavity is opened with a saw cut through the sternum (breastbone), and the liver, heart, and lungs are taken out. Next, the beef and bacon-pig carcasses are split into two halves down the backbone with power saws; lamb and pork-pig carcasses remain whole. Finally, the carcasses are weighed and transferred to refrigerated rooms or passed through chilling tunnels. The dressed carcasses may then be distributed to butchers for subsequent jointing, but there is an increasing tendency for further processing to be carried out at the slaughterhouse (on a production line basis), providing finished cuts that are then vacuum packed or frozen.

At various stages the carcasses and variety meat are inspected by qualified meat inspectors for signs of disease that might render the meat unfit for consumption. They are empowered by government regulations to condemn such meat.

Poultry

Table birds are slaughtered in specialized packing stations, where they are stunned, bled, scalded, and mechanically plucked. A light singeing removes the remaining small feathers, and after evisceration (removal of the entrails), the giblets are cleaned in a separate section to be repacked later inside the trussed carcasses. Spin chilling is employed to cool the great number of birds involved. In this process, the carcasses are tumbled in rotating drums filled with iced water. For poultry that is to be sold frozen, the last operation before weighing and packing is to pass them through freezing tunnels.

Ritual slaughter

The shechita method of slaughter prescribed under the Jewish religion is broadly similar to the Muslim method and originates from an early awareness of the need to achieve complete bleeding and the avoidance of ailing animals. No stunning is allowed; having turned the live animal onto its back (by means of a casting pen in the case of cattle), the shochet, or cutter, recites a prayer before severing the carotid arteries, the jugular veins, the trachea (windpipe), and the esophagus (food passage) in one clean stroke of a razor-sharp knife. The knife edge must be absolutely unmarked and the incision completed without pressure or any stabbing movement. If the animal fails to show violent reactions during or after slaughter, it is not considered suitable for Jewish food and will not receive the kosher seal. The lungs of the animal are inspected for abnormalities after slaughter, and if any are present, the meat is not passed as kosher.

By-products

The by-products of slaughtering are of great value economically and medically. The following list is by no means exhaustive.

Cattle hides are sold to tanneries for leather manufacture. The inner layer may be converted into edible sausage skins. The hair can be felted, and the ear hair makes fine brushes. The fleeces from sheep and lambs are sent to fellmongers, who convert them into wool and sheepskin, and pigs' hair can be used for paint brushes or curled and rubberized for use in upholstery.

Hooves, horns, and inedible bones are made into glue, while edible-quality bones, together with feet, produce gelatin. Good-quality fat is rendered into lard or dripping; low-grade fat, such as that derived from the gut, can be used in soap manufacture.

The small intestines are subjected to a cleaning and salting process that makes them into sausage skins. Ox stomachs are cleaned, bleached, and cooked to become edible tripe. The thymus gland, called sweetbread, is regarded as a delicacy. Processing techniques allow the total removal of meat from the bones and the variety meat in the form of a slurry. This slurry is then reconstituted into various meat products.

◀ Removing particular cuts of meat from a carcass requires the specialized skills of a trained butcher, who uses large, sharp knives to separate out cuts like the loin, tenderloin, and shoulder.

SEE ALSO: AGRICULTURE, INTENSIVE • AGRICULTURE, ORGANIC • FOOD PROCESSING • FOOD PRESERVATION AND PACKAGING

Sleep

Sleep is a period of rest that is essential to all humans and most kinds of animals. Most adult humans sleep for about seven to eight hours per night, but some people can do with much less or need much more. Generally, people need less sleep as they get older. Sleep patterns differ widely among animals, however. Of the vertebrates, only reptiles, mammals, and birds experience true sleep, some for short periods every day, others for one long period. Fish and amphibians, on the other hand, do not experience sleep in our sense of the word: they merely become less aware than at other times of what is happening around them, and, unlike mammals, they do not dream. Invertebrates such as spiders and insects have rest periods but do not seem to sleep or even to lose any sense of awareness during their rest periods.

▲ Sleeping like a baby—newborn infants spend an average 16 hours of every day asleep. Babies spend a lot of their time in REM sleep, which is thought to be important in the development of the central nervous system. By the time this baby reaches old age it may need as little as five or six hours of sleep a night.

Measuring sleep patterns

We all know that sleep restores energy to the body, especially to the nervous system and brain. But what actually is sleep? One way of finding out more about it is to monitor the brain's activity during periods of sleep with an electroencephalograph, or EEG. This device is simply a multichannel amplifier and recorder of minute electric potential differences that either exist within the brain itself or are externally supplied and then modified by the brain or bodily activity.

To measure brain activity with an EEG, a set of small cupped-disk electrodes is fixed to the scalp surface by a collodion adhesive or by double-sided sticky tape, depending on whether the adhesive area lies above or below the hairline. When the electrodes have been fastened securely into place,

a conducting jelly, made of agar-agar and saline solution of the same concentrations as that found in body tissue, is injected into the space between the disk and the scalp. It forms a highly efficient contact between the scalp and the fine, chlorided silver wires within the disk leading to the EEG's electric amplification system.

In monitoring brain activity, the aggregate of the electric discharges from the cells in the outer layers of the cortex forms the brain waves. These impulses are then amplified and displayed on the moving-pen graph recorder. Each brain cell shows activity as its head, or axon, fires electric energy to the receptor areas, or dendrites, of neighboring cells. The discharge of this energy by the axon lasts only one to three milliseconds and cannot be repeated until a short period of time has elapsed for the cell to recharge.

The dendrites, on the other hand, transmit energy continuously as they spread over a larger area and interact with many axons at once. As a result, the dendrites effectively smooth out the abrupt axon discharges. It is this comparatively smooth pattern of electric activity, averaged over a large number of nerve cells working in unison, that gives rise to the oscillations that are displayed on the EEG record.

There is nothing absolute about a particular EEG recording. It need not include any unit of measurement, except that of time, allowing the investigator to record cycles per second and compare amplitudes in different parts of the same record. Amplitude is relative, depending on the position of the electrodes. The EEG measures differences in electric potential, rather like differences of water levels at sea, which can be estimated by observing the difference in height between any two buoys out of a number floating on the surface, but which are themselves at different heights.

The onset of sleep

The EEG pattern of relaxed wakefulness when the eyes are closed shows what is generally termed the alpha rhythm of the brain—a fairly steady sinusoidal wave of about 8 to 12 cycles per second (cps), during which time the muscle tone, measured generally at the neck, is high.

As sleep commences (stage one of sleep), the muscles relax somewhat, and the eyes begin to move slowly from side to side. The EEG shows the development of desynchronized, mixed-frequency waves of varying voltage. As sleep deepens (stage 2), sleep spindles appear on the EEG. These spindles are bursts of 12 to 14 cps waves superimposed on a low-voltage, mixed-frequency background. Muscle tone decreases, and rapid eye movement (REM) ceases. At the third and fourth levels of sleep, the EEG shows higher-voltage, slow-wave (about 1 to 2 cps) activity of different intensities. In deep sleep, the waves are more continuous and of higher amplitude. Some eye movement also occurs.

Dreaming

Clearly, there is a difficulty in investigating the dreaming process directly. The sole witness to a dream is the dreamer, so investigators have had to generate a technology that can readily identify when dreams are occurring, preferably without having to awaken the dreamer.

However, as we know, the activity of both the brain and the body offers many small clues suggesting that part of the time we spend asleep is qualitatively different from the rest. When infants fall asleep, their eyes move continuously under their lids long after they appear to be fast asleep. Adults, too, display this rapid eye movement when they are asleep. If the sleeper is awakened at this stage, he or she will nearly always report a dream. REM sleep periods last several minutes

▼ The sleep/wakefulness center is located in the brain stem. Stimulated by information including physical sensations, it passes messages to the cerebral cortex, which determines whether we fall asleep or stay awake. It also responds to signals from the cerebral cortex, and thus, a worrying thought can keep us awake; equally, a quiet mind, warmth, and drugs such as alcohol or sleeping pills will induce sleep. The brain waves change as we become drowsy, sleep, and then return to wakefulness again.

before the dream ends and the cycle of deepening sleep repeats itself. In adults, this activity takes place at regular intervals, occurring first about an hour after the onset of sleep and then at approximately 90-minute intervals during the night.

The EEG record shows that REMs are by no means the only change in body and brain activity that occur during the hours of sleep. Varying levels of muscle tone, temperature, pulse rate, respiration, and vascular congestion—as well as the general pattern of electric activity within the brain—all accompany the REM dreaming periods throughout the night. Breathing is particularly affected by the stages of sleep, diminishing during slow-wave sleep and becoming erratic during REM sleep. The reduction in ventilation causes the amount of carbon dioxide in the blood to rise slightly, with a corresponding drop in oxygen. If the oxygen level drops too much, the body is triggered into waking.

As dream periods seem to occur about every one-and-a-half hours throughout the night, each individual will have four or five dreams—not just occasionally but every night. The knowledge that each of us experiences some 30 dreams per week may come as a surprise to those who confidently claim not to dream. However, if awakened during a dream period, even the most convinced non-dreamers are converted to the idea that they too have their share of nightly fantasies. It is simply that some people are very much better than others at recalling the details of their dreams.

Dream action

The intensity of REMs bears a relationship with dream action subsequently reported, but only in part. A dream of watching a pendulum, for example, produces oscillations on the EEG tracing, but of the wrong shape and at the wrong speed. Another curious finding has been that talking and walking during sleep occur mainly when the subject is not dreaming.

Other experiments have demonstrated that events in dreams occur at about the same speed as they would naturally (in the waking state), thus countering the popularly held view that dreams happen in a flash. An ingenious way to demonstrate this is to hypnotize a subject and give him or her a posthypnotic suggestion to describe while still asleep any dream experienced without waking up. In addition to providing a check on the speed at which dream events proceed, this method makes it possible to learn the true content of the dream before it has undergone the process of rationalization and integration (and lapses of memory) that the conscious mind inevitably performs on it when the subject awakes.

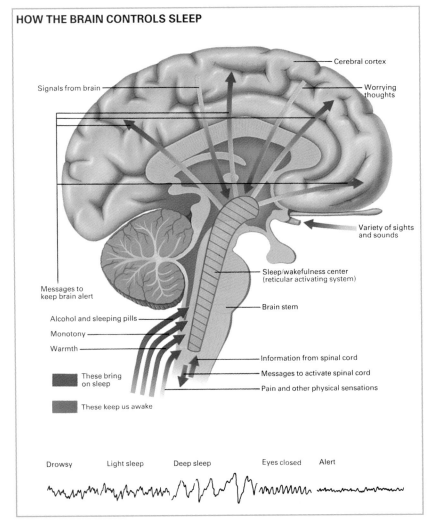

HOW THE BRAIN CONTROLS SLEEP

Cerebral cortex

Signals from brain

Worrying thoughts

Variety of sights and sounds

Sleep/wakefulness center (reticular activating system)

Messages to keep brain alert

Brain stem

Alcohol and sleeping pills

Monotony

Warmth

Information from spinal cord

Messages to activate spinal cord

Pain and other physical sensations

These bring on sleep

These keep us awake

Drowsy   Light sleep   Deep sleep   Eyes closed   Alert

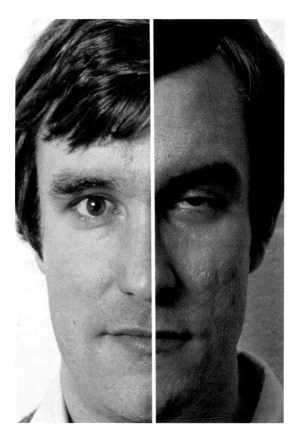

◀ Forcing someone to stay awake disrupts body as well as mind—the split pictures show a man before and after 72 hours without sleep.

The relationship between the dream state and external events is also interesting. Although people can respond to sound signals better during the first and second stages of sleep than during dream sleep, names presented during REM sleep (especially if well known to the sleeper) will often be incorporated into the subsequently reported dream. Alternatively, subjects taught to respond posthypnotically to verbal commands such as scratching their nose or hitting their pillows do so even when the command is given during dream sleep.

Sleep deprivation

One way to test the need for and functions of sleep has been by depriving subjects of all or part of their sleep cycle. Experimentation on rats that were totally deprived of sleep for periods between 6 and 33 days resulted in severe debilitation and, in some cases, the death of the animals. The longest period of sleep deprivation undertaken by a human was 11 days by a 17-year-old student volunteer. Researchers observing the student witnessed a number of symptoms, including blurred vision, slurred speech, irritability, confusion, and memory lapses, as he tried to stay awake. The student suffered no long-term effects as a result of being awake this long but experienced longer periods of stage 4 and REM sleep during his recovery. Symptoms observed in other studies include fatigue, hallucinations, and an inability to concentrate. Lack of concentration as a result of

▶ Lack of sleep affects the brain more than the body; this subject could no longer do the jigsaw puzzle after 72 hours of being awake (bottom).

sleep deprivation can prove fatal, as exemplified by the many long-distance drivers who have momentarily fallen asleep at the wheel.

The need for stage 4 and REM sleep has been investigated through selective sleep-deprivation studies in which both animals and humans were awakened just as they were about to enter these phases of sleep. REM sleep is usually associated with active dreaming, though the Austrian physician Sigmund Freud's view that it was essential for emotional well-being has been reassessed since the discovery that dreaming can also occur during the lighter stages of sleep. In some cases, suppression of REM sleep has been used in the treatment of depression.

New theories of the use of REM sleep suggest that it may be needed for cognitive processing, as experiments on the ability of REM-deprived animals to learn and remember new tasks appeared to be impaired. Another possible role of REM sleep is the regulation of certain drive functions—some animals showed increased sexuality or agressiveness when deprived of REM sleep. Unlike animals denied any sleep at all, there was little long-term effect, and the animals soon returned to their normal sleep patterns.

Sleep disorders

Most people will experience problems with their sleeping pattern at some point in their lives. Insomnia (lack of sleep) and hyposomnia (too lit-

◀ Dreaming occurs during periods of REM sleep, but one curious fact that researcher have discovered is that sleepwalking occurs during stage 4 sleep, disproving the old theory that sleepwalkers are acting out a dream.

rare in adults. Talking in one's sleep consists mainly of incoherent mutterings rather than articulated speech and is characteristic of stage 2 sleep. Nightmares happen to people of all ages during stage 4 or REM sleep. In adults, anxiety or stress from the waking hours becomes manifest during dreaming and leads to spontaneous arousal from the REM state. These dreams often recur as long as the original source of stress persists.

Drugs given to relieve sleep problems generally work by altering the proportion and length of REM sleep. Many of the ill effects felt by the withdrawal of sleeping pills result from the body's attempts to catch up on REM sleep.

▶ This subject's reactions during a period of enforced sleeplessness were tested on Wilkinson's vigilance machine—his ability to press a key in response to a noise became progressively worse (middle), until finally, this simple task became too much to cope with (bottom).

tle sleep) are usually the result of stress or psychological disorders. Sufferers actually get more sleep than they suppose, but research has shown that REM sleep stages are shorter and an increase in alpha waves (waking rhythms) disrupts the other stages of sleep; thus, a person may feel that he or she has not had enough sleep.

Narcolepsy is an extreme condition in which a person falls into a very deep sleep but can be easily awakened. It is believed to be caused by abnormal functioning of the sleep regulatory centers of the subcortex of the brain. Some of the effects of narcolepsy can be frightening both to the sufferer and to anyone watching. One of them—cataplexy—causes the sufferer to suddenly lose all muscle tone and fall down after receiving a momentary startle or shock. Alternatively, a narcoleptic may wake to find that he or she cannot move any muscles voluntarily for a period of several seconds to several minutes, an experience known as sleep paralysis. Hypersomnia is the name given to excessive length of sleeping and often involves the urge to sleep for long periods during the daytime. Though neither narcolepsy or hypersomnia shows any abnormality in EEG tracings, both are thought to be linked to failures in the mechanisms that turn sleep "on" or "off."

Minor sleep disorders, such as sleepwalking, nightmares, and talking, occur during the non-REM stages of sleep. Sleepwalking is most common in children and is thought to be linked to the maturity of the central nervous system, as it is

SEE ALSO: ANESTHETIC • BODY SCANNER • BRAIN • ELECTRONICS IN MEDICINE

Smell and Taste

◀ A professional wine taster examines a Beaujolais by using his sense of smell—a wine aroma may evoke grapes, cedar wood, or even fresh bread.

The sense of smell is one of the most important and probably the oldest of humankind's five senses. It is even more important for animals who use the sense of smell to recognize their home territory and other animals, to find food or a sexual partner, and to avoid getting caught and eaten. Even primitive species have well-developed smell and taste capabilities. Insects and some other animals communicate with their own species by secreting a substance called a pheromone. Silk moths, for instance, can attract mates by this means when several miles apart, and a salmon can smell its way thousands of miles to its birthplace.

In humans the sense of smell is much weaker than in animals. A dog can follow the scent of a human for miles across country, even through all the other scents that crisscross the trail. Humans rely much more on sight, hearing, and touch.

Detecting smells

The scientific term for smell is olfaction, and the mechanism by which humans smell is known as the olfactory system. Humans detect smells by breathing or sniffing air that carries odors—molecules of gas that have been released into the air from different substances. These molecules stimulate receptor cells deep inside the nose. The nasal membrane has about 20 million smell-sensitive olfactory cells packed tightly between supporting cells and glands that secrete mucus to keep the surface of the membrane moist. Each olfactory cell is a nerve ending specially modified for smell detection, with six to eight microscopic hairs, or cilia, that spread out in the mucus. The

rest of the olfactory cell tapers back into a nerve fiber that runs through holes in the cribriform plate to the olfactory bulb (or lobe) in the brain. In dogs and some other vertebrates, the olfactory lobe is large, but in humans, it is quite small. The size of the lobe is a good indication of how important the sense of smell is to its owner. From the olfactory lobe, the nerve impulses travel to the forebrain, the front part of the cerebrum, where they are translated into information about the odor—it is only then that an individual will recognize it.

Scientists have been able to work out roughly how the sense of smell works, but many details remain unexplained. For example, they do not know exactly how different smells are distinguished. Most people can correctly identify hundreds of objects by their smell alone and can even describe a new smell because it is very much like another already known. One explanation is that molecules of certain odors become more quickly and more strongly attached to mucus at a particular place on the nasal bones (called conchae) than do other molecules. In other words, molecules of certain kinds of odors always stimulate the same receptor cells on the conchae, so humans distinguish odors by how fast and where the gas molecules become attached to the receptor cells.

An American scientist in the 1950s, J. E. Amoore, postulated that there are seven basic smells: camphoraceous (mothballs, for example), peppermint, floral (flowers), musky (some aromatic plants), ethereal (kerosene), putrid (bad eggs) and pungent (vinegar). Different amounts of these basic smells make up all the odors it is possible to smell. Each of the basic smells is recognized in one of two ways. The first five smells—camphoraceous, peppermint, floral, musky, and ethereal—are recognized by the size and shape of the particles that go to make up the smell gas. Each of the five particles fits into its own special place on the cilia, like a piece in a jigsaw puzzle. The cilia then in some way count up the number of particles that belong to each basic smell. The other two basic smells—putrid and pungent—are recognized by their electric charge. For example, the putrid particles are negatively charged and so are attracted only to the positively charged parts of the cilia.

Smell and taste

Although humans have come to think of taste (gustation) and smell as being related, they are in fact separate—only at some point in the brain are the separate senses combined. This fact can be proved by blowing very clean air into the nose at the same time that food is put into the mouth. When this experiment is done, the subject cannot identify some foods and beverages (such as chocolate and coffee) although he or she still tastes them. Some substances categorized as smells, such as chloroform, have been found to be tastes.

In practical terms, however, taste and smell are closely linked. Human taste buds differentiate only between bitter, sweet, salty, and sour—when an individual experiences a taste sensation, it is in fact detected by the sense of smell. The link between taste and smell has another common effect. The smell of good food automatically triggers the hunger reaction.

The relationship between the sense of smell and taste is dramatically highlighted during a bad cold, when the nose is blocked. Food tends to lose much of its taste because vapors from the food are unable to travel up to the nose to the smell-sensitive regions of the nasal cavities. For the same reason, it is almost impossible to tell the difference between finely grated apple, potato, or onion on the tongue without chewing it if the eyes are closed and the nose is blocked. Chewing a food agitates some vapors to the olfactory region in the nose, where it is recognized.

To have a smell, a substance must give off particles of the chemical of which it is made—it must be volatile. A saucepan of boiling chicken soup smells more strongly of chicken than a plate of cold chicken because many more chicken particles escape from the broth than from the cold meat. Thus, a smell gets stronger closer to its source because the vapor cloud gets denser.

Particles of a smelly substance must stay in the air to be inhaled and must be soluble in water before they can reach their receptors. Traveling over the olfactory membrane, some particles dissolve in the mucus layer and come into contact with the smell-sensitive surface of the membrane.

Wetness also generally heightens smells. As the water evaporates from the wet surface of an object, it carries some particles of the substance with it. A wet dog is smellier than a dry dog, and wet earth smells more earthy than dry earth, for this reason.

Adaptation

The sense of smell wanes rapidly with exposure to an odor. A worker in a coffee shop is more or less oblivious to the strong smell of fresh coffee that greets the customers. Similarly, it becomes possible to tolerate an unpleasant smell.

This apparent change in sensitivity to a smell arises because of a phenomenon of adaptation in

THE SENSE OF SMELL

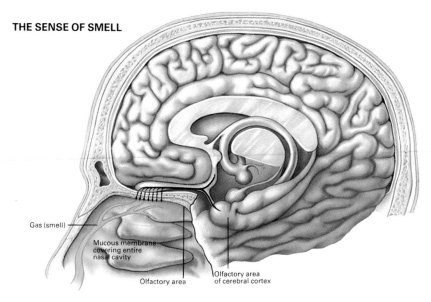

Gas (smell)

Mucous membrane covering entire nasal cavity

Olfactory area

Olfactory area of cerebral cortex

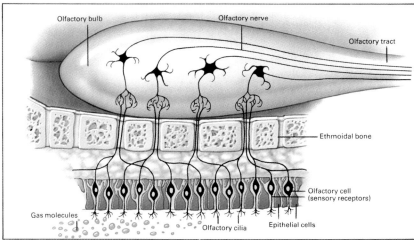

Olfactory bulb

Olfactory nerve

Olfactory tract

Ethmoidal bone

Olfactory cell (sensory receptors)

Gas molecules

Olfactory cilia

Epithelial cells

which the odor receptors become occupied by odor particles. The detection of a smell depends on the interaction between the chemical units of the smell and their receptor sites in the nose. When all the receptor sites are filled, the olfactory region stops signaling that the smell exists.

Communicating messages in smells

The sense of smell is more than a mere sensory decoration. The chemical communication of messages between individuals is used for an astonishing variety of purposes. They include territorial, social and sexual behavior and defense or escape from predators, as well as the more obvious applications of food location and selection and the avoidance of poisonous substances. Smell serves as a valuable early warning system if there are no auditory or visual clues. It is possible, for example, to smell the smoke of a fire before the flames appear. A smell had to be added to odorless natural gas when it was introduced for domestic use so that people would be able to smell potentially dangerous gas leaks.

Throughout the animal world, smells play an important part as a means of communication

▲ Gaseous substances are dissolved in the mucus surrounding the cilia. A chemical reaction then takes place that stimulates the olfactory cells into electric activity. These messages are passed across ethmoidal bone via sensory nerve fibers and into the olfactory bulb. Here the information is processed and then passed along the complex circuitry of the olfactory nerves to the cerebral cortex. At this point an individual will become aware of the smell.

between individuals and as a means of influencing behavior. Humans use artificial smells such as perfumes to express their sexuality.

Each person has his or her own distinctive natural smell. Body odor arises largely from the action of bacteria on the chemicals in sweat. There are two kinds of sweat glands on the body—those associated with cooling and temperature regulation and those (differing between the sexes) producing a fatty substance that bacteria attack. Masking these natural body odors with deodorants and antiperspirants may also smother the communication of fear, hostility, nervousness, or sexual excitement.

It is possible to identify and isolate the chemicals responsible for the characteristic smells of different substances. They can be reproduced in the laboratory and substituted for the natural substance. Because smells are closely linked to emotions, they are very memorable. The smell of a place or a person can be very evocative. In the same way, good and bad smells have a stronger effect on one's feelings than any other sensation.

Smell in animals

A chemical sense is found throughout the animal kingdom, although it is only among the vertebrates (fish, amphibians, reptiles, birds, and mammals) that smell and taste are distinguished through the existence of separate receptors, nerve pathways, and brain centers for olfaction and gustation. At the lowest level of animal life, single-celled organisms such as amoebas can detect chemical substances that impinge upon their sur-

face membranes and as a result can direct themselves through chemical gradients toward higher concentrations of substances they need to maintain life or away from noxious substances.

Seawater provides an ideal medium for a chemical sense, and the simplest animals to have specialized olfactory cells are the marine-living coelenterates—sea anemones, jellyfish, and hydra. Crustaceans such as prawns and lobsters use highly sensitive receptors in the hairs attached to their antennules and legs to detect amino acid concentrations as low as one part in a million and in this way are led to the decaying animals and plants that form a large part of their diet.

Nearly all vertebrate species possess a distinct olfactory organ consisting of an area of tissue packed with nerve cells specially adapted to the detection of chemical substances. Usually the cells bear several hairs or cilia (hairlike vibrating organs), the surfaces of which are thought to contain receptor sites for odorous substances. The cells are all connected by means of long nerve axons—filaments carrying nerve cells—to two protuberances in the brain, the olfactory bulbs.

In reptiles, birds and mammals, the olfactory organ is situated within the animal's respiratory tract so that olfaction is an inevitable accompaniment to breathing. In fish, however, the organ is separate from the gills and consists of a chamber through which water is forced to pass because of the fish's motion through the water.

Many terrestrial vertebrates also possess an additional olfactory organ, called Jacobson's organ, sited in a pouch leading off from the respiratory tract at the back of the mouth. In snakes and other reptiles, it detects odors that waft from substances and are picked up by the tongue.

The territorial behavior of many species depends on each member of the species staking out an area by urinating around its perimeter; other members of the species are then warned off by the odor given off by the urine. Within groups of animals, individuals may recognize one another by their different odors, and chemical communication may be used for such purposes as establishing dominant/submissive relationships or indicating sexual availability and receptivity.

In many species, a substance given off by one member triggers some specific behavior when smelled by another of the same species. These substances are pheromones, from the Greek words *pherein*, "to transfer," and *hormon*, "to excite."

The human nose

The odors of certain substances are influenced by factors other than the substance's effect on the receptor cells of the olfactory organ. For exam-

▼ A fly lured by its senses to the mouth of the pitcher trap of a *Sarracenia* plant, where it is in danger of losing its life. Insects are attracted by a bright red color inside the pitcher or by the smell of a viscous sugary fluid secreted near its entrance. The insects fall into a digestive fluid and are unable to get a foothold in the long, downward-pointing hairs of the plant, so they drown.

THE TONGUE

The human tongue allows us to suck, chew, and swallow. It also contains numerous taste buds and is an aid to speech. The tongue comprises a set of interwoven muscles, in between which are glands and fat, all covered with a mucous membrane. The top surface, known as the dorsum, has many projections from the mucous membrane known as papillae. These contain the taste buds, which sense flavors, and serous glands, which secrete some of the fluid found in saliva. In the upper rear portion of the tongue, these papillae are absent, being replaced by serous and mucus-secreting glands. The undersurface of the tongue is smooth and also contains no papillae. Humans are able to sense four basic tastes using four receptors found in specific areas of the tongue. Salt and sweet flavors are tasted at the tip of the tongue, bitter flavors at the tongue's base, and sour (or acid) along the edges. The array of small taste buds located on the top surface of the tongue transmit these flavor sensations to the nervous system.

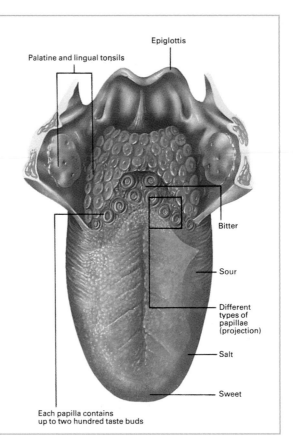

Palatine and lingual tonsils

Epiglottis

Bitter

Sour

Different types of papillae (projection)

Salt

Sweet

Each papilla contains up to two hundred taste buds

ple, the irritation caused by ammonia, the cool sensation of peppermint, and the tickling sensation of onions—all important features of their smells—may be due to stimulation of pain, cold, and heat receptors, respectively, in the supporting cells of the olfactory organ.

Many of the interesting features of our sense of smell can be appreciated by examining which substances have strong smells and which ones are virtually odorless. Since olfaction operates through the inhalation of air containing odor molecules, one obvious property of smelly substances is that they must be either gases or volatile liquids or capable of existing as fine suspensions in the air, perhaps dissolved in some other substance.

A second important quality is that they must be water soluble, since to gain access to the receptor hairs in the olfactory organ, they must first dissolve in the watery mucus that covers the hairs. A third quality is that they must have some rarity value; substances commonly impinging on the receptor cells of the olfactory organ cannot be smelled because any receptors for these substances would be permanently occupied. Fourth, many smelly substances, though by no means all, carry some biologically significant message—for example, they may lead to sources of food or they may warn of danger.

Putting these facts together, it can be seen why some substances have strong odors and others do not smell at all. Gases that form a significant pro-

portion of the air we breathe, such as oxygen, nitrogen, carbon dioxide, and the noble gases, are odorless, whereas less common and toxic gases, such as hydrogen sulfide, sulfur dioxide, and ammonia, smell strongly. Water, an integral element within the body, also has no smell or taste to human perception. Inorganic solids with lattice structures, such as most salts and metals as well as organic polymers and plastics consisting of long chains of molecules, cannot be smelled since their constituent atoms and molecules are firmly bound into the parent material.

Evolution

One striking feature of most smells is that they are usually either universally and instinctively liked or disliked: flower scents and cooking smells generally fall into the former category, the stink of rotting eggs or other putrefying material, into the latter. These positive and negative responses can be partly explained in terms of evolutionary pressures to avoid poisonous substances and to seek food sources: for example, it is likely that individuals that were put off by the smell of rotting meat have survived better than individuals indifferent to the odor, and these survivors have passed the trait on to their offspring.

SEE ALSO: CELL BIOLOGY • PHEROMONE • REPRODUCTION • SKIN

Soap Manufacture

◀ Soap flakes at this manufacturing plant are created by adding brine during the manufacturing process. The flakes are then pressed into shape and packed.

Soaps are salts of mixed fatty acids, and they are prepared mainly by reacting fats with caustic alkali (saponification). Alternatively, the fatty acids may be split from the fats and then saponified. The properties of the resultant soap will depend on the mixture of fats (or fatty acids) used, the kind of caustic alkali, and the postsaponification processing the soap undergoes. As an alkali, caustic soda, caustic potash, or mixtures of the two may be used, but usually it is caustic soda. Potash produces a more readily soluble soap and is reserved for soft soaps and shaving soaps. The fat–caustic reaction can be written thus:

$$
\begin{array}{ccccc}
CH_2COOR & & NaOCOR & & CH_2OH \\
| & & + & & | \\
CHCOOR' & + 3NaOH \rightarrow & NaOCOR' & + & CHOH \\
| & & + & & | \\
CH_2COOR'' & & NaOCOR'' & & CH_2OH \\
\text{fat} & \text{caustic soda} & \text{soap} & & \text{glycerin}
\end{array}
$$

R, R′, and R″ represent organic groups containing only carbon and hydrogen atoms, for example, the palmitic group, $C_{15}H_{31}$. Both animal and vegetable fats are used, but many of the marine animal and vegetable fats are too soft to yield usable soaps directly. They must be hardened by a process of selective hydrogenation to a more useful state. (Hydrogenation of a fat is the addition of hydrogen atoms to its molecules in the presence of a catalyst.)

History

The treatment of fat with alkali has been practiced in the Middle East for at least 5,000 years. The art was brought to Europe by the Phoenicians about 600 B.C.E. Its purpose, right through to the second century C.E. was solely medicinal, for example, for the treatment of scrofulous sores. Soap making disappeared from Europe with the decline of the Roman Empire. It reappeared in the eighth century, but reached Britain only in the 11th, probably as a result of the Norman invasion. It remained a relatively primitive art till the 16th century, when techniques that provided a purer soap—the conversion of potash (literally made from wood ash in an iron pot) to caustic alkali by means of quicklime and the salting out of soap—were developed. In the 17th century, the French industrial chemist Nicolas Leblanc produced caustic alkali from common salt and thereby eliminated a major stumbling block to expansion. (Today it is made by an electrolytic process.) In the 19th century, the French chemist Michel-Eugène Chevreul described the constitution of fats and put soap making on a sound basis. At the turn of the 20th century, methods for the hydrogenation of unsaturated compounds were discovered, and these methods were applied to the hardening of fats. In the first half of the 20th century, the crystalline states of hydrated soaps—which affect product performance—were elucidated, the bleaching of fats was perfected, and deodorization of fats was introduced for the highest-class products.

Manufacture

Soap may be made either in batches or continuously, but the batch process is now mainly reserved for small-scale outputs. In batch working, a molten premixed fat charge is pumped to a steel pan fitted with open and closed steam coils and runoff facilities. The fat is heated with open steam as the caustic solution (lye) is added slowly and intermittently over a period of hours. Half-spent lye is pumped in during the early stages to aid emulsification. At the end of saponification, brine is fed in until the soap separates as a curd. The underlying lye, which contained the glycerin, is run off. The soap is washed by boiling it up with a quantity of water, and a second lye is removed. There is now a finishing stage to ensure complete saponification. For this stage, a calculated quantity of caustic is added, and the mass is boiled gently for around five hours. More caustic is then added till the soap separates as a loose curd, leaving half-spent lye. Finally the soap is "fitted" by boiling it up and adding brine carefully until it flakes in a particular manner, readily recognized by an expert process worker. On settling—which may take up to four days—it separates into three layers: pure neat soap uppermost; next, an impure nigre soap; and at the bottom, a nigre lye. The neat soap is skimmed off for further processing. The nigre soap goes to be reworked. The whole process requires about a week.

By contrast, the more recently introduced continuous process takes only 15 minutes, but it requires a large throughput to be economic. The sequence of treatment—saponification, salting out, washing, and fitting—is the same, but all stages are carried out in totally enclosed vessels. Control is maintained by monitored feed.

Fat and caustic are fed concurrently by proportioning pumps into a saponification column, which is fitted with stirrers and operated at high pressure and at a temperature of 266°F (130°C). The saponified mass leaving the column passes to two centrifuges (or two pairs of duplicates) where it is washed alternately by spent lye and brine to remove the glycerin. The washed soap then enters a fitting column concurrently with a brine and caustic solution and from there passes to three centrifuges working in parallel that separate neat soap from nigre. Alternatively, the fat may be split and the freed fatty acids purified and reacted directly with caustic or carbonate alkali at a concentration that yields the equivalent of a neat soap.

Types of soap

Soft soaps are made from fats with a high proportion of unsaturated acids (organic acids that contain double bonds in their hydrocarbon portions) and are saponified with caustic potash. They are made by a special cold process in which the only heat involved is that of the reaction itself, and the glycerin is not removed.

Shaving soaps are made from fats with a minimum of unsaturated acids—stearine, tallow, and coconut oil—saponified with caustic potash or a mixture of potash and soda to promote easy lathering. A cold process may be used, but more likely a semiboiled process—one in which the initial reaction is promoted by external heating and continued by the heat of reaction. Again, the glycerin is not removed.

Soap powders are formulated products designed to facilitate the removal of fatty and particulate dirt from fabrics with minimum of physical effort. Ancillary constituents deal with chemical stains and general yellowing. Soap provides 50 percent of the product. The washing aids are sodium carbonate, sodium silicate, and sodium tripolyphosphate, but the silicate also helps to produce a readily pourable powder. All are mixed to a paste with molten soap and blown into a cooling chamber.

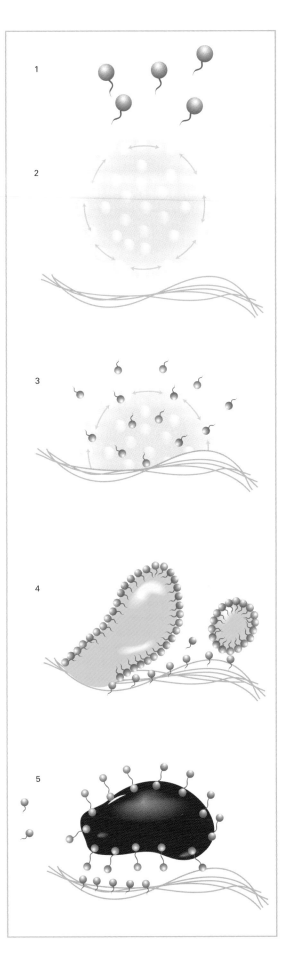

▶ A typical surfactant molecule (1). Soap and detergent molecules consist of a salt and a hydrocarbon chain that are polar at one end and nonpolar at the other. These electrical properties enable the surfactant to trap different types of molecules that may be soiling the material. Surface tension pulls a drop of water into a near-spherical shape (2), but when a detergent is added to it, the polar ends of the surfactant molecules reduce its surface tension so that the drop collapses and the detergent can then penetrate the fabric (3). Detergents remove grease from fabrics by breaking it into droplets coated with the nonpolar ends of surfactant molecules that lift it off the material and leave it suspended in the water (4). Soluble stains, such as rust, attract the heads of the surfactant molecules, which lift the dirt by coating it with a double layer of molecules joined tail to tail (5).

SEE ALSO:	ATOMIC STRUCTURE • CATALYST • DETERGENT MANUFACTURE • DRY CLEANING • HYDROCARBON • LAUNDRY

Soft-Drink Dispenser

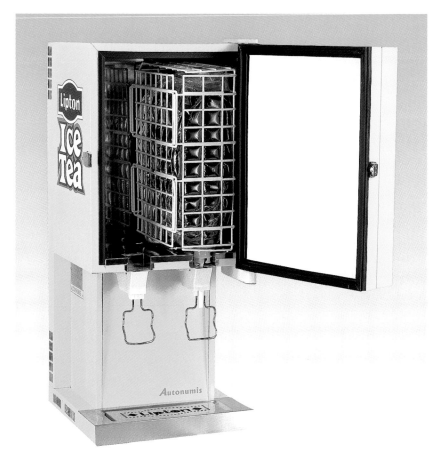

The soda fountain, located in an ice cream parlor or drug store, was for many years common in the United States and other countries. Ice cream sodas were made in a tall glass with ice cream and carbonated water, which causes the melted ice cream at the bottom of the glass to become fizzy. Soft drinks are also made with carbonated water. (Soft drinks are also called pop or soda pop in some parts of the United States, since the days when the bottles were sealed with corks, which made a popping sound when they were pulled out.)

Carbonated water was invented in the 18th century by Joseph Priestley, an English scientist, politician, writer, and Unitarian minister. It is a solution of carbon dioxide in water under pressure and acts as a preservative as well as supplying flavor and fizz. In its early manufacture, it was generated from sodium bicarbonate with an acid and has been called soda water ever since, although it has little to do with soda in the chemical meaning of the word.

Ice cream sodas are now rare because of the dominance of fast-food merchandizing. Today the equivalent of the soda fountain is the soft-drink dispenser, which can be either a postmix or pre-mix machine; coin-operated vending machines

▲ This bag-in-basket drink dispenser holds a disposable drink bag in a reusable cradle.

that deliver soft drinks can also be of either type. A premix machine has the drink already mixed in containers, such as cans, or delivers the drink from containers, such as disposable bags. The postmix machine, however, mixes the drink as it is delivered to the cup.

Postmix dispensers

The typical soft-drink dispenser uses a cylinder of carbon dioxide gas at a pressure of as much as 3,000 psi (206.8 bar), depending on the temperature. The gas is fed to a container of water called the carbonator, a regulator on the cylinder lowers the pressure on the gas to about 70 psi (4.8 bar), and there is a check valve on the delivery side of the carbonator to prevent migration of the gas.

The carbonated water is pumped through the lines of the system through a cooling unit and delivered to the dispensing heads, of which there may be several, each delivering a different flavor of syrup along with the carbonated water. Each dispensing head has an activating lever operating the valves so that the operator need only push the cup against the lever to operate it and a nozzle to combine the flow of the two valves, one for the syrup and one for the carbonated water.

Water is available to the carbonator from a pump at a rate of 100 gallons (455 l) per minute, and another pump delivers the carbonated water to the head at the same rate. The heads deliver the mixture at a rate of about six drinks per minute. There is a return line for the carbonated water, and if the draw rate exceeds 100 gallons (455 l) an hour, a system of valves ensures that no warm carbonated water reaches the heads.

Some machines use the pressure of the carbonated gas to push the syrup out of the containers. The cooled carbonated water can be piped around the rest of the system for more efficient cooling, or the cooling machinery may be built into the carbonator to make a heat exchanger. Some designs also have filters to clean the incoming water in case it is so heavily treated with chemicals as to affect the taste of the drinks. The dispensing heads can be located up to 300 ft. (91 m) away from the rest of the system for convenience, and the delivery lines are made of flexible plastic tubing, which can be tucked away under floors, counter tops, and so forth. Beers and wines can be dispensed by the same system.

SEE ALSO: CANNING AND BOTTLING • PACKAGING • VENDING MACHINE

Soil Research

The study of the structure and behavior of soil began in the early 19th century with attempts to understand the dead and decaying organic matter called humus. The sciences of soil engineering and analysis have since developed to provide advice for farming and engineering on the best ways to use the land and to monitor the sometimes destructive treatment soil undergoes. In this way, humans can learn how to avoid causing damage both to the soil and to themselves, for all living creatures ultimately depend on the soil. Soil science also provides methods for the rehabilitation of land damaged by industrial pollution.

Farmers think of soil as the raw material of their livelihood, necessary for the growth of plants and, through plants, the rearing of animals. For civil engineers, soil is literally the foundation of their structures. They dare not design or build without fully understanding the way the soil will perform. They think of soil in terms of the engineering properties of an aggregate of particles.

In one instance where a study of the soil was not made, a contractor in the south of the United States built a store and parking lot, and to create the necessary flat area, he had a section cut away at the foot of a hill. The consistency of the soil seemed sufficiently firm to support a straightforward excavation, but within a few months, a corner of the building started to lift, and the hillside began to slide.

A concrete retaining wall was built to halt the earth slide, but it had no effect, nor did the steel sheet piling then driven between building and hillside. The rate of advance remained constant. The contractor next constructed a horizontal reinforced concrete beam between the piles. The whole edifice of wall, piling, concrete beam, and steel supports continued to advance inexorably.

A correct soil analysis undertaken in the first place would have shown that the soil consisted of a swelling clay that was very sensitive to water. The cut-away hillside was already at the steepest stable slope, and excavating the toe of the slope had merely oversteepened it.

The soil invading the property was then removed and put back on the top of the slope. Of course, doing so only served to aggravate the problem. A street, a house, and a gas main were all destroyed by the moving hill. Eventually the owner was forced to have a professional soil survey made, and as a result, a drainage system was installed that gradually reduced the water content of the swelling clay and brought the expensive slow-motion landslide to a halt.

◄ Treating this Montana wheat field with fertilizers, herbicides, and pesticides will result in much higher yields, but many environmentalists are concerned that widespread use of these substances will result in a buildup of chemicals in the soil, damaging it permanently.

Soil

For engineers, soil is a three-phase assemblage of solid particles, liquid, and gas. The relationships between these three phases enable them to describe a given soil. In most soils the gas is air and the liquid is water. The solids are usually inorganic particles, but in the topsoil, the particles include the decaying organic material of great importance to agriculture.

To analyze soil structure, the soil is weighed both when wet and after oven drying, and from these statistics, the relationships between the phases can be calculated. The void ratio relates the volumes of the voids and solids, the water content relates the weights of the water and solids, and the degree of saturation relates the volume of air and water in the voids.

Clays, silts, and sands

Engineering soils are broadly divided into clays, silts, and sands. The granular sands are described by their grain size and range from fine sand at the limit of visibility to the naked eye to the coarse gravels of torrential rivers. Silts are very fine flourlike soils but with no cohesion. Clays are even finer soils than silts; in clays, the attractive forces of water adsorbed on the surfaces of the particles cause them to bind together.

In order to predict the performance of sands, silts, and clays for civil engineering works, tests have been devised that model in the laboratory the way in which these different soils will perform on the site. The results differ considerably according to which soils are tested.

In granular sands the sphericity and angularity of the grains affect performance. Flaky particles allow them to shear easily, and the sands themselves crush under pressure. Relative density is an important property of granular material. Loose sands with a low relative density will compact to a dense state and high relative density under foundation loads. Sands are particularly susceptible to this settlement under vibrating loads. They are highly permeable soils that allow the easy flow of water. This property is also measured in the laboratory for the design of drainage blankets in dams.

Clays are very fine, platelike particles with a grain size less than 0.0039 mm across. They are colloids with properties controlled by the layers of water adsorbed on their surface. The cause of adsorption is the electric charge on the clay mineral and in the water molecules. Water molecules are polar, having a positive charge and a negative charge at either end of a dipole. The positive dipole is attracted to the negatively charged surface of the particular clay mineral—a process known as electrostatic bonding. The water can also be held by the sharing of hydrogen atoms with the clay (hydrogen bonding).

Electrostatic charges on clay minerals may result in attractive or repulsive forces. If the clay particles are attracted, the structure is flocculated (the particles collect together in bunches); if they repel, the structure is dispersed. The ions of the water influence the charges. Clays deposited in salty water in a flocculated state may suddenly collapse to the dispersed state and liquefy after being saturated by fresh water. The quick clays of Scandinavia and Canada have created large landslides because of this very phenomenon.

Electrostatic bonding, however, normally creates cohesion in claylike soils. These soils are plastic and will deform without disintegrating, in contrast to the cohesionless sands. The engineer describes the plasticity of a particular soil by applying laboratory tests known as the Atterberg limits. The liquid limit defines the point at which wet clay will flow as a liquid, and the plastic limit defines the point at which the dry clay becomes crumbly. Many clays in their natural state fall between these two limits.

While the strength of granular soils is related to their relative density, the strength and compressibility of clay soils are related to their water content. As clays become drier their strength increases. Soft mud and hard bricks are merely

◀ Testing soils and fertilizers in a laboratory. Regular analyses of the soil are becoming increasingly necessary in agricultural regions to ensure that the soil is correctly balanced.

two extremes of strength for the same clay minerals. Clays are very impermeable, allowing water to flow through them only very slowly. For this reason, they are used for the cores of dams.

When loads, such as foundations, are placed on saturated clays, the load is carried by both the solid soil skeleton and by the water in the voids. The foundation load slowly squeezes out the water until the solid particles carry the load; thus, the loss of the water leads to settlement of the foundation. Engineers calculate the speed and amount of this settlement from laboratory tests on the permeability and compressibility of the clay.

The soils described above are typical of temperate climates, but in the tropics, soil structures may differ appreciably. Some 150 miles (250 km) north of Phnom Penh, in the tropical forests of Cambodia, stands the ancient city of Angkor Thom, a relic of the great Khmer civilization that flourished between the 9th and 16th centuries. With minimal signs of aging and weathering, the towers, temples, staircases, floors, and walls of Angkor Thom still stand firm, built from a combination of sandstone and an amazingly durable substance called laterite made from lateritic soils.

Lateritic soils

Laterite is an earth rich in minerals that turns rock hard when exposed to tropical climate and air. Although a remarkable building material, still used for the construction of roads and buildings in many parts of the world, its very nature makes it highly unsuitable for agriculture. A failure to analyze lateritic soils in areas being converted from jungle to productive agricultural land can result in the twin disasters of failed agricultural programs and ruined forest lands.

Lateritic soils are confined mainly to tropical and subtropical regions, although the rain forests themselves effectively deter the lateritic hardening of the soil by insulating it from the climate. When forest cover is removed, however, laterization, which is always in progress to a limited

▼ The relationship between soil phases enables engineers to calculate the volume, void ratio, and so on, of the soil sample being analyzed.

extent, is greatly accelerated. Rich iron and aluminum contents characterize lateritic soils, and they are, in fact, an important source of ores for these metals.

In temperate zones a typical soil profile (cross section) might have a top layer or layers, known as horizon A, containing very great amounts of organic material, silica, and undecomposed minerals. The next section down, horizon B, would hold an accumulation of material leached down from A, and the bottom of the profile, horizon C, would be the parent rock of the soil, continually breaking down through weathering and chemical reactions to form the soil above.

Lateritic soils do not follow this typical profile. Heavy rainfall and extreme temperatures will have broken down and leached out the majority of the organic material in horizon A. Most minerals necessary to plant life will also have been leached away, particularly potassium, calcium, and phosphorus. The top layer of the exceptionally porous soil consists largely of oxides of iron, aluminum, and other minerals, and oxidation can take place because of this porosity. Consistent high humidity and heat encourages a dense population of bacteria, insects, and other organisms that aerate the soil as they feed on and break down the organic material. Oxygen from the air moves easily through this porous layer to oxidize the iron and aluminum.

If laterization were not confined mainly to the tropics and inhibited by tropical vegetation, there would be a real threat to Earth's atmosphere. It has been estimated that if only a small percentage of Earth's ferrous iron deposits were to be oxidized to become ferric iron, all available atmospheric oxygen would be used up.

The lush jungles, rain forests, and savannas of the tropics have led many to believe that they stand on richly fertile soils capable of supporting intensive agriculture. Nothing could be further from the truth. The lush and rapid growth of the tropics is for the main part very specialized, owing its bulk and rate of increase to abundant moisture rather than to nutrient-rich soil. Yet massive projects are undertaken to turn rain forests into arable land, only to result in disaster.

Soil management

The need for careful and regular soil analysis in agricultural regions is not confined to the tropics. All agricultural activity depletes the soil progressively unless a systematic return of minerals and humus is made in the form of manures, fertilizers, mulches, and so on. Other soil conditions, such as compaction and anaerobic (airless) soil layers, can adversely affect crop production.

RELATIONS BETWEEN SOIL PHASES

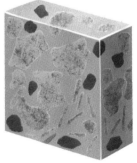

Element of natural soil

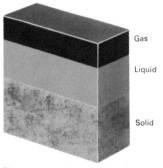

Gas

Liquid

Solid

Element separated into phases

◄ An engineer measures the amount of soil settlement on a freeway construction site.

Plowing and other mechanical operations in wet weather can compact some soils to the point where root growth is drastically restricted. In certain clays, wet-weather plowing creates a smear effect along the bottom and sides of furrows, thus sealing off many of the natural water channels in the soil and increasing the tendency to waterlogging at surface levels. Flowing of otherwise stable soils can ensue, whereby soil fissures become choked with fine silts, creating anaerobic conditions in which plant growth cannot take place.

All agricultural produce, whether crop or livestock, represents a mineral loss to the farm soil. Calcium and phosphorus particularly are depleted on stock-rearing farms where little or no fertilizer is added to the soil. While animal dung is a valuable part of the soil cycle, even it will not correct mineral deficiencies in isolation.

▼ The world over, trees and soil exist together in a delicate balance: the soil feeds the trees, which in return protect the soil from erosion and from drying out. The diagram shows what happens when the trees are felled: rain washes the thin layer of fertile topsoil down the slope. In the Amazon Basin, for example, it is estimated that even if the extensive tree felling stopped now, it would take at least 150 years for the soil to regain its fertility.

Crop farmers also have to consider soil type in relation to the crops grown. Root crops demand far more potash, more phosphate, and slightly more nitrogen than cereal crops. Shallow-rooted plants have a low food-assimilation power and need to be fed heavily in their early stages. Leguminous crops such as beans and peas and also clovers need little or no nitrogen supplements, as they can convert atmospheric nitrogen to their own use and fix it in the soil. The farmer's skill lies not only in knowing what each crop needs in the way of mineral supplements but also in estimating what the previous crop has added to or subtracted from the soil.

Pollution and soil damage

A problem that began to emerge in the 20th century is the pollution of soil by chemicals such as salts, sulfur, and other toxic substances used in industry. Many of these chemicals have long-term effects on plant life and therefore make the soil unsuitable for farming. Particularly harmful chemicals are so dangerous to humans that they may even render land unsuitable for housing or indeed for any human use. Pollution is also caused by excessive use of certain chemical fertilizers and pesticides. Some of these may leach from the soil into rivers, where they cause damage to freshwater ecosystems.

The soil of any region is a delicate constituent of that region's ecological balances. All activities involving soil use, whether intensive farming or building skyscrapers, alter and destroy those balances. Humans, therefore, need to use the soil sciences to understand the effects they have on the health of soil and ensure that their activities cause as little damage as possible.

FACT FILE

■ *In an earthquake at Niigata, Japan, in 1963, the repeated strains of the shocks on a sand deposit beneath the town increased the pressure on the sand grains until the soil structure failed, producing in effect a dry quicksand into which a large apartment building suddenly dropped to the depth of one story.*

■ *The ancient Babylonians built cities on flood plains by raising them up on earth pads and distributing the loads created by placing buildings on stone mats above the weak soil. Settlement damage was minimized by jointing the walls.*

SEE ALSO: AGRICULTURAL SCIENCE • AGRICULTURE, INTENSIVE • AGRICULTURE, ORGANIC • EROSION • FERTILIZER • FORESTRY

Solar Energy

◀ The NASA Helios experimental aircraft is a remote-controlled solar-powered wing capable of flying at altitudes of around 98,500 ft. (30,000 m). Solar-powered aircraft have the potential to remain airborne for many months at a time, and it is possible that one day such aircraft will be used as communication or weather satellites.

Earth receives enormous amounts of radiant energy from the Sun, which directly or indirectly sustains all living things. Anxiety about dwindling supplies of fossil fuels and about the problems that accompany nuclear power has led to rapidly growing interest in the possible ways of harnessing solar energy in ways useful to humans.

Energy available

The Sun radiates energy at a constant rate of 3.8×10^{20} MW (380 million million million MW). This prodigious amount of energy is generated by nuclear fusion reactions deep in the heart of the Sun. The nuclei of hydrogen atoms are smashed together at a temperature of about 27 million °F (15 million °C) to build the element helium. However, an atom of helium is lighter than the sum of the hydrogen nuclei used to build it. The mass discrepancy appears as radiated energy, the exact amount given by Einstein's famous equation $E = mc^2$, where c is the speed of light. The staggering scale of the continual fusion processes in the Sun can be appreciated when it is realized that the Sun turns about 4 million tons (3.6 million tonnes) of its mass into energy every second.

The orbit of Earth around the Sun is not a circle but an ellipse, so the solar intensity just outside the atmosphere varies slightly from 1,399 MW per 0.38 sq. mile (1 km²) at the closest (January 3) to 1,309 MW at the farthest (July 4). The energy distribution in sunlight as seen outside Earth's atmosphere approximates fairly closely to a blackbody radiator at 6000 K, but this spectrum is modified as the sunlight passes through Earth's atmosphere. (A blackbody is one that absorbs and radiates energy perfectly.) The ultraviolet component is cut down by absorption in the ozone layer at about 30 miles (50 km) altitude, and parts of the infrared are absorbed by water vapor and carbon dioxide. Moreover, some light is scattered out of the beam by dust particles and molecules of the air. Most of this scattered light reaches the ground in diffuse form, however, and since short-wavelength light is the most strongly scattered, the sky generally appears blue. The extent of all these effects depends on the height of the Sun above the horizon and local atmospheric conditions. The insolation, or solar intensity, at any point on Earth's surface therefore varies with the season and the time of day in a regular way and irregularly with cloud cover. The maximum intensity, about 1,000 MW per 0.38 sq. mile (1 km²), occurs when the Sun is overhead in a clear sky, but average figures are lower than this. Highest annual insolation occurs in the tropical desert areas (near the equator insolation is somewhat reduced by high humidity).

Solar water heating

When solar energy falls on a black object, which absorbs the light, the object is warmed, and in this way, radiant energy can be readily transformed into low-temperature heat. One of the simplest, as well as the most widespread, applications of solar heat is the provision of domestic hot water, using flat plate collectors. The units generally consist of a metal plate with a blackened surface through or over which water flows in pipes or corrugations. The plate is insulated behind to prevent heat loss by conduction, and in front of it, there is an air gap of an inch or so and then one or two glass cover plates, which help to prevent convective heat loss.

Solar radiation (both direct and diffuse) passes through the glass cover plate and warms the metal surface, which in turn warms the water flowing through the plate. The water is circulated from the hot-water storage tank either by convection or by a small pump. With appropriate thermostat controls to switch the system off when the insola-

tion is too weak to make a useful contribution, solar water heaters can readily provide a reliable and virtually cost-free domestic supply of hot water in consistently sunny areas of the world.

The average thermal efficiency—the ratio of heat falling on them to useful heat extracted—of these collectors is generally in the region of 45 to 65 percent. The main heat losses occur from the front surface of the collector itself, provided all other parts of the system are well lagged. The glass cover assists in minimizing these losses, since glass is transparent to visible radiation but opaque to infrared. Thus, solar radiation passes through it, but the long-wave thermal radiation from the warm collector plate cannot pass outward through the glass. The system can be made more efficient by means of a vacuum between the glass and the metal plate, so that heat is not lost through conduction or convection through the air (just as a thermos bottle keeps hot), and by using suitable spectrally selective surfaces on the metal. These are surfaces with properties opposite to those of glass. They absorb visible radiation efficiently, so they are black to sunlight, but they do not absorb infrared radiation appreciably. Consequently, they do not emit the latter wavelengths either and so cannot radiate heat, and therefore a spectrally selective superblackbody reaches a higher temperature in sunlight than does a normal uniformly blackbody.

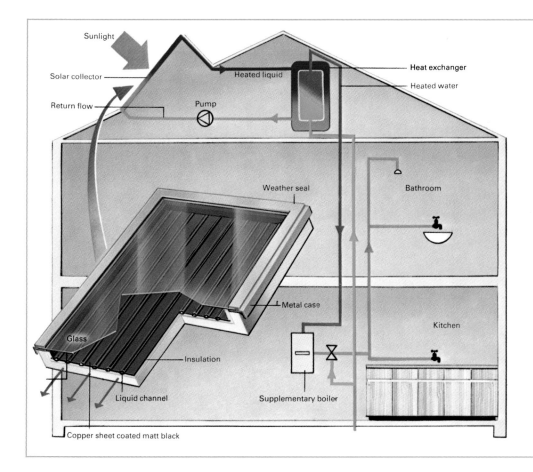

SOLAR-HEATED WATER SYSTEM

Solar collectors, mounted on the roof of a house, use the energy from sunlight to heat water. The water flows in channels under a black plate and is heated by the Sun. Above the black plate is a layer of glass, which prevents the loss of infrared radiation emitted by the plate, while insulation under the plate prevents heat loss into the roof, thus increasing the system's efficiency. After the water passes through the plate, it circulates to the hot-water tank where it may be stored. A supplementary boiler is usually fitted into solar-heated water systems to provide heat on cloudy days. Systems such as these are increasingly common in countries such as Israel and Australia.

It is also possible to use solar water heaters to provide space heating and cooling in a building. Larger areas of collectors than needed simply to provide hot water are required, and the solar-warmed water is stored in large tanks for circulation in the central heating system. In climates where summertime cooling is required and night skies are generally clear, the same collectors can be used to chill the water very effectively during the night by pumping it through the collectors, which radiate heat to the sky. The chilled water can then, through an appropriate heat exchange system, be used to cool the house the next day.

A similar system, which uses a shallow reservoir of water on the roof of the building, has been developed in California. When winter heating is required, the reservoir is covered during the day by a black sheet that absorbs solar energy and warms the water beneath. Thermal insulation is rolled over this sheet at night to prevent upward heat loss to the sky, so the warm water warms the house beneath. During the summer, this insulation, which is white, is placed over the pond during the day to prevent the water from being warmed by the Sun, but it is rolled back at night, and the water is chilled by radiation loss and evaporation, and the house is subsequently cooled as interior heat is transferred to the cool reservoir.

Other thermal uses

Solar distillation of brackish or saline water (desalination) is carried out quite successfully on a small or medium scale in several countries, and solar water or air heaters are in use for crop drying and timber curing. To obtain higher tempera-

◄ Solar power used to distill brackish water by causing it to evaporate. The water vapor condenses on the glass plates ready for collection.

tures, it is necessary to focus sunlight by means of lenses or curved mirrors. Only direct sunlight, not diffuse daylight, can be focused in this way. In consistently sunny parts of the world, there is some use of focused collectors to boil water to raise steam. The steam can then be used to generate electricity by conventional means or to provide mechanical power, for example, for uses such as pumping irrigation water.

A similar arrangement, such as that at White Cliffs solar power station in Australia, is used to focus sunlight onto solar cells to provide large amounts of electricity.

Solar furnaces are another means of harnessing solar energy in which sunlight is reflected by mirror onto a concave reflector, which then focus the light onto a small area. This technique may produce temperatures capable of melting metal and so is often used in high-temperature research. The largest solar furnace in the world is in France at Odeillo and is over 130 ft. (40m) high. This facility is capable of producing temperatures in excess of 7200°F (4000°C).

Making electricity

The necessity for continuous electric power generation on space satellites led to the development in the 1950s of the solar cell at the Bell Telephone Laboratories in the United States. These devices, which are generally made from thin slices of highly pure single-crystal silicon, produce electric power from radiant energy. Wavelengths in the range 400 to 1100 nm (nanometers) are the most effective, and about half the solar spectrum falls in this range. The actual conversion efficiency of silicon cells is, however, much less than 50 percent, owing to various internal losses. The best cells available today are made from gallium indium phosphide or gallium arsenide and convert sunlight to electric power with an efficiency of about 32 percent (the remainder of the energy is degraded to heat in the cell and lost). This rate is still, however, a big improvement on the solar cells most commonly used, which are often capable of only around 18 percent efficiency. These improved cells, potentially useful for powering satellites, were developed by the National Renewable Energy Laboratory (NREL) in conjunction with Spectrolab in California. Scientists hope to be able to further increase efficiency to around 40 percent in the next few years.

These cells contain added dopants (usually boron and arsenic) in small amounts to create in the crystal slice a junction between an n-type and a p-type semiconductor region. This junction creates a gradient of electric potential within the crystal, and when light falls on the crystal and

◄ Clear glass balls cover the surface of an experimental solar pond at Golden, Colorado.

excites electrons in it, creating electron–hole pairs, the junction separates the electrons and the holes, and a DC current flows. These cells have no storage capacity, and for terrestrial applications, they are used in conjunction with electric storage batteries. They are at present too expensive for widespread use on Earth, though new manufacturing methods being developed in the United States may greatly reduce their cost.

Even if the cost were low, one disadvantage would still be the low efficiency. To operate a 500 W electric heater would require 27 sq. ft. (2.5 m²) of cells even with maximum sunlight shining directly on them. Unless a large-scale method of energy storage or transmission of electricity is employed, this power would have to be used fairly close to its source of production, where it is probably not needed anyway. One possible solution to this problem in the future may be to equip a satellite with large arrays of solar panels generating power that would be transmitted to Earth by means of microwaves. These microwaves could be picked up by receiving stations consisting of arrays of wires even on cloudy days at fairly high latitudes, where the energy is required.

Solar-powered vehicles

Solar cells have been used to power piloted aircraft such as the Solar Challenger, which flew across the English Channel in 1981. The problem, however, with using a pilot to control the aircraft is that the pilot's weight adds a considerable burden to the amount of power the solar cells need to provide. Therefore, one of the most important areas of development in solar-powered vehicles is the use of solar cells on unpiloted aircraft. Recent research has shown great improvements in the design and performance of such experimental aircraft. In 2001, for example, the NASA Dryden Flight Research Center successfully flew its prototype Helios aircraft to an alti-

tude of 96,500 ft. (29,410 m), breaking the altitude record for a propeller-driven craft held by another experimental NASA craft, the Centurion. In ideal conditions, Helios is expected to reach altitudes of more than 102,000 ft. (31,000 m). The Helios is basically a remote-controlled flying wing, which at 256 ft. (78 m) in length has a longer wingspan than a Boeing 747. The upper surface of the wing is covered in 65,000 bifacial solar cells, which, under conditions of flight, are around 19 percent efficient in converting solar energy to electricity and provide a maximum output of around 35 kW, enough to power the wing's 14 propellers. NASA hopes to reach still higher altitudes with this craft and to be able to fly the Helios for months at a time without landing. During the night, power will be provided by hydrogen–oxygen fuel cells charged during the day by the solar cells. If such long flights are sustainable, solar-powered aircraft could be used as semipermanent weather satellites or communication satellites. NASA is also working with UCLA and Rockwell to create smaller pilotless solar-powered aircraft that would fly in a V formation, like migrating geese. This arrangement takes advantage of certain aerodynamic effects that reduce the amount of energy necessary to sustain flight. These aircraft could also be used for communication and weather prediction.

▶ The storage layer in this solar research pond at the University of New Mexico can reach temperatures of 225°F (107°C).

▶ An overall view of the solar pond at Golden, Colorado. The glass balls on the surface prevent evaporation of water during the day and act as insulation at night.

SEE ALSO: Energy resources • Energy storage • Heating and ventilation systems • Mirror • Semiconductor

Solar System

The Solar System is a complex structure of planets, moons, asteroids, and comets orbiting a central star called the Sun. Together they sweep out a disk-shaped region of space that is 9 trillion miles (15 trillion km) in diameter. The Solar System is believed to have formed out of a huge cloud of spinning gas and dust called a solar nebula five billion years ago. The Sun, which contains more than 99 percent of the system's mass, formed first, and planetary bodies gradually coalesced out of the remaining gas and debris over the next 500 million years to leave the nine planets in the positions we know them today.

The four planets nearest the Sun—Mercury, Venus, Earth, and Mars—are known as the terrestrial, or inner, planets. All are comparatively small and have rocky compositions and densities greater than 3 g/cm³. By contrast, the four outer planets—Jupiter, Saturn, Uranus, and Neptune—are giant balls of gas and ice surrounding tiny rocky cores with densities less than 2 g/cm³. At

▲ A composite image of the planets in the Solar System, looking back from Neptune (in the foreground). As we discover more about our own system, we can begin to understand how planets form around other stars and the conditions on them that are necessary for life.

the farthest reaches of the Solar System lies Pluto. Much debate has arisen over whether Pluto should in fact be classified as a planet. Smaller than the Moon, it is an icy, low-density body that resembles a satellite of one of the outer planets or the core of a comet.

Even before the advent of the space probe, a surprising amount was known about the physical and chemical characteristics of the planets. Earth-based observations of their orbital motions and relative distances enabled astronomers to calculate the diameter, mass, and degree and axis of spin. The introduction of the telescope revealed features such as rings, satellites, and large clouds on the large planets. New instruments, including spectroscopes and radio transmitters, followed, giving glimpses of the composition of planetary atmospheres and surface features such as craters, valleys, and mountains.

The space age transformed our knowledge of planets other than our own. With every new space probe sent deep into the Solar System, many questions have been solved, but entirely new questions have been raised. The exploration of space is a long-term business: spacecraft such as *Voyager 2*, launched in 1977 and containing technology that in any other field would be considered obsolete, was still able to return remarkable pictures of Neptune in 1989. *Pioneer 10*, sent out in 1973 to take pictures of Jupiter, was still sending signals back to Earth in 2001, as it traveled out of the Solar System.

Since the 1990s, in addition to spacecraft such as *Galileo*, targeted at Jupiter, and *Magellan* in orbit around Venus, the Earth-orbiting Hubble Space Telescope (HST) has proved itself capable of taking detailed planetary images. One of the most remarkable sights it has witnessed was the comet Shoemaker-Levy 9 crashing into Jupiter in July 1994. NASA and the European Space Agency (ESA) have plans for new probes to study some of the more unknown worlds in our Solar System in more detail, especially comets, asteroids, and the moons of Jupiter.

The Sun

As our nearest star, the Sun provides an excellent opportunity to study the processes that provide us with heat and light and gain insight into the workings of other stars in the cosmos. A number of probes were put into orbit around the Sun during the 1990s and have sent back spectacular pictures of the flares and eruptions that constantly shoot out from its surface. One of the probes,

SOHO (Solar and Heliospheric Observatory) has taken a good look at the Sun from the inside out and revealed that the Sun pulses over a 16-month cycle, as currents of gas beneath the surface speed up and then slow down. The movement of these currents creates a dynamo, which is believed to cause sunspots and magnetic explosions that loop across its surface. These magnetic loops are also the reason why the Sun's atmosphere is hotter than its surface. By the laws of physics, thermal energy cannot flow from the cooler surface to the hot corona, but each magnetic loop can carry as much energy as a hydroelectric plant can generate in a million years. When two loops hit each other, they effectively short circuit and discharge the energy to the corona, heating it to a temperature of several million degrees.

Ice on Mercury

No probe has visited Mercury since 1975, and half the planet remains unimaged. Mercury is a rocky planet with a thin, tenuous atmosphere. Its slow rotation exposes the side nearest the Sun to temperatures over 700 K, yet recent observations using radio telescopes have suggested that there may be ice at the bottom of deep craters near the poles. Ice is highly reflective to radar, and bright spots on the surface that can be correlated with known craters have been picked up by the Arecibo telescope. To survive, this ice would need to be kept in permanent shadow, but not enough is known about the depth of Mercury's craters, particularly near the poles, for this theory to be proved. A new probe, *Messenger*, due to be launched in 2004, will take a closer look at the polar craters and search for any water ice and frozen volatiles that they may contain.

Volcanic Venus

In August 1990, after a 15-month journey, the *Magellan* spacecraft went into orbit around Venus. Its arrival marked the return of the United States to planetary exploration after a gap of 11 years. *Magellan*'s task was to map the surface accurately, using radar to penetrate the planet's constant, very dense cloud cover, which hides the surface from view. Its only instrument was a synthetic aperture radar system, which mapped the surface, determined the height of surface features, and measured natural thermal emissions from the planet. From its elliptical orbit that took it around Venus in 3 hours 9 minutes, *Magellan*'s radar was capable of "seeing" surface features only 400 ft. (360 m) across, ten times better than ever before. With the spacecraft passing nearly over both poles, around the very slowly turning planet, *Magellan* took 243 days to complete its first map, covering 84 percent of the surface.

In early 1991, *Magellan* began a second mapping cycle to fill in the gaps in the first map and look for any changes occurring on the surface. During a third cycle, its motion was carefully

▶ The striking images sent back by the instruments on board *SOHO* have revealed the spectacularly violent eruptions that happen on the surface of the Sun. A major discovery was the formation of magnetic loops, seen on the far right and left of the picture. When these loops cross each other, they discharge an enormous amount of energy into the corona, heating it to several million degrees.

◄ Newton Crater on Mars was formed by an asteroid impact. On its north wall are many gullies scientists now think were formed by a liquid, probably water, flowing into the crater. Estimates based on the volumes of the debris flows at the bottom of the crater suggest that 660,000 gallons (2.5 million l) of water may have been involved in each event.

▼ This enlargement of an area on Jupiter's moon Europa shows large cracks in its icy surface. Experts believe that beneath the ice lies a huge ocean of slush or even liquid water. NASA is planning to send a probe to Europa equipped with special "hydrobots" that can melt their way through the surface and explore what lies underneath.

monitored to find anomalies in the planet's gravitational field caused by regions of higher density rocks beneath the surface. The main aim of the mission was to find out if the processes shaping the surface of Venus are similar to those occurring on Earth. Large structures on Venus appear to be caused by the upwelling of hot molten rock, or lava, from far below the surface rather than by plate tectonics, the process that produces the major land and undersea features on Earth.

Huge rolling plains cover 65 percent of Venus, with lowlands accounting for 27 percent and mountainous regions just 8 percent. Venus is pockmarked by craters, many over 30 miles across, though they are mainly volcanic rather than the result of impacts from space, suggesting that the surface of Venus is geologically young. There are no small craters because the smaller rocky bodies colliding with the planet burn up in the dense atmosphere before hitting the ground. Large areas are covered by volcanic ash, and there are lava channels over 3,700 miles (6,000 km) long. *Magellan* found that some volcanoes on Venus may still be active. The second highest peak, Maat Mons, which is 5 miles (8 km) high, seems to have been covered with fresh lava.

Further evidence for volcanic eruptions on Venus came from the *Galileo* spacecraft, making a flyby of the planet in February 1990 en route to its rendezvous with Jupiter in December 1995. Among its instruments were detectors that picked up intense, short-lived bursts of radio noise, possibly due to lightning flashes in the atmosphere of Venus. Such lightning flashes can occur in the cloud of ash spewed out by an erupting volcano.

Return to the red planet

Mars is the most investigated planet in the Solar System other than Earth. Although it is much smaller than Earth, its surface area is roughly the same, because it possesses some of the biggest mountains and deepest canyons in the Solar

System. One mountain, Olympus Mons, stands 78,000 ft. (24,000 m) above the surrounding plain and is more than twice the height of Mount Everest. Although it was once a volcano, there is no evidence of volcanic activity now, but it is highly probable that tectonic movement occurred in the planet's past. Data from the Mars *Global Surveyor*, launched in 1996, has revealed that, in the northern hemisphere, Mars' crust is only 22 miles (35 km) thick but is 50 miles (80 km) in the south. The southern plains are older and more heavily cratered than those in the north and stand several miles higher where the two meet. Why they are so is unknown, but some scientists have speculated that it may have been the result of a large impact shortly after the planet formed.

Whether there is water on Mars has been hotly debated ever since the U.S. astronomer Percival Lowell thought he saw canal-like structures on its surface. While the idea that they were engineered structures has been disproved, there is an increasing amount of evidence that there may once have been large bodies of water on Mars. In June 2000, *Global Surveyor* sent back pictures of features resembling the gullies formed by flash floods on Earth. These gullies are comparatively young and are found on crater and valley walls in the southern hemisphere. If they are recent, scientists believe the water may lie below the surface at depths between 300 and 1,300 ft. (100–400 m). More significantly, in December 2000, a series of high-resolution pictures revealed layers of sedimentary rock typical of those formed in shallow seas and lakes on Earth. Areas of these rocks are scattered all over the surface, suggesting that there may have been numerous water bodies about 3.5 billion years ago. Another possibility is

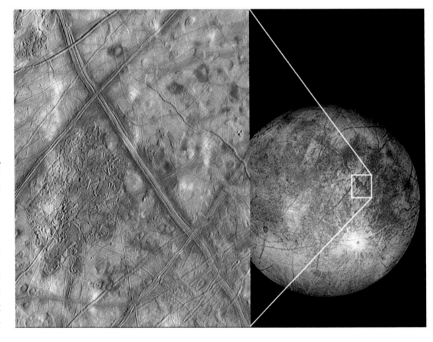

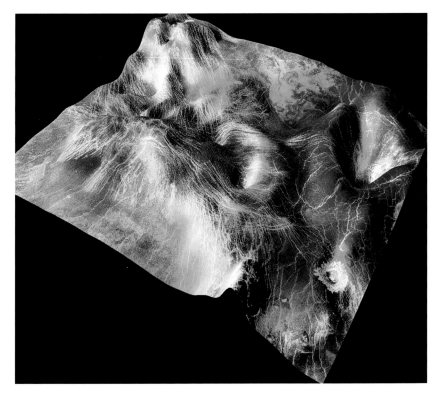

that these sediments were formed by winds, but such an occurrence would have needed a much more dense atmosphere than Mars has now.

Sedimentary rocks may provide the answer to another debate that has raged over the red planet—whether life has ever existed on or beneath the surface. Analysis of a Martian meteorite in 1996 revealed the presence of organic compounds. Further examination found a number of structures in the rock that could be the fossilized remains of microorganisms. As yet, the theory is controversial, but examination of the recently discovered sedimentary rocks by a robot explorer mission planned for launch in 2003 should give scientists more clues.

New studies of Jupiter

Jupiter is the largest planet in the Solar System and is twice as massive as all the other planets put together. It has a rocky core, but the bulk of its mass is a layer of liquid metallic hydrogen that lies just above the core at pressures exceeding 4 million bars. The outermost layers are a gaseous mixture of ordinary molecular hydrogen and helium with small quantities of carbon dioxide, methane, water, and other simple molecules.

Jupiter's atmosphere has long been the subject of observation, in particular, its colored belts and Great Red Spot, a huge circulating storm system. The Hubble Space Telescope has observed fine detail in the clouds that cover Jupiter, including dark "j-shaped" clouds along the equator caused by very strong winds. HST observations made in ultraviolet light in February 1992 showed an

▲ The visit by *Magellan* to Venus revealed many interesting details of the topography of the planet. The circular depressions, called coronae, are unique to the lowlands of Venus and occur in clusters along major tectonic belts. Coronae are thought to be caused by hot spots below the surface that push magma upward. As it cools the magma contracts to form a depression that generates a pattern of fractures that can look like a spider's web.

aurora—equivalent to Earth's northern lights—around the planet's north pole.

HST observations of the Jovian aurora were made simultaneously with the Jupiter flyby of the joint NASA–European Space Agency probe *Ulysses*. *Ulysses'* instruments made important measurements of Jupiter's magnetosphere, the region of interaction between the planet's magnetic field and the solar wind. Both were on hand to witness the crashing of the fragments of a comet, Shoemaker-Levy 9, into the planet's surface in 1994.

The most recent spacecraft to visit Jupiter, *Galileo*, was sent to determine the chemical composition of its atmosphere and investigate the structure of the cloud layers. To their surprise, scientists working on the mission found that Jupiter's ratio of hydrogen to helium was very similar to that of the Sun, suggesting that its composition has not changed since it first formed out of the solar nebula. Slightly higher levels of carbon, nitrogen, and sulfur than are found in the Sun may have arrived from meteors and other bodies impacting the planet. However, far less water and fewer organic compounds were found than the *Voyager* missions had suggested.

Another unexpected result was that the atmospheric probe detected only one cloud layer rather than the three that had been predicted. Persistent wind speeds of over 400 mph (600 km/h) were detected below the cloud layer. This evidence suggests that the heating mechanism that drives the winds is coming from the interior rather than from solar warming. Perhaps because there is less water in the atmosphere, the incidence of lightning is only one-tenth that of Earth, though the strikes are ten times more powerful.

Galileo has also been taking a look at the four Galilean satellites of Jupiter. Ganymede has been found to have a magnetosphere, an unusual phenomenon that implies it may have a molten core. Jupiter's own magnetosphere is lopsided and leaky, which could explain the presence of highly charged particles streaming away from the planet. Ganymede and Callisto have both suffered extensive impact cratering, though Ganymede has undergone some resurfacing, suggesting it was volcanically active for longer than Callisto. The hottest volcanoes in the Solar System are found on Io, which is constantly erupting as it is pulled by the gravitational tides from Jupiter and the other satellites. *Galileo* has discovered that Io has a giant iron core overlain by a mantle of partially molten silicate rock.

Europa, the smallest Galilean moon, is of great interest to scientists because it is covered in water ice. In fact, it is believed to have more water

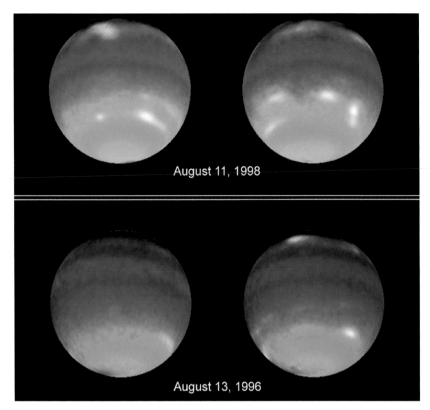

August 11, 1998

August 13, 1996

The outer giants

Beyond Saturn lie two slightly smaller gas giants, Uranus and Neptune. Both were targeted by *Voyager 2* on its journey out of the Solar System. The 1989 images of Neptune held a surprise. After the seemingly dull and featureless Uranus (imaged in 1986), Neptune turned out to have extremely active weather systems that are far more dynamic than those on either Saturn or Uranus. Neptune was seen to have high, wispy white clouds and a Great Dark Spot, a giant atmospheric storm comparable in size to Earth. Winds blow at around 900 mph (1,450 km/h), the strongest winds discovered to date on any planet. *Voyager* also discovered six new moons in addition to the two already known and found several rings similar to those around Jupiter and Uranus.

Since *Voyager*, HST has been pointed at both planets and has discovered more about their weather systems. Instead of being featureless, Uranus has pronounced streaks that appear to be seasonal. These streaks may be colored, but overlying methane is obscuring them. More surprising was the 1996 discovery that Neptune's Great Dark Spot had disappeared. A smaller spot also seems to be dissipating, indicating that Neptune's atmosphere changes rapidly. The biggest mystery is what is driving the weather, as it receives practically no energy from the Sun.

Pluto and Charon

Pluto, discovered in 1930, is by far the smallest and usually most distant planet. For 20 years of its 248-year orbital period it comes closer to the Sun than Neptune, as it did between 1979 and 1999. Nevertheless, its remoteness and small size have made it very difficult to study. Although no probes have been to Pluto, a cosmic coincidence has allowed astronomers to discover more about the planet. Between February 1985 and September 1990, Pluto and its moon Charon underwent a rare series of mutual eclipses, in which one body passed in front of the other. These eclipses allowed astronomers to measure their diameters: 1,444 miles (2,320 km) for Pluto and just 790 miles (1,270 km) for Charon.

Observations of Pluto's spectrum have confirmed that the planet has a surface layer of methane ice and polar ice caps that may vary in size as it orbits the Sun. In June 1988, Pluto passed in front of a relatively bright star. Observations showed that Pluto has a very thin layered atmosphere of methane gas that extends at least 125 miles (200 km) above its surface.

The best picture of Pluto and Charon was taken in 1994 by HST's Faint Object Camera. Precise measurements of such images enable their

than Earth, most of it as a salty ocean beneath the cracked and frozen surface. The edges of the cracks are brownish in color, indicating that a more liquid substance has risen to the surface in the past. Frictional forces arising from the gravitational pull of Jupiter may be keeping this subsurface ocean liquid, and the lack of impact craters suggests that it may still be mobile.

Saturn and Titan

Saturn and its rings has been one of the most fascinating objects in the heavens for centuries. The last probes to visit it were *Voyager 1* and *2*, which revealed that the rings were composed of over a thousand individual rings that were braided and had strange spokelike features within them. A new probe, *Cassini*, will reach Saturn in 2004 for a closer look at its atmosphere, rings, and some of its moons. One moon, Titan, will get particular attention, as a separate probe called *Huygens* will be dropped into its atmosphere by *Cassini*. Titan is thought to be the largest planetary satellite in the Solar System. Recent observations have shown that it has a small core and a very thick atmosphere, though its core is still larger in diameter than Mercury. Titan's atmosphere is so smoggy that it is thought to contain organic compounds such as methane and ethane. Bright patches seen by HST on its surface could be liquid hydrocarbons and will be investigated by *Huygens* as it descends. Most of its atmosphere is nitrogen, and scientists believe conditions could be similar to early life-forming processes on Earth.

▲ A time-lapse series of images show the complexities of Neptune's weather system. The planet appears to have clouds on several levels within its atmosphere and distinct zoning around its equator. How Neptune generates these features is a mystery. Unlike Earth, it receives very little energy from the Sun, which interacts with the atmosphere and oceans to produce weather systems.

masses and densities to be worked out. Pluto, with a density about twice that of water, probably has a rocky core surrounded by a mantle of ices. The combined mass of Pluto and Charon is only one-fifth that of Earth's moon. Pluto and Charon may be large planetesimals, icy bodies left over from the formation of the planets.

Comets and asteroids

Asteroids are the debris of the Solar System, comparatively small bodies orbiting between Mars and Jupiter. Comets have a very different appearance, with huge, glowing, gaseous heads and, sometimes, gas and dust tails. In recent years astronomers have found links between the two. These bodies may hold important clues to the origin of the Solar System.

The first closeup pictures of any asteroid were taken by the *Galileo* spacecraft in October 1991 while en route to Jupiter. Gaspra appeared roughly wedge shaped, with dimensions 12 x 8 x 7 miles (19 x 13 x 11 km) and very irregular. Its dark rocky surface was pitted with craters. There are surface fractures and evidence that Gaspra may be part of a larger body that broke up after a catastrophic collision.

The *NEAR-Shoemaker* probe was sent to take a closer look at another asteroid, Eros, which it encountered in May 2000. As it began to lose power, it was ordered to touch down on the surface and was able to send back information about its composition. To the surprise of many, the asteroid is covered with boulders and a layer of dust from meteorite impacts and is not as clean as expected. Some craters have bluish ponds of dust in the bottom that scientists have speculated may have been lifted from beneath the surface by electrostatic forces and flowed into the depressions. Fractures seen on the surface may be further evidence of impacts that have hit Eros but have not been strong enough to break it apart.

Great interest also surrounds Chiron, the unusual asteroidal object orbiting between Saturn and Uranus. The discovery in 1990 that it was sur-

▲ This false-color picture of Uranus shows its four major rings and 10 of its 17 satellites. Once thought featureless, Hubble has observed 20 clouds traveling across its surface, more than had been seen in all the years of observation that had gone before.

rounded by a cloud of gas and dust led to claims that Chiron is a giant comet. However, Chiron is very large for a comet, perhaps 120 miles (190 km) across. The cloud could be just the evaporation of icy deposits from the surface of a large asteroid as it passes its closest approach to the Sun.

There have been a number of attempts to fly probes into comets. In July 1992, the European spacecraft *Giotto*, which took the closeup pictures of Halley's comet in 1986, encountered a second comet. Its target, comet Grigg-Skjellerup, was a small, rather old comet, orbiting the Sun in about five years, and ejecting about 1/1000 as much gas and dust as the very active and "fresh" comet Halley. Although its camera was not working, *Giotto* detected a few impacts from dust particles, and measured the surprisingly complex interaction between the solar wind and the comet, which was more turbulent than expected.

The best look at a comet has come from *Deep Space 1*, which flew through comet Borrelly in September 2001. The pictures sent back revealed that the comet's nucleus was complex with rugged and smooth terrain, deep fractures, and very dark material. Instead of being centrally placed within the coma, it was set to one side, with the material forming the tail streaming off one side.

◄ The clearest picture of Pluto (left) and its companion Charon (right) was taken by the Hubble Space Telescope, enabling astronomers to measure their diameters more accurately.

SEE ALSO: ASTRONOMY • ASTROPHYSICS • EARTH • GEOPHYSICS • PLANETARY SCIENCE • SPACE PROBE • TELESCOPE, SPACE

Solenoid

A solenoid is an electric device consisting of a coil of wire. It can be made by simply wrapping wire around a cylinder. When a current passes through the wire, a magnetic field is set up that can be made to move a ferrous core to actuate switches and other devices. The solenoid is therefore a direct application of an electromagnet.

Outside the solenoid, the lines of magnetic flux behave in a fashion similar to those of a bar magnet. A solenoid freely suspended horizontally in Earth's magnetic field will set itself along a north–south line. Its ends behave like the poles of a bar magnet, their polarity depending on the direction of the current in the spiral.

The strength of the magnetic field within the solenoid is uniform for most of its length, but near the ends, the field diverges. At the poles, the field strength dies rapidly to about one-half of the strength in the center. Deep inside a thin solenoid, the magnetic field strength is very close to the value it would have in an infinitely long solenoid. More specifically, at a distance from one end of three-and-a-half times the coil's diameter, the field strength is 99 percent of the value from an infinitely long solenoid. Hence, in practice, a long solenoid should have a length at least seven times its diameter.

Relays

An electric relay is a form of switch that is generally operated magnetically or electromagnetically using solenoids, though solid-state electronic relays are finding increasing application. Changes in the input to the relay are used to alter the output, and they are widely used in the control and protection of equipment.

In a relay that uses a solenoid, a current flows through the relay coil forming a flux pattern in the surrounding space. Part of the "magnetic circuit" through which the flux passes includes the armature, which in the more conventional design, is mounted on a pivot with a separate return spring. The armature must be constructed from a magnetically soft material—that is, a material such as soft iron that will not retain any magnetism once the coil is deenergized. The armature moves in such a way as to minimize the reluctance of the magnetic circuit. It does not matter if the control current is DC or AC, because the armature will always move in the direction that minimizes the reluctance of the magnetic circuit. With AC operation, however, it is necessary to laminate the electromagnet iron core to reduce eddy currents for two reasons: first, eddy currents have an undesirable heating effect, and second, they slow down the operating speeds of the device.

Contacts

The size and shape of the contacts and materials used must be chosen to match the characteristics of the circuit to be controlled. For example, in power switch gear, arcing can damage the contact surfaces and lead to the contacts welding together. Consequently, in such applications careful design is necessary. On the other hand, contact resistance is an important consideration in low-voltage

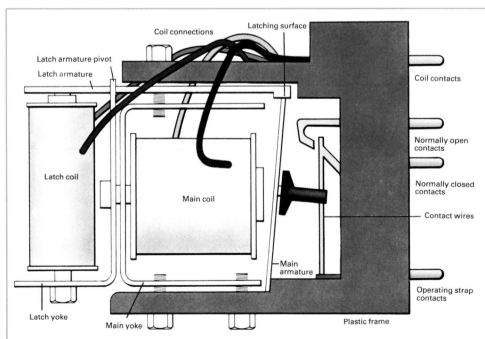

LATCHING RELAY

Conventional relays operate with the control current being turned on and off. The latching relay, however, needs pulses only to change over contacts. A common form of latching relay has two coils and two armatures. In operation, the main coil is energized in the normal way, but as its armature moves and closes the contacts, the other armature, mounted at 90 degrees to it, moves up to hold it in the closed position. To open the contacts again, the second coil is energized, moving its armature down to release the main armature and thus allowing the contacts to open.

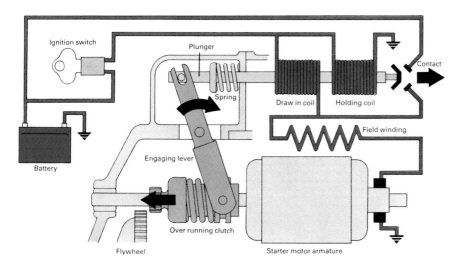

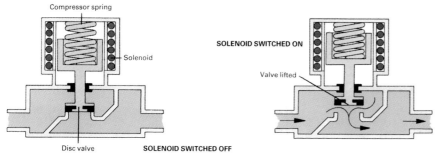

the other condition with the control current off. In some situations, however, it is useful to use control pulses, such that one pulse will change the relay state and a second pulse change it back again. Such a device is known as a latching relay. These relays often use two coils and two armatures rather than one of each.

Operating speeds

The pulling force of the electromagnet will determine the number of spring contact sets that can be operated—it is also one of the factors that will determine the operating speed of the device. Where high-speed operations are required, it is also necessary to reduce the mass of all moving parts (armature and contacts) and reduce the coil inductance. This latter feature is determined by the number of turns in the coil, which should consequently be made with few turns. The pulling force, however, improves with increasing turns, and so for high operating speeds, larger control currents are necessary.

In some situations, slow operating speeds are required. This objective can be achieved by increasing the number of coil turns, by adding an inductor in series with the coil, or by adding a capacitor in parallel with the coil. Other techniques include using a lag (or slugging) coil or an external time-delay relay. The lag coil is a separate coil of few turns mounted on the same iron core.

Applications

The ability of the solenoid to produce a magnetizing force leads to its use in starting devices and power-operated valves—only a switch need be turned to energize it. For example, solenoid switches are widely used to engage starter motors in cars. Here two solenoids, the draw-in coil and the holding coil, are mounted on top of the starter motor with a plunger running through the inside of both (thus operating in the region where the field strength is uniform and at a maximum). One end of the plunger is attached to a lever that engages and disengages the starter motor pinion with the flywheel. The other end of the plunger is connected to a switch.

In a simple power-operated switch, such as is found in a domestic central-heating system, the solenoid provides the power to open and close the valve disk. The disk is connected by a rod to the core of the solenoid. When the solenoid is deenergized, the disk is held against the aperture, and the valve is off.

applications. Where relays are used in conjunction with electronic circuits, contact bounce, where the contacts make and break several times before settling down, is a problem. In purely electromagnetic relay systems, this is not so great a problem because operating speeds are usually slower than the bounce rate, but in conjunction with electronic circuits, whose operating speeds are far greater, this bouncing is detectable.

With AC control currents, there are two instances every cycle where the current is zero, and the pulling force consequently is zero. If under these circumstances, the contact sets were constructed using rigid materials, they would be in continual bounce. They are made from a springy material, so the contact is made under tension.

The contact arrangements are classified by the required operating sequence—for example, make, break, changeover, make before break, and break before make are used in specific situations.

Types of relays

In the reed relay and the spring-suspended armature relay, the contact and armature functions are combined. The spring must be a good conductor of electricity, as it also acts as the contact conductor. When the coil is energized, the spring moves to the position of minimum reluctance, thus making or breaking the contact set. When the control current is removed, the spring returns to its original position. With conventional relays, one condition is maintained with the control current on, and

▲ Two applications of a solenoid. The starter motor arrangement for an internal combustion engine can be operated by two solenoids. When the ignition switch is turned, one solenoid draws in the clutch, and the other holds this position while the starter motor armature turns the engine. Solenoid valves are used extensively in industry as well as in home appliances for control purposes.

SEE ALSO: ELECTRICITY • ELECTROMAGNETISM • ELECTRONICS • FUSE AND CIRCUIT BREAKER • MAGNETISM • STARTER MOTOR • SWITCH

Sonar

Asdic (an acronym of Allied Submarine Detection Investigation Committee) is a device developed originally for detecting submarines by means of sound waves travelling through water. Since World War II, its usefulness has grown and applications now include detectors for shipwrecks and shoals of fish, navigational aids for ships, devices to measure the depth of water under a ship, and equipment for oceanographic research purposes.

Sonar (from *so*und *na*vigation *r*anging) has since replaced the term asdic. Another term, echo sounding, implies the principle of the system. Sound is normally thought of as being wavelike vibrations of the air, but water can also transmit vibrations. By analyzing waterborne echoes electronically, a picture of the area below the surface can be obtained.

In the basic technique, a short pulse of sound, which may be within the range audible to humans on a much higher frequency, is transmitted from the bottom of a ship, usually by way of a transducer mounted in a hole cut in the ship's bottom.

(A transducer is any device that converts electrical power into another form, such as sound, or vice versa.) The sound pulse travels downward until it strikes the sea bottom or a submerged object, which reflects it back to the ship. There it is picked up by another transducer, and the time taken for the pulse to travel down and back is measured. The speed at which sound travels in water depends on temperature, but it is approximately 4,800 ft. per sec. (1,460 m/s), over four times its speed in air. The distance the pulse has travelled can be determined from the measurement of the time it took to travel that distance.

Each pulse lasts anything from a few thousandths of a second to a few seconds, depending upon the range of the particular sonar (the longer the range, the longer the pulse). The pulses are emitted at intervals ranging from a fraction of a second to a few seconds or even minutes, again depending upon range. A typical shipboard echo sounder used for navigation has two range scales. On its shorter range it will measure depths up to

▲ This electronic sonar device is used to detect shoals of fish. Sonar is used by the fishing industry to locate potential catches and by marine biologists to monitor the health of fish stocks.

◄ Modern scanning sonars can build up a detailed image of the seabed using sonar-derived information processed by computer.

20 ft. (6 m) in steps of a fraction of a foot. On its longer range it will measure depths up to 100 or more fathoms (1 fathom equals 6 ft., or 1.8 m).

The time interval and therefore the range can be measured by a rotating disk carrying a neon tube that flashes when the reflected sound pulse (the echo) is picked up. The disk rotates at a constant speed, carrying the neon tube past a fixed circular scale graduated in terms of distance. The neon tube is at the top alongside the zero mark when the pulse is transmitted. If the echo sounder is set to a maximum range of 100 fathoms, the neon tube will be carried full circle, that is, halfway around. The scale at this point is marked 50 fathoms, since the signal has travelled twice as far as the depth. In some units a permanent record is provided by a rotating stylus that darkens electrically sensitive paper when the echo is picked up. Other units have a cathode-ray tube display similar to a TV screen. In all cases the distance is read directly from a scale that may be calibrated in feet, fathoms, or meters.

Military sonar

All merchant and naval vessels carry an echo sounder, the simplest form of sonar, used only to measure the depth of water. Fishing vessels also carry a sonar that shows the depth and location of shoals of fish, but naval and research sonar is con-

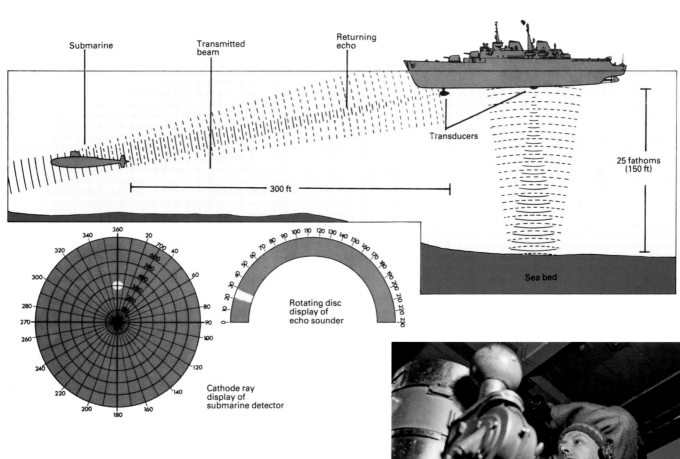

▲ A typical antisubmarine craft has two transducers. The signals from the fixed transducer are used to measure the depth—indicated on the rotating disk—and the forward array rotates through 360 degrees to locate nearby submarines—indicated on the cathode-ray tube.

▶ An asdic operator on an Allied convoy escort ship in 1943.

siderably more powerful and complex. The sound pulses are concentrated into narrow beams by mechanical horns in a manner similar to that in loudspeaker equipment.

Alternatively, the beams can be produced by placing a series of transducers in a line along the ship's bottom. Although each transducer sends out signals in all directions, the signals radiated from the different transducers interfere constructively and destructively with each other. In one particular direction, the interference effects are constructive, the signals add together, and a powerful beam is transmitted in that direction. In all other directions, the signals interfere destructively and cancel each other out so that very little energy is transmitted in other directions. The direction in which the beam points can be changed easily and quickly by altering the electrical timing of the signals fed to different transducers.

Sonar is essentially an intelligence-gathering device and, as such, does not have to be moveable or attached to ship hulls to be useful. In modern naval warfare, the capital ships are nuclear submarines, and hostile boats are hunted by both strategic and tactical sonar arrays.

The U.S. Navy is probably the only service to have a considerable strategic sonar capability. For many years, it has been seeding choke points in the oceans with passive, listening hydrophones (underwater microphones) that can record a ship's engine noises so accurately that they can tell one class of ship from another. The SOSUS (Sound Surveillance System) guards the edge of the American continental shelf and the entrance to the Atlantic through the Greenland–Iceland–Britain gap. It is backed up by SURTASS (Surveillance Towed Array) systems, in which standing patrols tow long arrays of passive sonar listening devices at slow speed over wide areas. Information from SOSUS and SURTASS is fed into the U.S. Navy Antisubmarine Warfare Center's Command and Control computers, which attempt to unscramble an overall picture of the numbers and general whereabouts of potentially hostile boats in the Atlantic.

DARPA (U.S. Defense Advanced Research Projects Agency) has experimented with immensely long linear acoustic sonar arrays that transmit their findings by satellite to a central computer. These devices hear a tremendous clutter of undersea noises, from snapping shrimps to ship propellers, and it is the computer's job to weed out the distant acoustics of a submarine's passage from all the other recorded sounds.

Sonar is also the backbone of tactical antisubmarine warfare, in which naval forces try to protect themselves and their sea area from submarine attack. Active transducers can send out pulses in a much finer beam if there is a long array of them; a technique devised to expoit this finding tows a line of sonars behind a submarine-hunting warship.

To increase a fleet's underwater reach, helicopters can be deployed both to drop passive, listening sonar buoys and to dunk active transducers in the sea. The passive sonar will radio back information about a ship's engine noises or returning sound pulses to the helicopter or a command ship.

Marine biology

Marine biologists also use sonar to monitor fish stocks and understand their movements. In addition, marine biologists use sonar in conjunction with the global positioning system (GPS) to monitor the health of coral reefs. The sonar provides information on the contours of the reef, while GPS provides accurate positioning. Together GPS and sonar enable the rapid creation of accurate seafloor maps; one use for this combined system has been in acquiring information on the effects of habitat fragmentation in coral reefs. Combined GPS and sonar may also have further applications in marine salvage and marine archaeology.

▼ Helicopters can move much faster than ships, and it is possible to make rapid searches or surveys of submarine activity by lowering sonar into the sea from a hovering helicopter. This is a horizontal scanning sonar device from which an array of transducers are positioned appropriately to generate a flat, horizontal beam.

Sorption

Sorption is a process whereby one substance—usually a gas or liquid—is taken in by another material. It has two forms—absorption and adsorption—that differ in a subtle way. In absorption, the absorbent—the host material—changes physically when it accepts the absorbate. This is the case when a cotton cloth mops up water, for example: water molecules penetrate the cellulose fibers that make up the cotton cloth, changing the physical properties of the fibers as they do so. In adsorption, molecules of a gas or liquid become reversibly attached to the surface of a solid, but that solid remains essentially unchanged.

In practice, absorption and adsorption often occur simultaneously, or it may be difficult to distinguish one process from the other. In such cases, it is appropriate to use the term *sorption* to describe a more general or indistinct taking in of one substance by another.

Some materials that have fine, porous structures appear to absorb large quantities of materials when they are in fact adsorbing material on the internal surfaces of their pores. Adsorption is also key to the catalysis of many chemical processes.

Adsorption

The study of adsorption on solid surface recognizes two distinct adsorption processes: physical adsorption and chemical adsorption, also called chemisorption. In physical adsorption, molecules of adsorbate attach themselves to the adsorbent surface by Van der Waals' forces. These forces are due to the coordination of motion of electrons in adjacent molecules or atoms; they tend to be stronger for inorganic solids, which are therefore better adsorbants. Van der Waals' forces are many orders of magnitude weaker than chemical bonds, and the phenomenon of adsorption is more akin to condensation than to any form of chemical reaction, an observation supported by the fact that the most easily liquefied gases or vapors are also the most readily adsorbed.

Physical adsorption is rapid and reversible—adsorbed gases can be removed by placing the adsorbent in a sealed vessel and attaching a powerful vacuum pump. Once an adsorbent has been stripped in this way, its surface area can be estimated by admitting a gas to the container and measuring the volume taken up by the adsorbent.

In chemisorption, adsorbed molecules are held by strong forces, similar to those that hold molecules together. Because of the strength of this bonding, chemisorption is less easily reversed than physical adsorption. Also, the formation of partial bonds between the adsorbed molecule and the adsorbent surface can withdraw electrons from bonds within adsorbed molecules, leaving them weaker than in unbound molecules.

Chemisorption can be recognized by studying the infrared spectra of adsorbed substances; infrared spectrometers measure vibrational energies of molecules, and the weakening of bonds in chemisorbed molecules appears as a downward shift in the frequencies of certain peaks in the infrared spectrum. Further information can be obtained by low-energy electron diffraction (LEED), which reveals changes in the surface of the adsorbent caused by adsorbed species.

▲ Chemical adsorption occurs during the catalytic hydrogenation of alkenes on platinum. In this schematic representation, but-1-ene (C_4H_8, far left) and hydrogen atoms chemisorb on the surface of platinum (center left). The process breaks the double bond, making it easy for a chemisorbed hydrogen atom to form a C–H bond with the but-1-ene molecule to form a chemisorbed butyl radical (C_4H_9, center right). A second hydrogen atom bonds to form butane (C_4H_{10}, center right), which desorbs from the catalyst surface.

Chemisorption is the first step in fluid-phase reactions catalyzed by solids, because it can tease open bonds that are more difficult to break in the absence of catalyst. An example is the platinum-catalyzed hydrogenation of alkenes, where chemisorption helps break single bonds in hydrogen molecules and double bonds in alkenes.

Absorption

When a substance has been adsorbed onto the surface of a solid or liquid, it may further penetrate below the surface to become absorbed. The absorbate either dissolves in the solid or liquid, or it reacts to form a chemical compound.

Palladium has a remarkable ability to absorb hydrogen, its volume expanding by around 10 percent as the ratio of absorbed hydrogen atoms to palladium atoms reaches 0.6. One application of this trait is in purification of hydrogen by permeation through the walls of palladium tubes. Any impurities are larger than hydrogen atoms—the smallest atoms—and remain in the tubes.

Sorbent materials

Sorbent materials are characterized by highly porous structures, and they are classified according to the typical pore diameters. Macropores have diameters greater than 200 Å, or angstroms (20 nm), transitional pores have diameters of from 20 to 200 Å (2–20 nm), and micropores have diameters less than 20 Å (2 nm).

Activated charcoal. Activated charcoal is a porous form of carbon that has a surface area of around 7 acres per ounce (1,000 m²/g). To make activated carbon, an organic (carbon-based) material, such as peat, wood, or coconut shell, is first carbonized at high temperature, and then the pore system is developed by reaction with steam at 1650 to 1830°F (900–1000°C).

The exact properties of activated charcoal depend on the choice of raw material for carbonization and the conditions of the activating treatment; charcoals with a wide variety of adsorptive properties can be prepared to suit different applications. Activated carbons are used to adsorb impurities from air and drinking water and to decolorize solutions of sugar during some sugar-refining processes. In some cases, used charcoal can be reactivated by heating to drive off volatile substances absorbed within its pores.

Silica gel. Silica gel is a glassy sorbent powder (the term *gel* merely indicates its condition at one stage of manufacture). It has a porous structure that enables it to adsorb as much as 40 percent of its own weight of water vapor. This porosity also makes silica gel useful as a the stationary phase in chromatography, whereby the components of

mixtures separate as they are washed through the stationary phase by solvents. Components repeatedly sorb and desorb on the gel as the chromatography proceeds, and those with the strongest tendency to be adsorbed travel slowest through the sorbent medium.

Zeolites. Zeolites are a class of aluminosilicate minerals; some are natural, others are synthetic. Their structures feature cages that are linked by tunnels, and the precise dimensions of these structural elements depends on the composition of the zeolite and the template compounds present during their synthesis.

Zeolites have strong affinities for water, making them useful as drying agents for gases and chemical solutions. The presence of alumina units within the cage structures of zeolites provides acid sites that can catalyze hydrocarbon reactions, such as isomerization and alkylation—two major oil-refinery processes. A zeolite favors products that most easily squeeze through its pores. For example, an appropriate zeolite can convert mixtures of dimethylbenzene isomers into high yields of 1,4-dimethylbenzene—the slimmest isomer—which is used to make a diacid for polyesters.

Ion-exchange resins. Some ion-exchange resins are polymeric materials that have anionic sites on their surfaces. In contact with water, these sites attract and adsorb ions responsible for water hardness—the cause of limescale in boilers and scum formation with soap—such as calcium and magnesium ions. When the water-softening capacity of the resin has been exhausted, it can be regenerated using a strong solution of common salt (sodium chloride, NaCl), which recharges the surface of the resin with "soft" sodium ions.

◀ In catalytic converters for automobile exhausts (left and below), a fine layer of platinum is adsorbed on a porous ceramic support (white cylinder at right). The catalytic reactions occur by chemisorption on the surface of solid platinum, so this construction saves platinum—a rare and costly metal—and boosts conversion efficiency by increasing the surface area per unit mass of platinum.

SEE ALSO: CATALYST • CHEMISTRY, ORGANIC • CHROMATOGRAPHY • HYDROCARBON • PLATINUM METALS • ZEOLITE

Sound

Sound is an oscillating disturbance that passes through matter in the form of pressure waves; the essential requirement for the propagation of such waves is the presence of a material medium that is to some extent elastic. Such a medium contains atoms and molecules that can pass on a disturbance—a sound wave—by bumping into their neighbors. Solids, liquids, and gases all propagate sound waves; pure vacuum does not.

The study of pressure waves is termed *acoustics*, and the term *sound* applies principally to pressure waves whose frequencies lie in the range 20 Hz to 20,000 Hz—the range of frequencies detectable by the human ear. When pressure waves reach the eardrum, they cause it to vibrate. The ear then converts these vibrations into signals that pass through nerves to the brain, where they are interpreted as sounds.

Acoustic waves of vibration frequencies below 20 Hz are termed *infrasonic*, and include most earthquake vibrations. Pressure waves at frequencies greater than 20,000 Hz are termed *ultrasonic*, and include vibrations produced by equipment for cleaning and therapeutic uses.

Production and transmission

When an object vibrates, molecules next to its surface are alternately pushed together and pulled apart—the medium is first compressed, then rarefied. As these molecules move back and forth, they collide with neighboring molecules in the medium. Those molecules then move back and forth with a slight time lag when compared with the molecules at the vibrating object's surface, and that time lag increases with distance from the vibrating object. As such, waves of compression and rarefaction spread through the medium from the surface of the vibrating object.

Speed of sound

The speed of sound is the rate at which pressure waves travel through a medium—solid, liquid, or gas—and this rate varies according to the medium and the prevailing conditions of temperature and pressure. One factor is the elasticity of the medium: the more elastic the medium, the greater the ability of one atom or molecule to nudge its neighbors into motion and the greater the speed of sound. Another factor is density: higher density indicates more massive particles, whose greater inertia makes their motions more sluggish, so the speed of sound is reduced. Temperature and pressure act indirectly by changing the elasticity and density of media,

thereby changing the rate of passage of pressure waves. In general, the speed of sound, v, is related to the modulus of elasticity, E, and density, ρ, by the formula

$$v = \sqrt{\frac{E}{\rho}}$$

In strict scientific terms, Young's modulus of elasticity, E, is the ratio of stress (force per unit area) to the resulting strain (change in length per unit original length). The force required to produce a given strain in steel ($E = 2 \times 10^{11}$ Nm^{-2}), say, is much greater than the force required to produce the same strain in rubber ($E = 10^7$ Nm^{-2}), so steel has a much greater elasticity than rubber in this sense.

▲ An anechoic chamber in use for testing an antenna for NASA. Sound-absorbing elements reduce echoes, and the shapes of these elements reflect sound into the gaps between the elements, where mutual cancellation of echoes occurs by interference.

THE COCHLEA

The cochlea is the part of the inner ear responsible for the ability to hear sounds. It is present in humans and other mammals, as well as in birds and some species of reptiles.

Sound waves reach the cochlea via the fenestra ovalis (Latin for "oval window"), a membrane that separates the middle and inner ears. They stimulate vibrations of the endolymph, the fluid that fills the cochlea, and these vibrations in turn cause vibrations of tiny hairs that protrude from the lining of the cochlea.

Hairs near the basal end of the cochlea vibrate in response to high frequencies, stimulating nerve impulses that originate in the sensitive cells that support them; hairs near the apical end of the cochlea respond to low-frequency sounds in a similar way. The brain interprets the impulses from the different types of cochlear cells to generate a perception of sound.

▶ The human cochlea, seen here uncoiled for clarity, has a spiral form resembling a snail's shell.

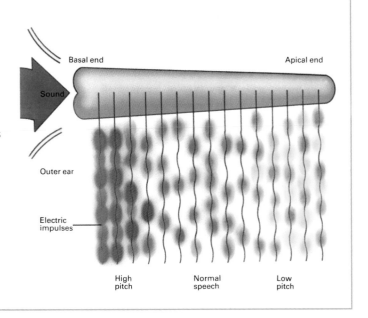

In general, the speed of sound is greatest in solids, less in liquids, and least in gases because the decrease in elastic modulus from solids to gases overwhelms the decrease in density. The speed of sound in steel is approximately 11,180 mph (5,000 m/s); in water, it is around 3,130 mph (1,400 m/s); and in air at room temperature and at sea level, it is 769 mph (344 m/s).

The effect of temperature on the speed of sound is much less pronounced in solids and liquids than it is in gases: values of elasticity and density change little with temperature in solids and liquids, whereas an increase in the temperature of a gas causes its molecules to move from collision to collision with greater speed, thereby increasing elasticity. The speed of sound in air, for example, increases from 741 mph (331 m/s) at 32°F (0°C) to 864 mph (386 m/s) at 212°F (100°C)—an increase of 17 percent.

Properties of sound

Audible sounds are characterized and compared in terms of pitch, loudness, and timbre. These are subjective properties that refer to the perception of sound by an "average" human listener.

Pitch. The pitch of a note depends on the frequency of the sound and is thus analogous to the color of visible light. Notes that differ in pitch by one octave differ in frequency by a factor of two, so middle C on a piano has a frequency of 261.2 Hz, whereas high C is 522.4 Hz, for example.

Loudness. The loudness of a sound is a function of the intensity of the transmitted sound wave—its power per unit area in a perpendicular plane to the direction of travel of the sound. Loudness also depends on frequency: sounds between 1,000 Hz and 5,000 Hz seem to be louder than sounds of frequencies outside that range. Increased loudness also influences perceived pitch, reducing the pitch of sounds below 1,000 Hz and increasing the pitch of sounds above 3,000 Hz, thus emphasizing the fact that pitch is related to the frequency of a sound wave but not identical to it.

Timbre. The quality of a musical note—often called its timbre—is the characteristic that enables a listener to distinguish between a note played on a piano and a note of the same frequency and loudness played on a violin. Timbre arises because sounds seldom consist of one pure frequency. When the hammer of a piano strikes a string, for example, it will cause the string to vibrate at its nominal frequency, or fundamental. At the same time, the hammer blow will excite overtones—vibrations whose frequencies are multiples of the fundamental.

Timbre depends on the profile of relative strengths of the fundamental and its overtones, and this profile is determined by the origin of the sound. In addition to the fundamental, a pipe organ produces only those overtones that are odd multiples of the fundamental frequency, for example, whereas even overtones predominate in the sound produced by a violin.

Wave properties

Sound is an example of a longitudinal wave—a wave characterized by vibrations parallel to its direction of travel—in contrast with transverse waves, such as light, where vibrations are at right angles to the direction of travel. Nevertheless, both types of waves are mechanisms by which energy moves from one place to another.

In addition to the characteristics of frequency and speed of propagation, sound waves are characterized by their waveforms. When a single frequency of sound passes through a medium, a plot of the displacement of any given particle from its average position is a sine wave, which is the simplest of all waveforms. The peak represents maximum displacement along the direction of wave travel; the trough represents maximum displacement in the opposite direction.

When two or more frequencies pass through a medium, the waveform becomes more complex, but it repeats at the rate of the dominant frequency. The complexity of the waveform is related to the perceived timbre of the sound.

Reflection and acoustics

Sound waves reflect off surfaces in a manner that resembles the reflection of light, losing some of their energy to the reflecting surface as they do so. The reflection of sound is responsible for echoes and acoustic effects, such as that at the Whispering Gallery at St Paul's Cathedral, London. There, a low-intensity sound emitted at one side of the gallery can be clearly heard at the other side, the sound bouncing around the walls at grazing angles that cause little loss of energy.

Reflection of sound is an important consideration in building design, and the sound-reflecting qualities of a space are called its acoustics. One element of the acoustics of an enclosed space is its reverberation time—the period for which echoes persist after the sound source has been stilled. In libraries and open-plan offices, reverberation times are kept short by using wall surfaces and flooring materials that absorb as much sound as possible, thereby creating a relatively quiet environment for work or study. Porous materials—cork, polystyrene foam, and soft furnishings—are all good absorbers of sound; hard, smooth surfaces, such as glass and glazed tiles, absorb very little sound, as do high-density materials, such as brickwork, plaster, and concrete.

In a concert hall, a short reverberation time—one of around 0.5 seconds, say—causes orchestral music to sound thin and lifeless, whereas an excessive reverberation time causes music to sound confused, as echoes drown out new notes.

The first systematic approach to acoustic design was developed

by the U.S. physicist Wallace Sabine in the last years of the 19th century. Faced with the poor acoustics of a newly opened auditorium at Harvard in 1895, Sabine set about making it useful as a theater. He found that the reverberation time depended on the volume of the room, the surface area, and the sound-absorbing characteristics of the surfaces. By 1898, he had developed a formula to link these characteristics.

Using such calculations, architects and designers can now predetermine the reverberation time of a new building by the judicious choice of the shapes of surfaces, construction materials, and furnishings. For certain purposes, such as the testing and design of loudspeakers, it is necessary to construct rooms whose walls absorb practically all the sound energy that falls on them. Such rooms, called anechoic chambers, are completely lined with blocks of highly porous materials.

Refraction

Sound waves change direction when they pass through regions where the speed of sound changes, mimicking the refraction of light through regions of changing refractive index. Since the speed of sound in a gas increases with temperature, atmospheric temperature variations can result in speed changes and consequent refraction of sound. This effect helps sound carry

▶ Schlieren photography detects small changes in refractive index, such as occur when sound waves pass through air. Here, the technique reveals the reflection of sound off a serrated surface.

▼ This schlieren image shows interference between beams of sound diffracted through slits.

► Schlieren imaging using laser light shows up the reflection of a planar beam of ultrasound, with a frequency of 3 MHz, from a horizontal surface (bottom right).

farther at night than during the daytime, for example. By day, high-altitude air is generally colder than air at ground level, so sound travels faster near Earth's surface, and sound waves refract upward. At night, air is colder near the ground, resulting in sound refracting back toward Earth's surface and maintaining its intensity at ground level over long distances.

Interference

Interference is another typical wave phenomenon exhibited by sound. One type of interference occurs when two sound waves of the same frequency arrive at the same point from different sources or via different paths.

If the waves arrive at that point in such a way that positions of maximum displacement in the same direction coincide, the waves reinforce each other, producing a loud sound; this phenomenon is constructive interference. If the maximum displacement in one direction of one wave coincides with the opposite maximum of the other wave, the two waves cancel one another, reducing the intensity of the sound; this is destructive interference.

Interference of two sound waves also occurs when the two waves have slightly different frequencies. The resulting sound has the average of the two frequencies, and its intensity rises and falls at a frequency equal to the difference between the two frequencies. These pulses of enhanced intensity, called beats, can be used to tune stringed instruments. A tuning fork produces the correct note for a given string, and the tension of the string is adjusted to make the beats slow down until they stop, that is, when the frequency of the string matches the true note.

Diffraction

In uninterrupted space, sound waves travel in straight lines. When they meet an obstacle, they bend around it, provided the size of the obstacle approximately equals the wavelength of the sound. This phenomenon is the equivalent of the diffraction of light but is more commonly observed because sound waves are normally between several inches and feet in length, so they bend around most commonly encountered objects. Low frequencies diffract more than high frequencies, and thus, the rumble of traffic is heard before higher-frequency noises when approaching a main road through an alley, for example.

Doppler effect

The Doppler effect is the shift in the pitch of a sound that occurs when the source of the sound and the listener are moving relative to one another. Common examples include the change in the pitch of a locomotive horn as it approaches, passes, and then recedes from the listener: the pitch drops suddenly as the train passes.

In fact, the true pitch of the horn is heard only at the instant when the locomotive passes in front of the listener. During the approach, the number of waves reaching the listener in a given time is increased by the relative motion of the source, so the frequency—and therefore pitch—increases. As the source recedes, fewer sound waves reach the listener in a given time, so the pitch drops.

Infrasonic and ultrasonic vibrations

Infrasonic waves include vibrations that cause slow oscillations—at 20 Hz or less—in the pressure of a fluid such as air or in any other wave-transmitting material. As such, they include seismic vibrations of Earth's crust. Artificial infrasonic pulses can be generated by the detonation of explosive charges buried beneath Earth's surface, and infrasonic signals can be generated by vibroseis, the use of "thumper" trucks that pound Earth's surface at an appropriate frequency.

Ultrasonic vibrations have frequencies greater than 20,000 Hz. They do not occur naturally but are commonly generated by piezoelectric oscillators. These exhibit the reverse piezoelectric effect, whereby the dimensions of an appropriately cut crystal of piezoelectric material change in response to an electrical field applied across opposing faces. The most widely used piezoelectric material is quartz. When a rapidly alternating electric potential is applied to such a crystal, the crystal expands and contracts at the frequency of the electrical signal. The amplitude of vibration becomes large when the frequency of the alternating potential coincides with the natural vibrational frequency of the crystal. In this condition, the amplitude of the vibration is sufficient for such a crystal to be used as an efficient source of compressional waves. The frequency of vibrations is selected by cutting the crystal to have the appropriate resonant frequency.

Applications of acoustic vibrations

Apart from the obvious uses in speech and music, there are many technical uses of compressional waves. Seismologists analyze infrasonic waves conveyed by the Earth's crust to locate and classify the seismic activity that caused them. Prospectors for natural reserves of oil and gas rely heavily on the information obtained by reflecting infrasonic acoustic waves to locate the types of rock formations that have previously been found to be likely bearers of such reserves.

▲ An acoustic microscope (right) examines a steel component for signs of deterioration brought on by exposure to radiation in the core of a nuclear reactor. The display at left shows the "view" through the steel component.

Sonar (*so*und *na*vigation *r*anging) uses high-frequency audible vibrations and near ultrasound for the location of underwater objects and shoals of fish, for example. The sound for this technique is generated by transducers, which vibrate in response to an electrical signal.

Ultrasonic vibrations have a wide and growing range of applications. Important among them are ultrasonic cleaning, and drilling and nondestructive testing of metal castings. When generated in liquids, ultrasonic waves produce cavitation by creating minute voids within the liquid giving rise to a vacuum effect within the liquid that is extremely effective in removing dirt and dust particles from surfaces requiring cleaning. The effect is also used for emulsifying immiscible liquids (liquids that will not normally mix, like oil and water) and for the removal of air bubbles from liquids prior to casting. Ultrasound may also be used to catalyze certain reactions, since the energy released by collapsing cavities is sufficient to activate reactions between molecules.

Holes of any shape can be bored in a surface by the action of ultrasonic waves imposed on a rod in contact with the surface to be drilled. The cutting action is achieved with the aid of abrasive powder, and the resulting hole is the shape of the vibrating rod. The reflection and transmission of ultrasonic waves provide the basis for the nondestructive testing for microscopic flaws, voids, cracks, and other irregularities deep within large metal castings. A similar technique underlies noninvasive ultrasound scans that are used to examine fetuses in the womb and to identify abnormalities in internal organs without surgery.

FACT FILE

- *NASA technicians once built a steel and concrete horn 48 ft. (14.5 m) in length, capable of producing a noise of 210 decibels, or 400,000 acoustic watts. Sound at this level can drill solid material.*

- *The opera house at Bayreuth, Germany, was designed by the composer Richard Wagner with a long reverberation time to emphasize the full, rich texture of his operas.*

- *Acoustic holography records the interference pattern of sound waves instead of those of reflected light. The hologram image is formed by the action of the ultrasound beams on a liquid surface.*

- *Scanning laser acoustic microscopy (SLAM) uses sound vibrations to search out defects in metal parts at the micron level. Sound waves beamed through the parts are altered by defects and impinge on a sheet of gold foil to produce distortions matching those of the defect. These distortions are revealed by a scanning beam of laser light.*

SEE ALSO: ACOUSTICS • DOPPLER EFFECT • DRILL • HEARING • OSCILLATOR • SEISMOLOGY • SONAR • ULTRASONICS • WAVE MOTION

Sound Effects and Sampling

Sound effects are indispensable tools of the film, radio, television, and theater industries. They reinforce the impression of reality—or the invented "reality" of science fiction—by providing sounds that match the audience's expectations deriving from what is seen on screen or stage; in radio plays, they give nonverbal clues that set the scene for the action. Sound effects also add atmosphere to films and to television and theater plays by signaling events outside the field of view—trains rattling past low-rent apartments, for example, or wind howling through trees on a stormy night.

In broad terms, there are three types of sound effects. The most straightforward type uses the sound of the event itself—thunder can be recorded and then played back at the appropriate cue, for example, while a gunshot can be produced by firing a blank round on cue. The second type uses mechanical means to produce sounds that mimic natural sounds; the film industry term for this effect is "Foley," named for Jack Foley, a U.S. sound engineer of the early 20th century. Foley developed artificial sounds to accompany the action in some of the first talking films.

The most recent addition to the sound effect engineer's armory is sampling. With this technique, natural sounds are recorded in digital format—as a sample—then manipulated to create new sounds. Sampling is particularly useful for giving voices to fantasy creatures and for producing credible noises for the futuristic vehicles and weapons of science fiction movies.

▲ This engineer produces sound effects for the British Broadcasting Corporation radio series *The Archers,* a soap opera set in rural Britain. The tools of his trade include creaking gates and a whole range of door knockers and locks.

Theatrical sound effects

The use of sound effects in theater started long before the advent of talking films. In many cases, the sounds were natural—an actor playing a blacksmith would hammer a real anvil, for example. In other cases, sound effects would be produced live offstage—three or four stagehands might march in a trough of gravel to provide a realistic trudging sound while "soldiers" march quietly on the boards of the stage.

Thunder. There are three categories of theatrical thunder: the sharp thunderclap, the prolonged distant rumble, and an intermediate noise that is sharper than the distant rumble while more prolonged than the thunderclap. Each of these thunder sounds is produced by a different machine.

The thunderclap machine consists of up to ten pairs of wooden slats hinged a few inches apart by a rope. Another rope is fastened to the last slat in such a way that, when sharply pulled, it brings all the slats progressively but rapidly together.

Distant rumbles of thunder can be simulated using a rubble of bricks and large stones in a cart fitted with uneven or eccentric wheels. When the cart is pushed along, its misshapen wheels cause the rubble to shift, emitting a continuous rumble whose quality and duration depend on how fast and how long the cart is pushed.

Another thunder sound is produced using a thunder sheet—a thin sheet of metal suspended by one edge. As with the rumble cart, the quality and duration of the sound depend on the degree of violence and length of shaking.

Wind machine. The traditional wind machine consists of a slatted wooden drum mounted on a standing frame so that it can be turned. A canvas sheet drapes over the drum; it is fastened to the frame on one side and tied down or weighted on the other. The drum is turned using a handle, and the scraping of the slats on the canvas produces a sound that resembles that of wind howling past a building or through trees. The pitch of the sound rises when the drum turns faster, and the sound can also be altered by adjusting the tension on the canvas. This type of wind machine has even been used in orchestral works such as *Don Quixote*, a tone poem by Richard Strauss.

Rainfall. The sound of rain falling on a metal roof can be simulated using a metal chute of zigzag form. Dried peas or shot poured into the top of the chute produce the sound as they make their way under the force of gravity through the various drops and gradients of the chute.

Whip crack. The sound of a cracking whip or of snapping wood is recreated using two thin strips of wood, each around 2 ft. (61 cm) long and 2 in. (5.1 cm) wide, screwed to either side of a flat wooden handle so that they are parallel and separated by a small distance. To make the sound, the engineer holds the device in one hand and smacks it against the palm of the other hand, causing the two long strips to smack together.

Train sound. The sound of metal wheels passing over the joints of a railroad track is such an established sound effect that it continues to be used even though modern continuous-welded tracks produce no such sound—an example of how sound effects are tailored to meet expectations rather than to be faithful to reality. This sound is produced using a roller skate pressed against a revolving metal-covered wooden drum. The wheels of the skate jump as they pass over two grooves cut into the surface of the drum and thus reproduce the sound made by two pairs of wheeled axles as they pass over joints in a track.

Creaks, groans, and squeaks. A variety of creaking noises can be made using a resin-impregnated rope in a barrel. One end of the rope passes through a hole in a piece of three-ply wood that closes one end of a barrel; the other end of the barrel is open, and the barrel acts as a resonator to amplify the sound. The rope is held taut inside the barrel and stroked using a piece of resinous leather, rather as a violin string is played by a bow. The sounds from such a device range from a squeak to a lion's roar, depending on the speed and abruptness of the action; the sound also depends on the part of the rope that is played.

Foley

The Foley technique applies the theatrical sound effects already described—as well as many others—to enhance the soundtracks of films. Such effects are necessary because the microphones used to pick up actors' voices are highly directional. Consequently, they fail to register incidental noises, such as slamming doors and footsteps on gravel, at the intensity that would be heard by an observer on the scene of the action.

Once the action has been filmed, the Foley track is created by artists working in a soundproof studio. This environment is acoustically dead, so it imparts no artificial ambience to the final soundtrack. The film is played silently on a screen in the Foley studio, so the artists can synchronize effects with the actions played out on the screen. Foley studio props include a variety of ground surfaces and flooring over which the artists walk in time with the actors, as well as doors, telephone sets, cutlery and crockery, and so on. The various components of the Foley track—walking and prop handling, for example—are recorded separately and then mixed together at the appropriate levels to create the Foley track that will later be mixed with dialogue, ambience, and music tracks to form the final soundtrack.

Sampling

Source materials for sampling include the sounds of voices, instruments, and animals, as well as more unusual noises produced by sound engineers working with props. Once recorded in digital form, each sample can be manipulated in pitch, speed, and duration, and various electronic filters can be applied to further modify the sound.

One of the main innovators in sampling technology is Skywalker Sound, founded by the U.S. film director George Lucas. This postproduction company used the sound of a taut guy cable being hit by a hammer as the source sample for the sound of laser blasts in the *Star Wars* films; various animal samples create the sounds of fantasy creatures and dinosaurs.

▼ A technician of the California-based company Dinamation International works on a sample-based soundtrack to create realistic sounds for a triceratops dinosaur.

SEE ALSO: LOUDSPEAKER • MICROPHONE • MOVIE PRODUCTION • SOUND MIXING • SOUNDTRACK • SYNTHESIZER

Sound Mixing

Sound mixing is the practice of setting the relative levels and tonal qualities of audio signals from two or more sources. Its purpose is to provide balanced audio signals for recording or broadcasting or for amplification through the public-address system of a concert hall, for example.

For sound mixing to be possible, each sound source must have its own transducer for converting sound into an electrical signal. Such transducers include microphones and guitar and piano pickups. In some cases, prerecorded sounds are played back along with the live performance. The signals from transducers and playback devices mostly reach the input channels of a mixing desk by cables, although microphones with radio links are sometimes used to increase performers' freedom of motion during live performances.

Mixing desk

Mixing desks vary enormously in sophistication and cost, and the choice of mixing desk for a particular event depends largely on the available funds and the amount of control required over the sound output. The simplest setups have only two or three input channels, each channel consisting of an input socket and a sound-level control and a similar number of output channels for supplying signals to amplifiers and recording devices. Such mixing desks are typically used for onstage mixing of small bands and solo artists.

The sound-mixing desks of recording studios and large performance venues are much more complex, typically having hundreds of switches and slider level controls for manipulating sound. A typical mixing desk of this category might have 20 to 30 input channels and 2 to 24 output groups.

Each input channel has an input preamplifier that can be switched into the circuit to boost low-level signals from microphones, for example, ensuring that all signals are of a suitable strength for the next part of the channel, the equalizer.

An equalizer uses electronic circuits to split an input signal into component signals that each span a narrow range of frequencies. In this way, the bass, midrange, and treble components of the signal are each split into three or four signals, and the levels of these signals can be adjusted individually, usually through slider controls attached to variable resistances, or potentiometers. Mixing engineers use equalizers to compensate for imperfect acoustics in the performing environment that favor one frequency range over another and to modify the tonal quality or timbre of an instrumental or vocal sound.

The next stage in the mixing desk is channel distribution, or routing. The routing unit makes the electrical connections between the input channels and the output mixing groups, sometimes after the signal from the input channel has passed through a main fader that controls its

▲ This engineer sets the sliders of this digital mixing desk as he would those of a conventional analog mixing desk. The manipulation of digital data streams rather than analog signals preserves sound quality throughout mixing and recording.

level. Each mixing group has faders that control the levels of signals from the various input channels fed to it by the routing unit. The sound engineer uses these faders to establish the required balance between the input signals, and an amplifier then boosts the mixed signal to a suitable level for recording or public-address equipment.

In addition to the main mixing system, mixing desks often have completely separate multichannel systems, each having a separate fader for each channel and its own master level control. Such auxiliary mixing systems are used for mixing together signals to be sent to echo plates or other special effects devices. The returning signals from these devices are fed back into spare input channels on the main mixer, thus allowing echo or special effects signals to be added independent of the original source signals.

Another auxiliary mixing system returns a mixed signal—the monitor mix—to the artists to help them synchronize their performances with one another. For live performances, the fold-back mix plays through monitor loudspeakers on the stage; in recording studios, this mix plays through the artists' headphones, or "cans." The monitor mixer is independent of the main mixing system and controls only the way in which the signals are heard by the engineer and the performers. As such, changes made to a monitor mix have no effect on the mix and equalization setup for the signals sent to recording devices.

Recording

The output from the mixing desk is frequently recorded for further manipulation after the performing sessions. For decades, these recordings were made on 2 in. (50 mm) wide magnetic tape, with up to 24 channels occupying parallel tracks on the tape. Now, most recordings are made on digital media using magnetic or optical data storage; nevertheless, the term "track" is still used to describe a single channel of a recording.

Mixing down

The end uses of sound recordings usually require fewer tracks than taken from the mixing desk at a recording session. A stereo compact disc requires only two channels—left and right—whereas a movie soundtrack might have five tracks, for example. The process of combining the channels of the mixer output for the final mix is called mixing down. It is the point at which final choices are made concerning the relative levels of performers and their position in the stereophonic sound field. Nevertheless, the mixing down process can be repeated if necessary, provided the intermediate multitrack recording is kept intact.

▼ The Neve 8108 sound mixer. Features include (1) control of incoming signals from the studio, (2) filters to eliminate unwanted sound, (3) parametric equilizers, (4) auxiliary assignment and multitrack controls, (5) secondary fader to adjust approximate sound, (6) mix-down control with pan potentiometers, (7) primary fader to control the main sound balance and volume, (8) interrogation switches to determine which microphones are feeding which tracks, (9) remote control panel, (10) touch pad facilities panel for quadraphonic listening.

Digital technology

As with many other processes, the introduction of digital technology has vastly improved the process of sound mixing. When recordings are made in digital format, they can be manipulated without any loss in quality, in contrast with analog mixing, where each change in level and equalization introduces distortion to the signal.

Whereas analog mixers use variable resistors to control sound levels and equalization, digital mixers manipulate streams of data to change their levels. Thus, mouse-movable screen images of sliders can replace the physical sliders of old. Furthermore, the whole mixing setup can be changed between preset configurations at the click of an on-screen button—an extremely useful feature for live performances that present several artists with different mixing requirements. For recording engineers, digital mixing offers features such as looping, whereby short recorded excerpts, such as drum tracks, can be repeated seamlessly as many times as required. Variable delay allows each track to start at a point that synchronizes it with the other tracks of the recording, and effects such as reverberation and compression, which reduces signal peaks, can be added at will.

| **SEE ALSO:** | AUDIO AND VIDEO RECORDING • SOUND • SOUND EFFECTS AND SAMPLING |

Soundproofing

◀ A cutaway model of a double-glazing installation. The space between the panels of glass is lined, on the sides, with sound-absorbing materials.

Soundproofing is concerned with the exclusion or reduction of sounds from a particular location. It might be an open-plan office or classroom, a room in a home or a factory, or the interior of a motor vehicle or ship.

When soundproofing is needed, three factors must be considered. The first is the source of the sound, its location, and power output. A second consideration is the path the sound takes to a listener. If the sound is airborne, it is called noise, and if it is propagated through material—for example, walls or flooring—it is referred to as vibration. Last, the effect of the various levels of sound on humans must be estimated in order to set tolerable levels—when sound pollution exceeds these levels, sleep loss, hearing loss, and stress-related illnesses may result.

Architecture

In the design of residential and commercial buildings, provision is made to minimize the transmission of unwanted sound between rooms. One way to do so is to make floors and walls thick and heavy, but this solution is expensive. Lighter panels have been developed that are very rigid, thus providing some sound insulation. Some panels are coated with viscoelastic materials, such as rubber or vinyl, which further damp the sound. Sometimes an air space of a few inches is provided between two adjacent panels. Some sound is always reflected back at the interface between two different materials. Further improvements in sound insulation can be provided by ensuring that even small gaps in a building structure are insulated and by using carpets and other soft materials on building interiors.

The same principles are used in windows for buildings. A single window pane of typical thickness (⅛ or ⅙ in., 3 or 4 mm) will reduce noise to about one-quarter loudness. If laminated glass is used, it will provide still more damping, and double glazing will cut the noise level by half as much again as a single pane. Sometimes the edges of the air space between two panes are lined with a soft fibrous material, to further reduce the problems by absorbing vibration.

Open-plan office space represents a real economic advantage as well as design flexibility, and open-plan classrooms make possible new teaching methods, but when such architectural space was first designed, noise levels proved to be a problem because of the way sound will travel along walls that are not interrupted by partitions. Movable partitions are now used to create acoustic environments, and soft, absorbent materials can be used in various places. Partitions and walls as well as floors can be covered with soft materials such as carpeting, felt, hessian, and so forth. The height and absorptive treatment of the ceilings are of great importance in controlling the direction and loudness of intruding sound. Absorbent ceiling tiles are widely used in building construction.

▶ A soundproofing baffle with glass beads. This type of insulation is used in the exhaust system of an industrial gas turbine driver.

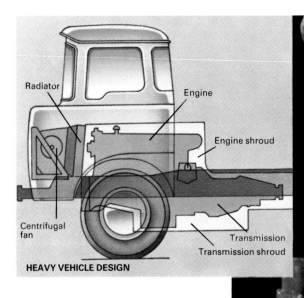

HEAVY VEHICLE DESIGN

▲ Minor design changes and adequate soundproofing of diesel engines can greatly reduce noise levels.

▶ Rigorous testing and monitoring of decibels are important factors in the manufacture of engines.

Factory noise

Industrial architecture is designed so that noisy areas will be insulated from noise-sensitive areas by space that is not as sensitive, for example, storage or warehouse space. It is important in industrial soundproofing to insulate the sound source from the floor so that offending vibrations are damped; a solution is to install a relatively flexible element between two rigid structures. Springs, soft rubber mounts, and cork are used to isolate a machine from the factory floor. In instances where these measures are insufficient to provide adequate soundproofing, protective ear pieces may have to be worn.

Motor vehicles

In cars, both noise and vibration control are necessary. At low speeds, airborne noise from the tires can be a problem, while at higher speeds, the noise from air flow in window cracks and around the body of the car can be intrusive. During sudden acceleration, engine and exhaust system noise can be excessive.

Noise control in the design of motor vehicles amounts to a surprisingly costly item; many countries have legislation setting permissible noise levels in commercial vehicles, though no such protection exists for private cars. The aerodynamic design of a vehicle body is important, and manufacturers test scale models of new designs in wind tunnels partly for this reason. The suspension of a car is designed to isolate the body as much as possible from road shock. The engine is mounted on pads of rubber to damp vibration; body panels may be attached to the car with rubber strips installed for the same purpose. The various parts of the car are designed so that one part will not be subject to sympathetic vibration with another; in other words, each part of the body shell should have a different resonant frequency.

Exterior noise from motor vehicles is increasingly regarded as a threat to the quality of life, especially in cities. Screens made of vegetation planted between roads and buildings provide some sound protection. More important, however, is legislation that requires proper maintenance of vehicle exhaust systems, in particular mufflers. In some cities the police are equipped with sound-level meters for noise measurement.

Airport noise is another increasing problem that, despite research into means of making the jet engine quieter, is impossible to solve to the satisfaction of those living around airports. Today the most common partial solution to the problem is the use of double glazing, but—like the use of air conditioning in commercial buildings so that doors and windows can be kept closed to keep out sound—it is a stopgap measure. The increase of noise pollution in our industrial society is likely to be of increasing concern in years to come.

SEE ALSO:	ACOUSTICS • AERODYNAMICS • AUTOMOBILE EXHAUST SYSTEM • NOISE MEASUREMENT • SOUND • WAVE MOTION

Sound Reproduction

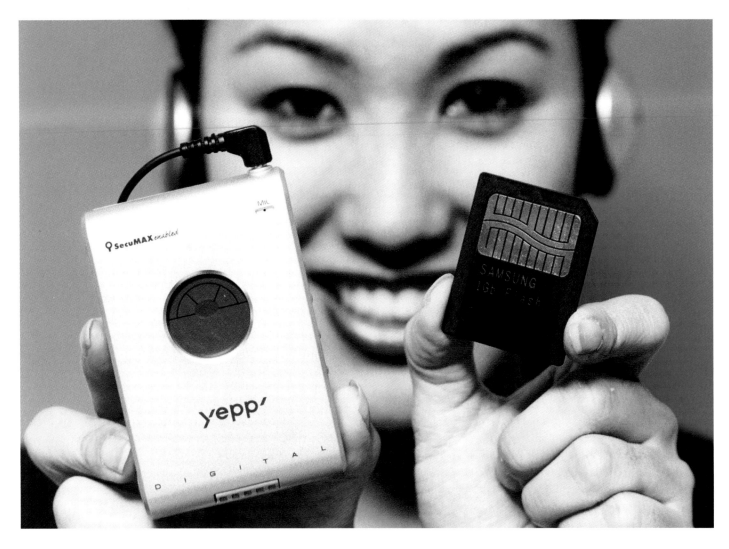

Sound reproduction encompasses processes that convert recorded signals into sounds that mimic those that would be heard by a listener at a live performance. The growth and diversification of technology for recording sounds has been accompanied by refinements in techniques and equipment for sound reproduction.

Hearing

Any person who has hearing in both ears has an inbuilt mechanism for determining the direction from which a sound comes because the different positions and orientations of the left and right ears combined with the shape of the human ear modify the sound that is heard according to the direction from which it originates.

A sound that originates from the left of a listener reaches the left ear earlier than the right ear and with greater intensity and tonal brightness. The difference in time of arrival is due to the greater distance that the sound must travel to reach the right ear, while the change in intensity and brightness is due to the fact that the sound

must diffract around the head to reach the right ear. Only a part of the sound energy diffracts in the direction of the ear, and the diffraction process favors lower frequencies over higher frequencies, resulting in a duller sound.

Sound is also louder and sharper when it arrives in front of the listener because the external structure of the human ear blocks sounds that come from the rear to some extent.

The brain uses differences in the timing, intensity, and brightness of perceived sounds as clues to determine the position of their sources. Sophisticated sound-reproduction technologies use these clues to trick the brain into forming the impression that recorded sound originates from a specific angular direction relative to the listener.

Stereophonic reproduction

The earliest sound recordings were monophonic—that is, all the sounds of a given recording were contained in one channel. The lack of spatial information meant that a listener would be aware of the position of the loudspeaker but not

▲ Portable sound systems are becoming ever smaller with the introduction of digital technology. This MP3 player uses a one gigabyte flash memory card to store 32 songs that are reproduced with the same sound quality as that of a CD player.

of the relative positions of the artists at the time of the recording. In stereophonic recordings, two sound channels—left and right—contain recorded sounds that differ between channels in a way that mimics the differences between the sounds that reach the left and right ears of a well-positioned audience member at a live performance.

When playing back such recordings, the two loudspeakers must be connected in phase so that both speakers compress and rarefy air at the same time. If not, the phase difference between the sound waves creates bizarre spatial effects, as interference between the sound waves from the two speakers cancels out certain frequencies. Also, the unnatural phase difference confounds the brain's mechanism for determining the spatial origins of sounds; the mechanism depends on the smaller phase differences that occur because sound takes longer to reach one ear than the other.

Dummy head

Experiments in stereo recording in the early 20th century used two microphones, one in each ear position on a model of a human head—a dummy head. When the sound from the two microphones was recorded and played back through twin loudspeakers on either side of a listener, that listener would be able to determine the positions of performers ranging from the right to the left. The stereophonic effect was found to be even more distinct when sound was played through headphones, since each ear would then hear only those sounds detected by the corresponding microphone in the dummy head.

The use of dummy heads had a resurgence in the late 1970s, particularly in West Germany. There recording engineers used a *Kunstkopf* (artificial head) to produce recordings that, when played back, enveloped the listener in a full 360-degree sound field.

Microphone techniques

Although the dummy-head system provides good stereo recordings, it is not very flexible in use; consequently, most stereo recordings use simple microphone arrangements. One of the pioneers of such techniques was the British engineer A. D. Blumlein, who showed in 1930 that accurate spatial effects can be created using intensity or time of arrival as locating clues. Such recording techniques therefore disregard the differences in brightness detected by the dummy head.

In one approach, Blumlein used two highly directional microphones, called coincident microphones, one mounted directly above the other in the same location. The microphones were set at 45 degrees either side of the straight-

▼ Two microphones in the ears of a dummy head (left) give good stereo recordings by detecting subtle differences in the intensity, timing, and muffling of sounds as they would reach the ears of an audience member. A pair of directional microphones (right) gives satisfactory results by detecting intensity differences alone.

ahead direction so as to be sensitive to opposite sides of the stage. Hence, a sound originating from center stage would be detected with equal intensity by both microphones, whereas a sound from one side of the stage would be detected with greater intensity by the microphone pointed toward that part of the stage. That intensity difference increased with the distance from center stage. There was no provision for recording differences in timing or for muffling sounds according to the positions of their sources, but the intensity differences were found to be sufficient to create a convincing stereo sound "image" when played through a pair of loudspeakers.

In another approach, two sound channels are recorded using a widely spaced pair of microphones, which may not be particularly directional. Once again, intensity differences arise because of the different spacings between sound sources and the microphones. However, there is also a difference in the time taken for sound waves to reach the microphones that does not occur with coincident microphones owing to their shared location.

Studio methods

The majority of sound recordings are done in recording studios rather than live venues. In studio recording, it is common for individual artists

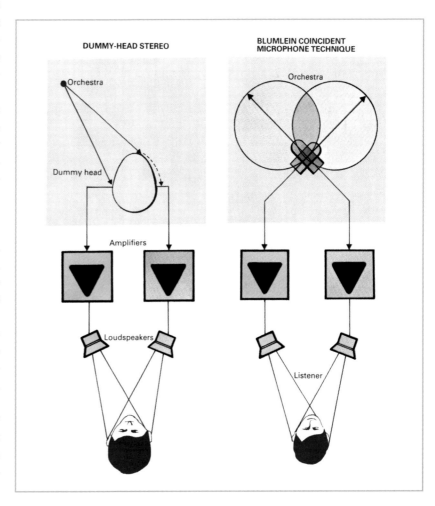

to record their contributions at separate times while listening to previous recordings of their colleagues' contributions to the same piece, so a guitarist might play while listening to a recording of the drum track on headphones, for example.

Each contribution is recorded monophonically, and then given a position in the stereo sound field during the mixing process. In analog mixing, sound engineers use a panoramic potentiometer, or panpot, which consists of two variable resistances attached to a single knob. As the knob is turned clockwise from the neutral position, the output to the left channel diminishes to place the track right of center in the sound field; turning the knob counterclockwise has the opposite effect.

Analog recording

The distribution of sound recordings occurs either by radio or television broadcast or in the form of playable media. For decades, the dominant playable media were gramophone records and audio tapes carrying analog recordings.

Stereo gramophone record. A gramophone first reproduces recorded sounds as vibrations of a stylus. A transducer system then converts those vibrations into electrical signals for amplification so that they become capable of driving the cones of loudspeakers or headphones.

Stereo recordings of this type are made as grooves cut in vinyl. The walls of the groove are at 45 degrees to the vertical—the inner wall corresponds to the left channel, while the wall closer to the edge of the disk corresponds to the right channel. The grooves are made using a cutting tool driven at 45 degrees to the vertical by one channel, while the other channel drives movements at 45 degrees in the other direction. Since the vibrations of the two channels occur at right angles, an appropriate transducer setup in the stylus mounting effectively separates the two channels.

If such a recording is played on a monophonic, or mono player, the sum of the two channels becomes the mono channel. Transducers of mono players detect only vertical oscillations of the stylus.

Audio tape. Audio tapes carry recordings in the form of variations in magnetization of metal oxides embedded in plastic tape. In analog systems, these variations correspond directly to the variations in an audio signal, and inductive loops embedded in metal playback heads convert the

---

STEREO BROADCASTING

Although radio could be broadcast in stereo by using separate frequency channels for left and right, such a process would cause unnecessary crowding of the airwaves and would require two receivers at the listener's end. Since 1967, all radio stations have used a form of multiplexing to transmit stereo signals on single frequency-modulated (FM) carrier signals.

In the Zenith-GE system, the sum of the left and right signals (L + R) modulates the carrier frequency in a way that can be demodulated by both stereo and mono receivers. The difference between the two channels (L − R) is first used to modulate a subcarrier at a frequency of 38 kHz, and that modulated signal is then used to add a further modulation to the carrier frequency. The subcarrier is at such a frequency as to ensure that the L − R modulation is above the audible frequencies of the sum signal.

A third modulation is added to the carrier in the form of a pilot signal at 19 kHz—half the subcarrier frequency. This signal activates the decoders of stereo receivers, sending the signal through circuits that strip the sum and difference signals out of the carrier and subcarrier frequencies, respectively. These signals are then added and subtracted to yield the stereo channels:

left channel: (L + R) + (L − R) = 2L

right channel: (L + R) − (L − R) = 2R

Mono receivers have no means of processing the subcarrier and pilot modulations, which are above the audible frequency range, so they have no effect on what the listeners hear.

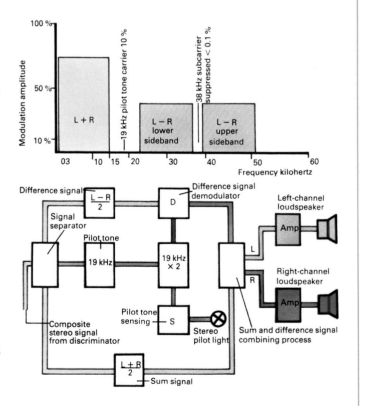

▲ The modulations of a stereo radio signal (top) consist of the audio-frequency sum signal, a pilot signal, and the difference signal modulated around a subcarrier. Filters separate these modulations (above), and matrix circuits then recombine as stereo channels.

QUADRAPHONIC SOUND

At the start of the 1970s, sound engineers developed techniques for improving the realism of recorded sounds by using four sound channels instead of the two sound channels used in stereophony. These techniques were known as quadraphony.

When attending a live performance, an audience member hears mainly the sounds emanating directly from the stage. These sounds are encoded in the left-front (L_f) and right-front (R_f) channels of quadraphony, which are identical to the left and right channels of stereophonic sound-recording techniques.

In addition to the sounds heard directly from the stage, the audience members hear weaker sounds that echo off the walls of the auditorium. These are the left-back (L_b) and right-back (R_b) channels of quadraphony, and they are played back through an additional pair of speakers behind the listening position.

The proliferation of quadraphonic sound systems was at first hindered by the complexity of recording and playing back the four signals using the twin-channeled analog recording media of the time—audio tapes and vinyl discs. Two approaches were used: matrix encoding and discrete encoding. Matrix encoding was the simpler and cheaper of the two methods, but it suffered from high levels of cross talk, whereby one channel contaminates another. Discrete encoding achieved better cross talk results by using the difference signals ($L_f - L_b$ and $R_f - R_b$) to modulate the sum signals ($L_f + L_b$ and $R_f + R_b$), a similar method to that used to combine left and right channels in stereo radio broadcasts. The resulting signals included frequencies as high as 45 kHz and required expensive demodulating equipment for playback.

The current descendents of quadraphony include surround-sound movie and DVD (digital versatile disc) soundtracks, which typically combine the four channels of quadraphony with a fifth track that emphasizes rumbles and other low-frequency sounds. Each track is recorded separately on the film or DVD, so there is no need for special decoding equipment.

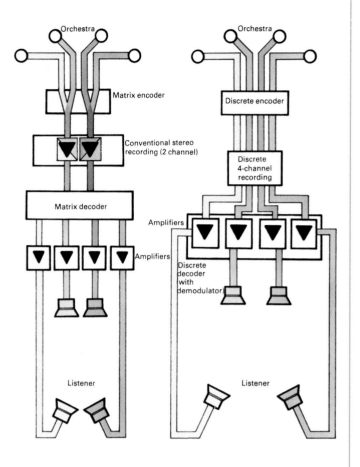

▲ Matrix quadraphony (left) combined front and back signals in both the left and right channels used for stereo recordings. A matrix decoder in the playback equipment would then separate the front and back components for amplification. Discrete quadraphony (right) borrowed modulation techniques from radio broadcasting to combine and separate the four channels. It gave better channel separation than matrix encoding but required more expensive equipment.

variations in magnetization into electrical signals for amplification. Each channel is present as a separate track in a tape recording, and the integrity of the stereo signals depends on how closely the playback head follows the track of the original recording head. Analog tapes are therefore prone to high levels of cross talk.

Digital recording

Digital recordings are superior to analog recordings in many respects. The overall quality of recordings is maintained by processes that identify interference and overlook it. The same processes also eliminate cross talk, which is simply a form of mutual interference between the left and right channels of a stereo recording.

Analog signals from microphones, guitar pickups, and other sources are first digitized by a process called sampling. This process measures the amplitude of the signal at regular intervals and converts it into a digital value. The sampling rate must be at least 2.2 times the highest frequency in the signal—a rule called Nyquist's theorem—to prevent the generation of false frequencies, called "ghosts."

The digitized signals can be recorded on various media—notably compact discs, digital audio tapes, and computer drives. In some cases, a process called compression is applied to remove redundant information and save storage space. This is the case with MP3 computer files. On playback, a processor called a digital-to-analog converter (DAC) reconstructs the original analog waveforms using data from the digital signal.

SEE ALSO: AMPLIFIER • COMPACT DISC, AUDIO • DIGITAL VERSATILE DISC (DVD) • LOUDSPEAKER • MICROPHONE • RADIO • SOUND MIXING

Soundtrack

Until recently, a soundtrack was simply the sound area on film used to show moving pictures. Film soundtracks are an established technology, but now with the increasing use of digital systems, many various new methods of recording the accompanying sound have been devised.

In 1906, a Frenchman, Eugene Lauste, who had worked in Thomas Edison's laboratory, became interested in adding synchronized sound to the then very new motion pictures. Lauste's method was to photograph a representation of the sound signal onto the picture negative. Inside the camera, he fitted an exposure lamp and a solenoid coil with a slit diaphragm to which he connected a telephone microphone. Speech signals from the microphone vibrated the diaphragm assembly, which he called a light valve, causing variations in the intensity of light falling on the film. Lauste also had to construct a special projector to reproduce this track, but since the audio amplifier had not yet been invented, he was unable to reach a wide audience.

In 1922, a U.S. scientist, Theodore Case, used an oxyacetylene flame to show the action of sound waves. He photographed the modulations of the flame caused by sound waves but soon abandoned the system as it was commercially unviable. In 1923, after inventing a photoelectric cell, he demonstrated talking films using a gas-discharge tube for recording, and his light-sensitive photocell coupled to an Audion amplifier and loudspeaker. Unfortunately, at that time film laboratories were unable to give consistent results, and the surface noise from the film was extremely high.

Al Jolson's *The Jazz Singer*, which appeared in 1927, was the first movie with a synchronized soundtrack. Early talkies either had the sound recorded on the film photographically or on a separate synchronized disc. The discs were 10 in. (25 cm) in diameter, played at 33⅓ rpm, and contained a start mark on the inside groove, because they played from inside to outside. There were 96 grooves to the inch, so each disc lasted for 12 minutes—sufficient time to accompany 1,000 ft. (305 m) of film running at 24 frames per second. The discs were made from shellac, and very few now survive.

Optical sound

Cameras for producing optical soundtracks are available in 35 mm, 16 mm, and Super 8 (8 mm) formats. The fundamental design consists of a light-tight film chamber, a film transport system with flywheel and sound drum, a detachable magazine for holding exposed and unexposed film, and an exposure lamp with optical system and modulator, to expose a track that varies in step with sound vibrations.

Two types of modulators are used, a mirror galvanometer and a light valve. Both produce a variable-area sound negative, in which a white band in the center of a black strip varies in width. The galvanometer reflects light from the exposure lamp, via a V-shaped mask, through a narrow horizontal slit. The light valve passes light directly through to the slit. In both cases, an image of the slit is focused onto the film as it passes around the sound drum. A noise-reduction bias is applied to the modulator when there is little or no sound so that it passes the minimum amount of light and masks unwanted background noise.

The optical soundtrack is printed onto the picture film in such a way that it is in advance of its corresponding picture frame by 20 frames on 35 mm, 26 frames on 16 mm, and 22 frames on Super 8, because each frame of the film is held motionless for a fraction of a second as it passes through the projection gate. The film must be running as smoothly as possible for accurate sound reproduction, so the film is passed around a series of loops and rollers and a sound drum. The sound drum is quite heavy so that its inertia

▲ This technician is sitting at a mixing desk in a recording studio where a man is reading a narration script for a television program. The recording settings are computer controlled from the desk. Mixing desks improve the quality of the reproduced sound by recording it digitally in tiny packets of separate information so that when it is combined the sound mimics the subtleties of the original sound. Other sounds can be added to the soundtrack at this point before it is laid down on the finished film or video.

smoothes out ripples generated during the film's path through the gate.

The reproducer consists of an exciter lamp, slit, and optical system, together with a light-sensitive cell—either a photodiode or an integrated circuit consisting of a photodiode and amplifier—behind the film. Optical soundtracks have an overall frequency response of 50 Hz to 8 kHz on 35 mm, 80 Hz to 6 kHz on 16 mm, and 100 Hz to 4 kHz on Super 8.

Magnetic sound

Magnetic soundtracks were introduced in the United States in 1950, leading to almost silent backgrounds, extended frequency response, immediate replay after recording, and quick methods of making copies. All magnetic soundtracks originate on ¼ in. (6 mm) magnetic tape, using portable recorders such as Nagra, Perfectone, and Stellavox. In addition to the audio track, a separate pulse track is recorded, which provides a speed reference to the picture camera. The selected material is transferred onto magnetic film for editing purposes, and the pulse track is used for synchronizing the tape to the magnetic film recorder. A wide magnetic stripe—allowing up to three tracks—on clear 35 mm film base is preferred for editing, but fully coated magnetic film is used for recording up to six tracks on 35 mm film.

The component parts of a soundtrack—dialog, music, and effects—are synchronized to the edited picture and assembled into separate reels of magnetic film. There may be as many as 15 or 20 reels of sound for 1 reel of picture, and they are mixed together in a rerecording theater equipped with a sound-mixing console. Volume levels and sound quality are adjusted to the satisfaction of the producer, and a final three-track magnetic master is recorded with dialog on track one, music on track two, and sound effects on track three. This separation allows for other languages to be substituted and mixed with the existing music and effects or other alterations to be made to any part of the soundtrack if needed. The magnetizer master is then rerecorded onto an optical film negative for making standard-release prints.

Films with magnetic soundtracks offer better sound quality than those recorded optically. Films of this type have a magnetic coating consisting of an iron oxide lacquer applied to the film after printing, 35 mm films having three magnetic stripes and 70 mm films having six stripes, five of which feed loudspeakers behind the screen while one feeds the auditorium loudspeaker for surround sounds and special effects (such as the low-frequency earthquake sounds that enjoyed brief popularity in the movie industry some time back).

Projectors for 35 mm and 70 mm films have penthouse sound heads located between the upper spool box and the picture gate, rather than below the gate. This arrangement gives a picture-to-sound separation of minus 24 frames for 70 mm and minus 28 frames for 35 mm. With 16 mm films the sound reproducer is below the picture gate, and the synchronization separation is 28 frames.

Dolby systems

Dolby is a noise-reduction system that was originally invented by Dolby Laboratories for use in professional recording studios. However, its potential application for improving movie soundtracks soon became apparent, particularly in films that had optical tracks. Dolby A first came into use in 1965 and works by splitting the incoming audio signal into four separate bands. Each band is then boosted above 10 decibels, the level of ambient noise, by a technique called pre-emphasis. The signals are then sent to a compander, which compresses and expands them again before they are recombined. The resulting sound is much cleaner because the compander process eliminates most of the low-level noise on the track. The drawback with this system is that the frequency response is narrowed, leading to a much smaller dynamic range of sounds.

▼ This control unit for audiovisual presentations contains both an encoder and a recorder, enabling a prerecorded soundtrack to be synchronized with a slide presentation. The slide changing control information, which is held in the form of pulses or bleeps, is recorded on a separate track from the sound. This model plays in stereo using a built-in amplifier with separate loudspeakers. It can be operated with the remote-control handheld unit shown here.

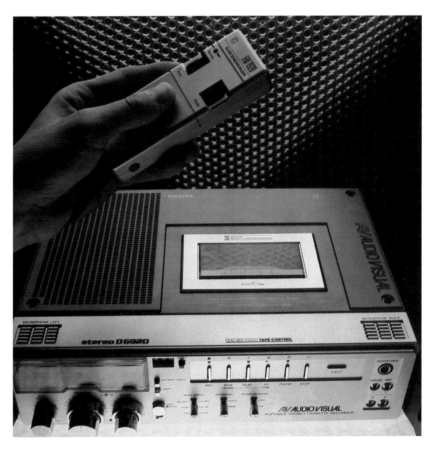

The next advance was Dolby Stereo, which uses two optical tracks on each film. Double tracks had been implemented with Dolby A but experienced noise problems when films were shown in "surround sound" theaters. Surround sound had been used mainly with magnetic soundtrack films, as it allowed the signal to be split into four or more channels linked to speakers placed at the front, back, and sides of the theater. Dolby Stereo uses a process called matrixing to split the two optical channels into four and distribute them to the relevant speakers by comparing whether the left and right tracks were in or out of phase.

Similar systems are used in home viewing systems where they go under the names Dolby Surround and Dolby ProLogic. If the system does not have a surround-sound decoder, the tracks are treated as ordinary stereo signals and sent to the right and left speakers. Dolby Surround creates a phantom-speaker effect that makes listeners believe that sound is coming from a central speaker as well as from right and left. With the ProLogic system, the central channel signal is sent to a central speaker located on the television or under the monitor or viewing screen.

Digital sound systems

Digitization offers the filmmaker the opportunity to split the soundtrack into many more discrete channels. One such system, first used on the film *Jurassic Park*, employs the DTS (Digital Theater Systems) process. DTS is similar to the old method of recording the sound onto lacquer discs but uses digital compact discs instead. The key to the system is an optical time code that is printed next to each frame of the film as a series of dots and dashes.

To read the code, the projector has to be equipped with a special reader, which the film passes through before it enters the projector. A light-emitting diode sends light through the time

code and is picked up by a photoelectric cell, which sends pulses to a computer. The computer controls three CD players linked to an audio system. Six speakers are arranged right, left, center, right-surround, left-surround, and subwoofer to correspond to the tracks on the CD. The code on the film is checked by the computer against the audio code on the CD, which is held in a buffer memory to avoid any time lag in accessing the CD and keeps the sound synchronized with the film. However, an analog optical stereo track is also laid down on the film as a backup in case the CDs are lost or in case the film is shown in a theater that uses a different system.

Dolby Digital also uses a code system but differs from DTS in that the soundtrack remains on the film. Again, there are two optical tracks on the film, but the system uses the space between the sprocket holes to put a digital track encoded as binary digits. A reader in the projector shines light through the film to a charge-coupled device, which sends the binary data to a digital processor to be turned into sound. Like DTS, this system sends the sound to six speakers, the subwoofer being used for low-frequency sounds, such as the booms of explosions and building collapses.

Another digital system that makes use of the empty space, this time on the outer edges of the film, is Sony's Dynamic Digital Sound (SDDS). The digital audio signal is laid down as a continuous stripe on one side of the film, but an identical though largely redundant stripe is laid down on

the other and serves for error correction. A laser is shone through the digital track as it passes through a reader where it is collected by photocells that convert the patterns of light and dark into a binary signal, which is sent to a proprietory processor. SDDS can produce an extra two channels instead of the customary six, and they are usually located at left-center and right-center.

Soundtrack elements

A film soundtrack can have four components: narration, music, sound effects, and dialogue. Narration is used to hold the visuals together, to provide an explanation of what is happening in the picture, or as a story-telling device. Two techniques are used, depending on how the narration is to be cut into the final soundtrack. In the first, known as "sync to picture," the narrator views the film and records his script live during the projection. In the second method, known as a "wild" track, the narrator reads the lines in a studio without seeing the picture, and the lines are recorded as isolated takes. The lines are then edited into the right place in the footage. Both methods are usually recorded in a professional studio but can also be recorded out on location without the cameras running so as to match the background noises behind on-screen dialogue.

Music is used to alter the viewer's perception of what is happening in the picture by invoking an emotional response. Most music in a film soundtrack is extraneous in that the people in the theater hear it, but the actors do not. Occasionally there is a practical need for the actors to hear music in the form of radio broadcasts or live musicians. While some music is prerecorded, or

▲ It is difficult to edit sound on a video because the sound is recorded onto the film at the same time as the pictures. The video film is duplicated so that the pictures can be edited and a time code added. The sound is copied onto a multitrack audio recorder where sound effects, music, and narration are added before the multitrack is mixed down to a mono or stereo track. The pictures and sound are then married together using the time code to form the finished video tape.

"canned," film scores are specially composed. During composing, the editor and the composer create a click track, which consists of clicks placed against a picture to guide the composer about rhythm and where the music should climax. When the music has been composed, it is recorded at a scoring stage, where the musicians can see the film and hear the click track as they play; the sound is recorded on a multitrack for later mixing.

Sound effects can be recorded live or added to the soundtrack during editing. There are libraries that supply many effects, but often the sound will have to be matched to a particular car or airplane that makes a recognizable noise. Sometimes a sound technician will be sent out with a specific list of sounds to record, but more usually the sounds are recorded in a studio by a Foley artist who uses a variety of props to create sounds to accompany the action taking place on film. Other sounds may have to be created if there is no live reference for them; for example, the sound of a dinosaur walking may be built out of a number of simple sounds that have been electronically manipulated.

The most vital part of any soundtrack is the dialogue. Words that an actor speaks while facing the camera is described as "lipsync," as the dialogue must match the movement of the lips. Speech by actors with their back to the camera or out of shot is regarded as wild and is less crucial during editing. Most dialogue is recorded during filming, though extra lines are often recorded off camera to replace words fluffed by the actors or to replace profanities if the film is to be recut for a more sensitive audience.

Occasionally the dialogue has to be replaced after shooting because of extraneous background noises or equipment malfunction during recording. It used to be necessary to physically cut loops of wrong dialogue out of the film and rerecord sentences on a separate track and then carefully align each frame with the new audio track. This looping process was replaced by a system of running the picture, original soundtrack, and blank audio track in synchronization and controlled by a computer. The computer is fed instructions as to the start and end of the sequence to be replaced and alerts the actor with audible beeps at the point where the line should be spoken. This process is repeated until the lipsync is perfect. When the film comes to be edited, it is then easy to splice in the new dialogue, as each frame is matched to the same point on the audio track.

SEE ALSO: Animation • Audio and video recording • Movie production • Solenoid • Sound effects and sampling • Sound mixing

Space Debris

Space is teeming with bits of debris—ancient debris thrown from the gravitational fields of planets and more recent junk left over from space programs. If it enters Earth's atmosphere, most of this material burns up through the heating effect of friction with air, but there are billions of objects that remain untouched in Earth orbits hundreds and thousands of miles beyond the reach of Earth's atmosphere. There, various-sized fragments of old launch vehicles, satellites, and space probes hurtle above our heads at speeds as great as 25,000 mph (40,000 km/h), equivalent to around 7 miles (11 km) per second. Some of these objects are intact—ranging from lost spanners to disused satellites—others are fragments, such as paint peelings, frozen coolant, and debris from on-orbit explosions of disused satellites. Some 200 such events have been recorded to date.

The risk
At 25,000 mph, a 0.01 oz. (0.28 g) fragment has 17.5 kilojoules of kinetic energy—in comparison, a 0.22-caliber round (mass 0.12 oz., or 3.5 g) travels at 2,100 mph (3,400 km/h) and has only 1.5 kilojoules of kinetic energy. If such a fragment were to collide with a space vehicle crossing its path, all its energy would be delivered in a fraction of a second, vaporizing the fragment in a flash of energy that could do untold damage to the equipment and pressure-containing skins of a spacecraft

▲ The solar panels of the space station *Mir* suffered many hits from particles of rock and debris during its time in orbit above Earth. At the end of its useful life, the space station was carefully moved into an orbit where it would burn up during reentry through the atmosphere. Several large pieces were seen to land in the South Pacific near Fiji.

if not adequately shielded. Current shielding technology can withstand impacts with objects up to 0.4 in. (1 cm) in diameter; larger objects must be avoided to prevent unacceptable damage.

Observation
There are two ground-based methods for observing space debris: visual and radar observation. It is also possible to monitor debris in space.

Ground-based visual observation detects sunlight reflected by debris, and its sensitivity for a given size of object falls off in proportion to the square of an object's distance from the observer (because the intensity of light reflected by the object decreases at that rate). Such observations depend on the contrast between an illuminated object and dark sky and thus take place near the horizon only for an hour or so just before dawn or just after sunset on clear days.

The main use of visual observation is for tracking whole rocket stages and satellites in high Earth orbits (HEOs). The most important HEO is the geostationary orbit at 22,240 miles (35,800 km) from Earth's surface, which is occupied by satellites that remain fixed over a point on Earth's equator. Using the best charge-coupled detectors to pick up light, the minimum diameter that can be observed at this distance is 2 ft. (60 cm).

In radar observation, the radar transmitter "illuminates" objects with radio-frequency radiation, and the receiver—often attached to the same antenna—detects its reflections. Since both illuminating and reflected radiation fade in proportion to the square of distance, the sensitivity of radar decreases with the fourth power of distance between object and observer. In contrast to visual observation, radar detection relies neither on clear skies nor on solar illumination.

Given its combination of restrictions and advantages compared with those of visual observation, radar is used to track small objects in low Earth orbits (LEOs). The limits of capability of current systems are 0.8 in. (2 cm) diameter objects at 311 miles (500 km) for NASA's Goldstone radar and 2.4 in. (6 cm) at 620 miles (1,000 km) for NASA's Haystack radar installation, although an experimental radar in Ukraine has already detected 1.2 in. (3 cm) objects at 620 miles.

Space probes have been set up to monitor debris, and retrieved objects and space shuttles can be inspected for signs of impacts with debris on their return to Earth. One example was the 108 sq. ft. (10 m²) sample of solar panel that had been exposed for 10 years when it was retrieved in

1998 from the Russian space station *Mir*. Such sources provide data about the distribution and number of small particles in space but does little to elucidate the positions of chunks of debris.

Catalogues and statistics

In 2001, an estimated 5,000 tons (4,535 tonnes) of debris—some 6 million pieces in all—were orbiting Earth. Of that total, only a tiny fraction of fragments are of such sizes and distances that they can be observed; the rest must be estimated from the numbers of strikes with spacecraft.

The current NASA catalogue of space debris classifies fragments as observable if they are greater than 4 to 12 in. (10–30 cm) in diameter. This classification is based on the past capabilities of radar and visual observation installations and will improve as such equipment becomes more sensitive. Where available, the catalogue lists for each object data such as orbital characteristics, mission data, masses at the start and end of a mission, radar cross section, and light reflectivity.

Data on the size distribution and quantity of particles at a given orbital radius are obtained by analyzing impact scars on retrieved equipment. For example, examination of the Hubble Space Telescope solar array, active between May 1990 and December 1993, revealed an annual impact rate of 0.02 per 1.2 sq. yds. (1 m²) by objects 0.04 to 0.08 in. (0.1–0.2 cm) in diameter; the rate was 1,200 per year for particles around 0.16 thousandths of an inch (4 µm) in diameter. The sizes of impacting objects are gauged by comparing their scars with those made in hypervelocity impact laboratory experiments. The debris density obtained by such experiments peaks at around 0.002 objects per cubic mile (0.0005/km³) at 560 miles (900 km) above Earth.

Implications

At the present levels of space debris, it is possible to plan journeys to avoid known objects and take measures to protect from impacts from unknown objects. Debris tends to orbit in the direction of Earth's rotation, so astronauts can protect themselves by performing extravehicular activities on the sheltered sides of their craft, for example.

If the amount of space debris continues to increase, however, it may soon become unacceptably risky for humans to journey into space. To avoid this scenario, it is necessary to retrieve or force the reentry of spacecraft at the ends of their working lives. Alternatively, fragment-forming explosions could be reduced by removing fuel and pressurized gases from decommissioned probes and by discharging their batteries and despinning their gyroscopes to extinguish all energy sources.

FACT FILE

- *There are currently an estimated 8,500 observable objects—fragments greater than 4 in. (10 cm) in diameter—in near-Earth orbits. Any one of them could cause disastrous damage by striking an active space vehicle head on or from the side.*

- *NASA's space shuttle orbiters have to make avoidance maneuvers to keep safe distances from known large objects and have suffered damage from impacts of unobservable small debris. The European remote sensing satellite ERS-1 was repositioned twice to avoid debris impact—in June 1997, and again in March 1998—and SPOT-2 also performed such a maneuver in July 1997.*

- *The first collision between two catalogued objects occurred in 1996, when a fragment from an exploded* Ariane *upper-stage rocket struck* Cerise—*then an active satellite. This type of collision will become more frequent as near space becomes more densely populated by space debris. Some experts fear that we are witnessing the start of a chain reaction, whereby fragments from one collision go on to strike other objects, producing more fragments, and so on.*

▼ This map of observable debris emphasizes the preponderance of such objects in geostationary Earth orbits (GEOs), some 22,240 miles (35,785 km) above Earth's equator. There the orbital period coincides with the period of Earth's rotation.

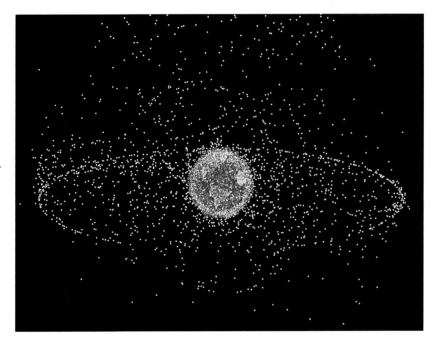

SEE ALSO: RADAR • SPACE PROBE • SPACE SHUTTLE • SPACE STATION • TELESCOPE, OPTICAL • TELESCOPE, SPACE

Space Photography

◀ In 1969, Neil Armstrong and Edwin Aldrin Jr. were the first astronauts to land on the moon. Armstrong took this picture of Aldrin in the Sea of Tranquillity using a 70 mm lunar surface camera. Armstrong can be seen taking the picture in the reflection on Aldrin's helmet.

Initially, space photography was almost an afterthought of space exploration. Only some 300 pictures were taken in the four orbital flights of Project Mercury in 1962. These photographs were widely distributed, and their value soon became apparent, not just for scientific purposes but also because of their immense publicity impact. Consequently, in Project Gemini in 1965–1966, 2,400 frames were exposed in ten flights. Over 10,000 photographs were taken in one later Apollo mission. Today space photography has developed into an important tool for space research, using digital cameras that store images in computer memories or transmit images by radio to receivers on Earth.

Camera modifications

For the Gemini flights, the basic camera for an astronaut was a Hasselblad. It was significantly modified, bearing little resemblance to a standard unit. The mirror and reflex viewfinder were removed to comply with NASA regulations limiting the amount of glass permitted on board. In zero gravity conditions, broken glass would float around a capsule and constitute a major hazard. Indeed, NASA had to grant a special dispensation to allow even the glass lenses to remain.

Extra large knobs were fitted to the Hasselblad exposure controls so that they could be operated by a crew member wearing space suit gloves. The modified cameras had either a nonreflective anodized black trim or a silver anodized trim for lunar surface work. The shiny trim served to reflect away heat and prevent the camera from overheating when outside the spacecraft. Inside the camera, conventional lubricants were replaced by oils that would not ignite in the cabin's oxygen atmosphere.

The standard movie camera used by the astronauts was the Maurer variable-sequence camera. Its main function, however, was not entertainment but data acquisition. Because of its slow framing rate, the Maurer produces a jerky impression of astronauts' movements when they are played back.

Film for space

For space photography, film was modified to give the maximum number of exposures per loading. To achieve this end, a special film base of Estar polyester was used, which has less than half the thickness of normal triacetate film base. It enables some 200 exposures to be made per loading of black and white film and around 160 per color film.

Film was processed under stringent conditions by the Photographic Technology Division (PTD) at the Houston Space Center. Every precaution had to be taken so that invaluable films brought all the way back from the Moon were not damaged during processing. The PTD's elaborate control and backup facilities ensured success.

Training for photography

Usually astronauts are not trained photographers. They are chosen for their ability to fly jet planes or because of their academic training in fields such as engineering or astronautics. While some astronauts have been keen amateur photographers, the authorities urge them to regard themselves as operators rather than free-ranging photographers. By encouraging astronauts to follow simple set procedures, the chances of error are reduced.

Training for scientific or experimental photography is conducted formally and in simulated mission conditions. General photography is somewhat more informal. Typically, a crew is issued cameras and other photographic equipment at least six months before the mission takes place so that they can familiarize themselves with them—astronauts due to land on the Moon practiced wearing Hasselblad cameras on their chest packs during training. Wherever possible, the pictures taken are analyzed and problems discussed with NASA photographic specialists.

In some cases, astronauts have been able to make a significant contribution to the formulation of the photographic program. Astronauts are the operators and are in a unique position to contribute their experience. The Gemini and Apollo veteran John Young, commander of the first shuttle test mission, persuaded the authorities to allow him to carry more film than was originally planned. His experience told him that a crew never minded having too much film aboard and that its members greatly regretted having to restrict their nonscheduled picture taking. It was often the informal shot taken in a spare moment that resulted in the most dramatic images.

▼ This image of the International Space Station was taken from the space shuttle using a 70 mm handheld camera.

Space guidelines

Initially, space photographic requirements were stated in general terms and were among the first to be deleted if problems developed during the mission. However, by the time of the Apollo flights, photographic tasks were included in the flight plan.

The Apollo crew found abbreviated but detailed photographic instructions in their flight plan so that the room for operator error was minimized. For example, CM4/EL/80/CEX(f/8, 1/250, focus) 5FR meant that the scene was to be photographed from the Command Module right-hand rendezvous window using the Hasselblad EL camera with the 80 mm lens fitted. Ektachrome film would be used and the exposure would be 1/250 of a second at f/8 with the astronauts focusing visually. Five frames of the magazine would be shot.

Exposure help

The most important task for the astronaut photographer is to obtain the correct exposure. However, the Hasselblad has no exposure meter, and the peculiar lighting conditions in space would, in any case, be likely to trick any metering device used.

Despite the difficulties, the astronauts had a high success rate—not because of successful metering but because they used exposure charts. They were built up using the accumulated experience of the early flights. The first missions normally used a fixed exposure time and an aperture size ¹⁄₂₅ of a second at f/11 on 64 ASA film. Any changes in exposure had to be related to differences in the brightness of the subject. Thus, scientists were able to analyze the images and calculate brightness levels for all types of subject and illumination.

Where specific and clearly delineated targets were to be photographed, special meters were used. Called spot meters, these are light meters that record over just a small part of the overall field of view. Unlike normal meters they are not fooled by the bias of peculiar space effects—such as the blackness of space, lunar shadows, Sun glint, or light scattered from Earth's atmosphere.

▶ The Wide Field Camera 3 (WFC3) is scheduled to be installed in the Hubble Space Telescope in 2004.

▼ The experimental remote-controlled Sprint camera was tested by NASA in 1997. Free-floating cameras, such as this one may one day be used to inspect the exterior of spacecraft to detect damage, thus avoiding the necessity for time-consuming and dangerous space walks.

Because the astronauts used Hasselblads that had been stripped of their viewing systems, they could not frame their subjects through the viewfinder. Instead, when working on the lunar surface, the camera was attached to the astronaut's chest. To take a picture, all the operator had to do was to point the camera in the right direction; the Hasselblad was equipped with a lens that took in a fairly wide angle of view, so the astronaut could be sure of capturing the object to be photographed.

Photography problems

Photography in space faces special difficulties arising out of unusual and often unforeseen circumstances. Photography seems to have been the last subject in the engineers' minds when designing spacecraft. Windows, for example, become surprisingly dirty from pollutants, such as engine gas, or fog over with internal condensation. Waste liquids dumped out of the spacecraft tend to follow the craft, glinting in the sunlight and partially obscuring the photographer's view.

On the Moon, surface dust has been a constant menace to photographic equipment. The absence of a lunar atmosphere has aggravated this problem. In a vacuum, dust has a tendency to stick to surfaces because of intermolecular attraction. The result has sometimes been a soft-focus effect that gave astronauts the eerie appearance of being haloed in strange glowing light.

Sometimes the problems are human. It would have been only natural to suppose that careful plans would have been made to ensure that Neil Armstrong—the first man on the Moon—was subsequently photographed by Aldrin with the Hasselblad. If Aldrin had done so, high-quality stills would have been obtained for posterity. As it is, none exist.

Digital images

Electronic techniques have now taken over from simple photography. Images are produced by television systems, or vidicon cameras, or by arrays of light-sensitive components called CCDs. The images are relayed to Earth by picture element (pixel) and then reassembled on arrival like the light and dark dots of a newspaper picture. This digital information may be image processed on a computer. Features can be computer enhanced to reveal details not visible in the raw images. Systems such as these are used by astronauts as handheld cameras and on satellites and probes where they are operated remotely.

Digital video cameras have also been deployed on an experimental free-floating remote-controlled camera called Sprint. This device, tested in 1997, is about the size of a basketball and was designed to view the outside of spacecraft, such as the International Space Station, to help detect damaged areas, thus avoiding the necessity for astronauts to make space walks. Twelve pressurized nitrogen gas thrusters are used to maneuver Sprint, enabling its two video cameras to take images that can then be relayed to Earth or to astronauts within a spacecraft.

The Hubble Space Telescope also uses a variety of remote-controlled instruments, such as the

European Space Agency's Faint Object Camera and the soon-to-be-installed Advanced Camera for Surveys, to create digital images that are then transmitted to Earth. Originally intended to operate till 2005, NASA made the decision in 1997 to extend the Hubble's mission till 2010. To improve the functioning of the telescope over this extended period, a new camera, the Wide Field Camera 3 (WFC3), is to be added in 2004 and will supplement the imaging capabilities of the Wide Field Planetary Camera 2 (WFPC2). This new camera is designed to be low cost and will include parts, such as the Selectable Optical Filter Assembly (SOFA), taken from the Wide Field Planetary Camera 1 (WF/PC 1), retrieved from Hubble in 1999. A new infrared channel and a visible channel that use CCDs to provide images with a format of 4,096 x 4,096 pixels will also be included, helping to improve the Hubble telescope's discovery efficiency by around a factor of 10. The wide field of view of this camera will also enable astronomers to take single pictures that would previously have required the piecing together of many different images.

▲ The astronaut Chiaki Mukai, representing Japan's National Space Development Agency (NASDA), changes a camera cassette during a space shuttle mission.

SEE ALSO: CAMERA • LENS • LIGHT AND OPTICS • MAPMAKING TECHNIQUES • PHOTOGRAPHIC FILM AND PROCESSING • SATELLITE, ARTIFICIAL • SPACE PROBE • TELESCOPE, SPACE

FACT FILE

■ In 2002, NASA intends to install a new camera in the Hubble Space Telescope called the Advanced Camera for Surveys (ACS). This camera will be able to produce images of galaxy clusters in deep space and thus aid our understanding of galactic nuclei and the way in which planetary systems form. The ACS will contain three different cameras; the Wide Field Camera (WFC), which will produce images of galaxies during the early formation of the Universe; the High Resolution Channel (HRC), which will improve the contrast of bright objects, allowing astronomers to study black holes and gaseous nebulae; and the Solar Blind Camera (SBC), which is suitable for observing faint far-ultraviolet images.

■ The Faint Object Camera (FOC), built by the European Space Agency and installed on the Hubble Space Telescope, is capable of producing images 100,000 times brighter than the object observed.

Space Probe

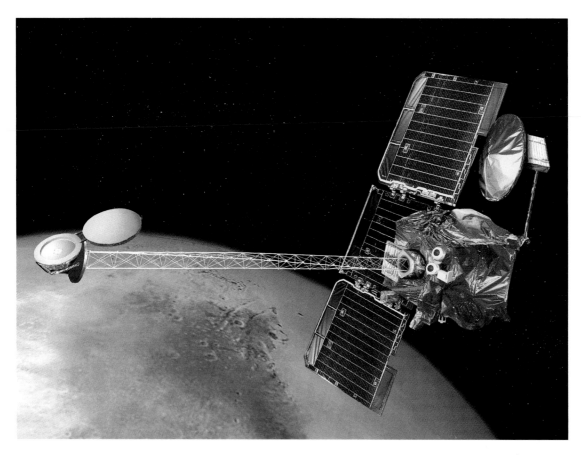

Space probes are some of the most complicated robots devised. They navigate their way between the planets and on arrival at their destination radio back the observations of their electronic eyes and other sensors. An Earth satellite sends back measurements and sometimes photographs of the terrain below it, but a space probe must often carry out precise maneuvers when at a vast distance from Earth. Probes have been sent to the Moon, Mars, Venus, Mercury, Jupiter, Saturn, Uranus, Neptune, and Halley's comet; they have orbited the Sun to investigate conditions in space on the far side of Earth's orbit, and they have detected particles of the solar wind at several points widely distributed through the Solar System.

Design

The design of any space probe depends upon its destination and what it has to do. All space probes and satellites have an elementary framework around which can be added the various experiments and systems, and all probes of a particular class, such as the Mariner probes, sent to Mercury, Venus, and Mars, have basic similarities.

Near the Sun there are few problems of power supply; panels of solar cells can provide an adequate supply of electricity for several years. In the case of probes intended for Mars and beyond, however, the solar intensity is much lower and power from solar panels is limited.

In the case of the Pioneer and Voyager craft that travelled to Jupiter and Saturn, no solar panels at all were used, since the solar intensity near Saturn is almost one-hundredth of that near Earth. Instead, four thermonuclear generators, producing heat from the radioactive decay of the plutonium-238 isotope, were used to provide 130 watts of power. This output deteriorates with time.

To protect the scientific instruments from radiation from these generators, the power units are located on booms pointing away from the instrument packages. Booms are often used on spacecraft when some particular instruments for collecting data may be affected by the others.

Another dominant feature of a space probe's design are the telemetry antennas. The transmitter power is usually very low, around a few watts, so to make the best use of it, the signals must be beamed back to Earth by a parabolic dish reflector, which gives a narrow beam. For the Pioneer and Voyager probes, this dish dominates the whole craft, being 9 ft. (2.7 m) in diameter. A less directional spike antenna is also provided for transmission at a low rate if the main beam is not exactly aligned with Earth. Very large parabolic dishes on Earth, such as NASA's Deep Space

Network of dishes positioned in California, Spain, and Australia, are needed to detect the very weak signals from space probes.

Stabilization

In order that the craft can point its antennas and experiments in the chosen direction, it must be stabilized in some way. The two methods available for any space vehicle are spin stabilization and three-axis stabilization. In the former, the craft is set spinning by a platform on the launch vehicle just before it is sent on its way into space. Like a gyroscope, it will tend to stay spinning in the same direction in space. Where rapid pictures are to be taken and where a number of experiments have to be pointed in different directions, this arrangement is unsuitable. For most space probes, therefore, three-axis stabilization is used in which the craft is kept in a particular orientation by means of attitude correctors. To achieve this goal, the orientation of the craft must be known, so Sun and star sensors are employed to detect the direction of the chosen object. As the brightest object in the sky, the Sun is easiest to find. Only one other star is needed to fix the orientation of a craft, and the star Canopus, the second brightest in the sky, is generally used because of its brightness and its large angle from the Sun.

Minor effects, such as the gravitational pulls of the planets, may disturb the attitude. In this case, the attitude is corrected by means of small gas (usually nitrogen) jets. Another method, with the advantage that it does not deplete gas supplies, is to arrange a set of reaction wheels inside the spacecraft. By spinning one of them, the probe can be made to turn slowly in the opposite direction.

Once the attitude of a craft is corrected, its orbit or path through space has to be corrected from time to time. A probe in space will follow an ellipse around the Sun unless its rocket is fired as predicted in the laws laid down by the 17th century German astronomer, Johannes Kepler. Firing changes the orbit, and as soon as the rocket stops, the probe will continue along a new, slightly different orbit. These course-correction maneuvers are carefully calculated when the orbit of the probe is known, and if carried out accurately, only one correction will be needed per mission. The craft is commanded to fire its rocket for a precise length of time at a certain instant. In this way, extreme precision of aiming can be achieved.

Landers

A number of space probes are designed not simply to travel past (fly by) a planet or to go into orbit around a planet but also to land on a planet or on the Moon. Some of the earlier probes made

▲ The Thermal Emission Imaging System (THEMIS) is one of the detectors installed on the *Mars Odyssey* probe. This device uses spectrometers to measure visible and infrared radiation emitted from the surface of the planet.

▶ Scientists work on the *Mars Odyssey* probe to prepare it for acoustic tests and thermal vacuum chamber tests.

little or no attempt to slow their velocity before striking the surface, and were known as hard landers. Some, such as the Ranger series, made no attempt to brake their progress and hit the Moon, taking television pictures as they went. Others, such as *Luna 9* and *Luna 13*, slowed their descent using retrorockets until they were very close to the lunar surface and then cut the rockets off, leaving the device to drop. The instruments were protected by being inside a ball-shaped capsule that was ejected from the main craft before impact to bounce and roll across the surface, coming to rest some distance away from the rocket. Four petals then opened out after an interval in such a way that the probe was forced upright and the instruments were revealed.

An improved technique was used by the Surveyor craft, five of which landed on the Moon in 1966 and 1967. They were equipped with controlled vernier rockets (small rockets used to adjust trajectory and velocity) to keep the spacecraft attitude correct; the main retro-rocket slowed the craft down and was then ejected, and the vernier rockets took the spacecraft down to a soft landing. An essential feature of this technique is an automatic onboard controller linked to a radar altimeter and velocity sensor working on the Doppler principle; it enables the craft to know how high above the surface it is and how fast it is moving. (Guidance from Earth would be difficult because of the two-and-a-half-second delay in the round trip of a radio signal between Moon, Earth, and Moon.). Another means of acquiring data is

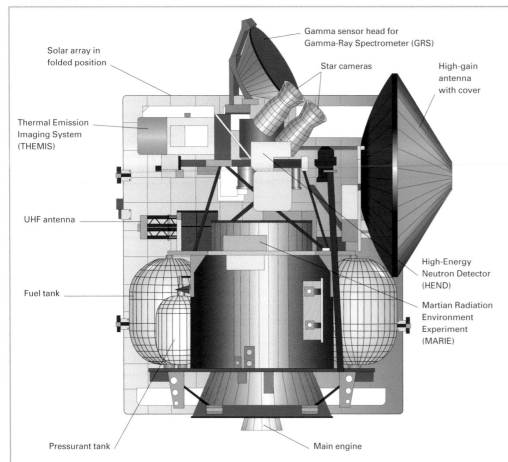

Solar array in
folded position

Gamma sensor head for
Gamma-Ray Spectrometer (GRS)

Star cameras

High-gain
antenna
with cover

Thermal Emission
Imaging System
(THEMIS)

UHF antenna

Fuel tank

High-Energy
Neutron Detector
(HEND)

Martian Radiation
Environment
Experiment
(MARIE)

Pressurant tank

Main engine

MARS ODYSSEY SPACE PROBE

This space probe contains a number of different instruments for studying the chemical and mineral constituents of Mars. The Thermal Emission Imaging System (THEMIS) measures electromagnetic radiation in the infrared region and thus measures the heat given off at different parts of Mars's surface. The Martian Radiation Environment experiment (MARIE) measures radiation from cosmic rays. This information will be used to calculate the dangers from radiation that will face astronauts on Mars. The Gamma-Ray Spectrometer (GRS) will use a neutron detector to collect data that will enable scientists to discover whether liquid water exists under the surface of Mars.

by using a rover. Because of the relatively fragile nature of rovers, they must be protected from too hard a landing. One of the most recent rovers was the *Sojourner* vehicle used on the Martian *Pathfinder* mission. This rover was released from the *Pathfinder* spacecraft, and its descent to Mars was broken by parachutes and then finally by air bags. The bags were then deflated and retracted to allow the rover to emerge from a protective metal casing.

Instruments

The point of sending space probes to the planets is to obtain details of conditions on the way and on arrival. The photographs sent back are the most spectacular results from probes, but scientific measurements of temperature, atmospheric pressure and composition, soil composition, magnetic field, and particle densities are also made and sent back to Earth.

The cameras used for photography are not simple television cameras. The Moon probes

◀ The payload module of the *Solar and Heliospheric Observatory (SOHO)*. undergoes checks.

▶ This image of the Sun taken from *SOHO* was formed from two images obtained by the Ultraviolet Coronagraph Spectrometer (UVCS) and the Extreme Ultraviolet Imaging Telescope (EIT).

Ranger and *Surveyor* had television cameras of a special design, though neither returned the sort of continuous signals that normal broadcasting stations send out. Instead, each picture took a short while to read from the face of the camera tube, one reason being that the bandwidth of the telemetry channel used could not send enough information in the time needed.

The Mariner craft sent to Mars, Venus, and Mercury were equipped with tape recorders to record the camera output for later transmission at a slow rate. *Mariner 9*, for example, sent back a total of 7,329 pictures of Mars over a period of a year from orbit. Two cameras were used with a variety of filters to measure color and polarization of the surface. In addition, an infrared radiometer was used to measure the surface temperature.

SOHO

In 1995, the European Space Agency and NASA launched a probe called the *Solar and Heliospheric Observatory (SOHO)* designed to study the Sun. *SOHO* contains a variety of equipment for studying the Sun's interior, the solar atmosphere, and the solar wind. The solar interior is observed using Global Oscillations at Low Frequencies (GOLF), Variability of Solar Irradiance and

Gravity Oscillations (VIRGO), the Solar Oscillations Investigator (SOI), and the Michelson Doppler Imager (MDI). These instruments are designed to measure solar waves, which pass through the Sun in a way similar to sound waves passing through air. The movement of these waves provides information on the temperature and composition of the Sun's interior.

To collect data on the solar atmosphere, many different instruments are used including the Solar Ultraviolet Measurements of Emitted Radiation (SUMER), the Large Angle and Spectrometric Coronagraph Experiment (LASCO), and the Coronal Diagnostic Spectrometer (CDS). These instruments measure the density and velocity of ionized gas at different temperatures at the surface of the Sun.

The solar wind is also measured using a variety of instruments including the Charge, Element, and Isotope Analysis System (CELIAS) and Solar Wind Anisotropies (SWAN), which together acquire data on the magnetized plasma blown out from the sun.

Since *SOHO* came into operation, it has provided some remarkable images of the Sun and, more important, invaluable information to astronomers on the Sun's structure and behavior.

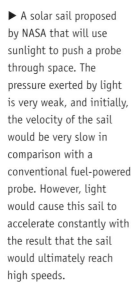

▶ A solar sail proposed by NASA that will use sunlight to push a probe through space. The pressure exerted by light is very weak, and initially, the velocity of the sail would be very slow in comparison with a conventional fuel-powered probe. However, light would cause this sail to accelerate constantly with the result that the sail would ultimately reach high speeds.

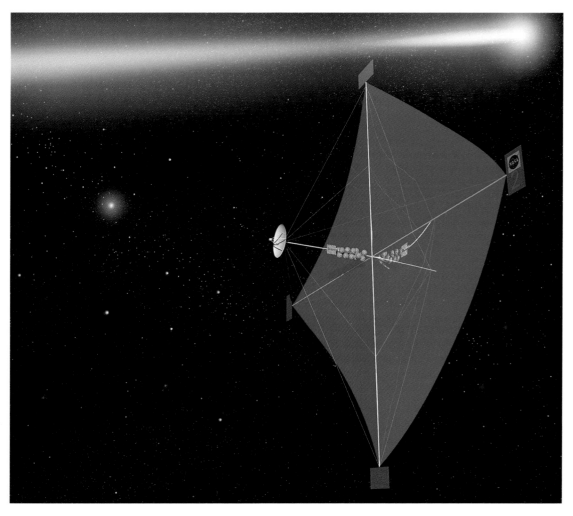

element to emit a unique wavelength of gamma ray, thus enabling scientists to identify the general profusion of elements over a given area without actually having to take rock and soil samples. A neutron detector on GRS will also enable scientists to detect whether there is any water on or just under the surface of Mars. Neutron detectors are highly sensitive to hydrogen, and the form in which hydrogen is most likely to exist on Mars is as frozen water. A spectrometer on MARIE will measure the levels of radiation from cosmic rays to give some indication of the amounts of radiation and therefore the possible health hazards likely to be experienced by astronauts landing on Mars.

The final use of the *Mars Odyssey* probe is as a communications satellite between Earth and a variety of future Mars landers.

Cassini and future probes

The *Cassini* spacecraft flew past Jupiter in 2000 and on to Saturn, where in November 2004 it is to release a probe that will land on one of Saturn's moons, Titan. *Cassini* has already sent many images of Jupiter back to Earth, and the Titan probe will provide important information about Titan's atmosphere and surface.

In the future, NASA hopes to send a probe to one of Jupiter's moons, Europa. This moon is particularly interesting because it is covered with a thick surface of ice under which there may be free water. Scientists believe that this environment may also contain thermal vents suitable for supporting life. Consequently, the Europa probe will have to be able to carry out many functions. Not only will it have to melt its way through the thick ice surface, but it will also have to propel its way through water, survive extremes of temperature, carry out experiments to detect life, and be able to send all the resulting information back to Earth. It may be many years before such a probe is actually sent to Europa, but already scientists and robotics engineers are working on prototypes for this difficult task.

Another area of research is in methods of propulsion. One of the problems that faces many space probe missions is providing enough energy to power the vehicles and their instruments over the vast distances and long periods of time necessary to arrive at their destinations. Scientists are therefore exploring alternative means of propulsion, such as solar sails powered by the pressure exerted by sunlight.

Mars Odyssey

The *Mars Odyssey* is a probe designed to orbit Mars and collect data on Martian chemicals and minerals, to look for water, and to measure levels of radiation. When the probe arrived at Mars, it entered a 25-hour orbit, but over the next 76 days, the probe gradually moved closer to Mars until it finally entered an orbit taking only two hours. This orbit was achieved by a process called aerobraking, using atmospheric friction to lower its position, thus avoiding the necessity for extra fuel. Once in this orbit, the probe spent a Martian year, the equivalent of 29 months on Earth, mapping the surface of Mars and collecting scientific data.

The *Mars Odyssey* contains three primary data-collecting devices: the Thermal Emission Imaging System (THEMIS), the Gamma-Ray Spectrometer (GRS), and the Mars Radiation Environment Experiment (MARIE). All of these devices contain spectrometers, which measure the intensity of wavelengths in the electromagnetic spectrum. THEMIS is designed to measure waves in the infrared region emitted by the surface of Mars. Differences in wavelength and intensity indicate the types of minerals existing on different parts of the Martian surface. THEMIS also takes images in the visible part of the spectrum to provide detailed knowledge of the surface to help plan future landing sites and further understanding of where liquids once existed on the surface.

GRS measures the levels of gamma rays emitted from Mars. The elements on Mars are constantly bombarded by cosmic rays that cause each

▲ In the future, NASA hopes to send a robot probe to Jupiter's icy moon Europa. This probe will melt its way through Europa's thick layer of ice until it reaches free water. A robot will then be released that will propel itself through the water, collecting data as it travels. Some scientists believe that this environment may contain thermal vents suitable for the evolution of life.

SEE ALSO: ROBOTICS • ROCKET AND SPACE PROPULSION • SATELLITE, ARTIFICIAL • SOLAR SYSTEM • SPACE PHOTOGRAPHY

Index

Page numbers in **bold** refer to main articles; those in *italics* refer to picture captions.